The Death of Francis Stevens

Randy Maizuss

Thanks to Faith Pantel at Precision Services Group

&

Nichole Hill at Inspired Creations

Artwork and cover design by Yukari Vlasaty

ISBN 978-0-692-21624-8

For my mother on Earth,
and for my father up in Heaven.

PROLOGUE

Shit, shit, shit.

Fuck, fuck!

In her bedroom, Abigail lifted her shirt and slid a razor across her stomach three times. "I have a cunt of a mother," she thought as she dropped the razor on the floor after the fourth cut. She laid on her bed and felt the "joyful" pain and she stared in a "daze" at the circles of yellow ceiling light above her.

Ruth typed on her laptop, in her home office, writing the first draft of her first novel, *The After Life*. She drank another glass of Scotch.

She was alone in the house. She felt a draft. She heard the floor creak in the room.

Someone was there.

Francis was a happy man. He lived. He died young.

What else matters?

DEATH

CHAPTER 1

The night of the horrible and bloody murder, Abigail pleaded with her mother to see her father's body. Ruth sat on the edge of the bed, near a circle of yellow lamp light, in her bedroom. She held a glass of Scotch in her trembling hand and turned and noticed Abigail in the doorway.

"I want to see him," Abigail said. "I want to see him for the last time."

"No, absolutely not!'

"Why not? I have to see him!" Abigail pleaded.

"Look, Abby, I'm not going to argue about it right now. Just do what I say!"

"Then don't argue, but I'm going with you!"

Abigail left her mother's bedroom on that dreadful night and closed the bedroom door. Ruth was distraught and weak; and so she did what her seventeen year old daughter asked for; and the next day, Ruth and Abigail rode the elevator down to the morgue of The Crenshaw District Hospital to identify the body of Francis Stevens.

The place was cold and sterile and the pathologist pulled the sheet back from the victim's face followed by his entire body and the moments felt slow. Abigail waited to see the end result of a horrific murder, as if this was a macabre hobby; but that very moment represented the death of her forty-seven year old father.

Ruth and Abigail couldn't believe what they had witnessed that day, in the morgue. Francis was nearly unrecognizable. He had been stabbed over twenty-five times, in the chest, arms, neck, and face. The most experienced homicide detectives were shocked at the human carnage they discovered in the parking structure of The Crenshaw District Hospital, where the warm body was originally found by a Hispanic nurse, named Carmen Espinoza.

And every news station in southern California reported on this horrible and unfortunate story; and why not? This top story was "horribly" fascinating, and "fascination" equaled high-ratings for the networks. The story had an interesting "hook." A white wealthy surgeon from Santa Monica was "sliced and murdered" at dusk, in the parking structure of The Crenshaw District Hospital, which was the city's largest HMO Hospital.

The incident became the top story among the daily news, which garnered the highest ratings on the various network and cable stations. The incident had the tragedy people loved and feared. A white surgeon was murdered in a hospital parking structure. The graphic image of a bloody corpse covered by a white sheet next to a white blood splattered Mercedes appeared on the front page of newspapers throughout most of the state; and people wanted to know where in the hell was security during the atrocious incident? And how come a security camera only "caught" grainy footage of a black man, in a green hoodie, running by a vending machine. And then the media "sabotaged" the hospital's reputation for the second time in twenty years.

The following days of the murder, television anchors ambushed black elderly patients as they wobbled from the hospital lobby in a walker or who were wheeled out in a wheel chair and were asked if they felt safe at The Crenshaw District Hospital.

"Yeah, I feel safe. Why not? Why wouldn't I feel safe? I been comin' here since I was ten years old," a black elderly patient said. A black middle age patient replied "Safe in this hospital? Hell yeah' I feel safe. Stuff happens everywhere, especially when you're near the hood."

And what made this unfortunate story more eventful was that the suspect was free to "strike again." Fear and interest filled the minds of millions of residents throughout Los Angeles. All the media really knew was that an "eyewitness" noticed a "black man" in a green hoodie running from the parking structure around the time of the murder; and so the entire city was on "alert" for a black man in a green hoodie.

Most "white" citizens in L.A. were more cautious of their surroundings, as they were afraid of being another victim of this vicious black man in a green hoodie. Phone calls "poured" into police stations from anonymous callers from "all colors." There was a call that a black man wearing a beanie was "loitering" in front of a Starbucks "talking to himself." And there was a phone call that a black man in a green bandana was yelling obscenities into a cell phone in front of a Vons Supermarket and then there was a report of a black man with a shaved head who was aggressively asking people for change on the corner of so and so. Thousands of "panicked calls" led to nowhere.

Racial tensions increased and blacks were "singled out" more than usual in the wealthy neighborhoods of Santa Monica, Beverly Hills and Brentwood. There were intense debates on network TV; and on cable stations, there were political shows that featured white politicians and black community leaders in which they discussed the life of Dr. Stevens, the wealthy white surgeon, who had the "perfect wife," Ruth, and the perfect teenage daughter, Abigail, the pristine, beautiful blue eyed sandy blond hair girl, who resembled a model in a pageant; and this was the teenage girl who attended St. Susan Catholic High School, and wore a checkered skirt, a white button up blouse covered by a black sweater with the school mascot of an eagle stitched on the right hand corner.

And so this perfect "white" family was instantly torn apart by this bloody brutal murder. Ironically nobody knew the truth about Ruth and Abigail. They despised each other before the murder; and now years of silent tension opened old wounds.

Abigail should have been attending history class and it was only two-fifty three p.m., on a Tuesday afternoon. Instead she sat on a green couch, listening to Motorhead, and snorted cocaine on a glass table, in the living room of her boyfriend's apartment. She cut each line of coke with precision and snorted the line through a rolled up twenty dollar bill. She loved this "shit" and she touched her nose after her last "line" and swallowed the drug as it seeped from her nose to the back of her throat and she grimaced, as the drug tasted like aspirin. Abigail was only a "cokehead" for nearly ninety days and her dumb fuckin' boyfriend, Danny Ruiz, introduced her to the drug; and Danny was a twenty-eight year old high school "dropout" with brown shoulder-length hair. He loved the English heavy metal band Motorhead and their 1980 album, Ace of Spades, which was currently playing from a "shitty ass" stereo.

Danny worked as a waiter in a Chinese Restaurant, in Hollywood; and Danny wanted to be a great theatre actor, and he cherished his green 1973 Pontiac Trans Am, and he "adored" his underage girlfriend, who was currently sitting on his green couch, snorting cocaine on a glass table and listening to Motorhead; and Danny entered the living room and sat on the green couch behind Abigail and put his arms around her flat stomach, as she finished another line of cocaine and she finally said "I fuckin' love this stuff."

"Not as much as I love your tits," Danny said. He fondled her large chest. She turned around and kissed Danny; and then Abigail resumed cutting another "line" with an expired credit card on the glass table.

A few weeks earlier, Abigail's mother was still sleeping when her phone rang and Ruth jolted from her "dream" at eleven thirty-four a.m. and she answered the phone and she heard an unfamiliar voice from the administration office of Grant High School. Ruth realized that Abigail was in "trouble" again at the public school that she now attended. Ruth had to get the "fuck up" and shower and "shake off" the hangover; and before she showered, she vomited in the toilet and walked to the sink and splashed water on her face; and she could barely stand and she said something like "Why did you leave me, you bastard!" and the bathroom door opened wider, but Ruth didn't have time to think about this "weird shit" happening. Now in the shower, her head pounded and her back was stiff. She felt dizzy and wasn't in any "condition" to speak to any "responsible" person, but she had to. And as Ruth washed her body, she wondered what Abigail could have done since "this was the second time" that would prompt one of the administrators to call her. "She never used to get into trouble," Ruth thought as she stepped from the shower and dried her body and private area with a large blue towel.

Forty-five minutes later, Ruth drove to the public high school and mistakenly parked in a reserved parking space and she walked through an empty hallway and found the administration office that smelled like Pine-Sol and mothballs. She instantly noticed her daughter, Abigail, brooding on a wooden bench by the door. Ruth glared at her daughter, but before she could "bitch" at her, a Chinese administrator ushered Ruth Stevens into the principal's office and then Ruth met with the vice principal and then Ruth finally met with the high school counselor, Norm Jacobs, whom she never met before, but since it was Abigail's second time in trouble at school, Ruth had to "talk" to Norm. He was a calm man, in his mid-forties, who had the same hair cut since he was a teenager; and he usually "brown bagged" his lunch to work five days a week and he usually wore thick argyle sweaters, even during the summer months.

Ruth sat in a chair and listened to Norm read something "offensive" that Abigail had written in a "blue test booklet" in English Class, for a midterm; and then Ruth nervously began to fidget with her wedding ring.

"As you know, there was a recent death in the family," Ruth said. Her voice was soft and barely audible and she averted eye contact with Norm.

"Did Mr. Newmark give Abigail a three day suspension?"

"Yes, yes, he did," Ruth said slightly raising her voice.

"I'll see if I can reduce her suspension to two days," Norm said.

"I think my daughter needs professional help," Ruth said. Her voice was now at a normal level but she still "fidgeted" with her wedding ring and she still averted eye contact with Norm.

"Why would you say that?" Norm asked.

"I just think, I just think she's out of control," Ruth said.

"I know I'm the counselor and I should agree with you, but you should see what some of these students do in these schools nowadays," Norm said and he paused for a moment and finally continued "Well, if you have anymore questions, please give me a call anytime." Norm handed Ruth his business card and she took it and stood up and placed the card carefully in her purse. Norm stood up and they shook hands and she finally looked at Norm.

"You're a nice man," she said.

He smiled and said "Thank you" and she averted eye contact again and left his office and thought about having "another" glass of Scotch before she made dinner for that "little bitch" that waited on the wooden bench in the administration office that smelled like Pine-Sol and mothballs.

And now weeks after the murder of her husband, Ruth usually sat in her home office most of the day drinking Scotch and writing her first novel, *The After Life,* and it was a title that she took from a eulogy that her daughter wrote for her father.

Now Ruth had to raise Abigail alone and Ruth felt lonely and this loneliness followed her everywhere, whether it was in the kitchen, or in the supermarket to buy more Scotch, or at church, where she prayed alone, or at night, in her moonlit bedroom, where she "tossed and turned" in the empty bed.

She was alone at forty-three years old and she prayed repeatedly not to be alone anymore and then fate "temporarily" intervened and Ruth became romantically involved with Norm Jacobs; and this was the high school counselor who "brown bagged" his lunch and had the same hair cut since he was a teenager. Ruth and Norm spent weekends and some weeknights together. Although Ruth enjoyed being with Norm, she could not stop thinking about her dead husband.

During a visit to the mall, on a Saturday afternoon, Ruth and Norm moved through a thick crowd of people and entered an expensive clothing store and Ruth found the most beautiful brown suede jacket and they found her size and Norm helped her put it on. She loved the feeling of the eight hundred dollar brown suede jacket. She started to forget about her "loss" and her "rotten" daughter; and Ruth walked to a mirror in the expensive clothing store and posed in the brown suede jacket and felt "sexy" again and then she discovered something horrific behind her in the mirror.

"I can't do this," Ruth said. She peeled off the jacket and threw it at Norm and stammered from the expensive clothing store.

"Wait, Ruth!" Norm yelled. He quickly hung up the expensive brown suede jacket and followed Ruth into the mall. "Talk to me, Ruth? Is it Abigail?" Norm asked when he caught up to Ruth and he was now partially out of breath.

Ruth stopped and turned and faced her "new" love interest.

The first time Abigail got suspended from Grant High School, she was considered a "loner" and she was unable to "fit in" at the public school, in Santa Monica. She was used to the "white culture" at St. Susan Catholic High School, located in the yuppie neighborhoods of Brentwood.

Now at Grant High School, Abigail was "lost" in a culture of urban diversity. She didn't "fit in" with the white girls who "tried out for the drill team" and dated black guys from the basketball team. And Abigail didn't "fit in" with the Hispanic girls who stenciled their eyebrows and smoked pot in the school bathroom, and she didn't "fit in" with the black girls who wore weaves and pierced their "super "long fingernails with diamond studs. And these female "cliques" disliked everything about Abigail, including her long blond hair, which they assumed were hair extensions. They hated her blue eyes which they thought were colored contact lenses and the "female cliques" believed that her "ass was too perfect" and her chest "way too big" for her "skinny ass" frame. And the "female cliques" believed that she had a bad attitude and so a group of Hispanic girls decided to unleash Patty Sanchez, on "the white bitch." Patty was the most feared girl, at Grant High School; Patty had a large obese body and patches of ripe acne on her face. So one morning when Abigail was trying to leave the girl's bathroom Patty "bumped into her."

"What the fuck!" Abigail said. Yet surprisingly, Abigail was not intimidated.

"What's up, bitch!" Patty said. She raised her flabby arms.

Abigail instantly scratched Patty's face and Patty instinctively punched her in the shoulder and a "white" male teacher rushed inside the girl's bathroom and broke up the fight, which lasted nearly forty-five seconds, and the "white bitch" survived the fisticuffs with Patty Sanchez. There was talk of a "rematch" between Abigail and Patty but it never occurred; however after the forty-five second confrontation, the "white teacher" walked Abigail and Patty to the administration office where they were both suspended for two days.

And that was the first time that Abigail was suspended from Grant High School. However the night before the "bathroom scrap," Abigail was arguing with her mother, in the kitchen, and the arguing was constant since the night of her father's murder.

CHAPTER 2

Two days after the murder of Francis Stevens, Abigail wrote her father's eulogy and it wasn't easy since she didn't know what to write; and all she knew was that she had "lost" her best friend; so she wrote what she felt about life and it was only three lines that dealt with different parts of life. And after she wrote the short eulogy, she tried to sleep and she tossed and turned in her bed the night before the funeral; and then the unfortunate day arrived; and Abigail stood in front of a podium, at the Westwood Cemetery. Abigail wore a black dress and her hair was in a ponytail. She held the handwritten eulogy in her shaking hand. She averted eye contact from the thick crowd that gathered under a canopy tent. She thanked everyone for coming and she mentioned her father and how great he was and how loving he was and then she read her handwritten eulogy.

> *"Birth and death are like a puzzle. What actually comes first? Who really knows? Every moment, every part of life feels out of order; but, in the end, life and death come together, within the after life."*

Relatives and friends were intrigued by the short eulogy and some of them thought Abigail may have "ripped it off" from a famous poem, yet, nobody knew which poem she could have "taken" it from, but nothing mattered to Ruth and Abigail at that moment. They were overcome with grief, as they stared at the coffin that lowered Francis Stevens in the ground. Ruth felt someone "touch" her shoulder and she turned but nobody was directly behind her. She was slightly puzzled. She turned around and focused on the coffin that contained her dead husband; and among the growing afternoon shadows, Abigail remembered the night when she was studying for a midterm on "life and death" at St. Susan Catholic High School, in Brentwood. Ruth entered her bedroom pale and distraught and said frantically "It's Francis, he's gone!' Those words continued to echo through Abigail's mind as her father lay in a casket.

So after the funeral, relatives and neighbors gathered at Ruth's house and Ruth was cooking in the kitchen, preparing small appetizers she bought from Costco; and her mother, Louise, leaned against the counter drinking a soda while watching Ruth scurry from the refrigerator with a plate of appetizers.

Ruth was frantic at that moment. All she "really" knew that her husband was gone and she had to feed her guests inside her house, as the media celebrated her misfortune by waiting halfway down the street hoping to film some "unfolding" debacle on the front lawn so they could report it on the ten and eleven o' clock news.

"Abigail tells me you need help," her mother said. She continued to drink her soda.

"Yes, she's right. Why don't you start by taking out the appetizers from the oven."

"That's not what I was talking about," Louise said.

"I'll do it!" Ruth put on a green pot holder and took out the burnt appetizers from the oven. "Now look at these! What am I going to do with these?" Ruth slammed the baking tray on the counter and the relatives and other guests in the living room were suddenly quiet.

"Why don't you give them to the media people parked down the street?" Louise asked and resumed drinking her soda.

"I'm glad you think this is a joke," Ruth said. She tossed the green pot holder in the sink and walked into her bedroom and slammed the door. Louise calmly followed Ruth into her bedroom and closed the door behind her. Ruth was fidgeting with her wedding ring, in front of the mirror above the dresser.

"You're not going to get rid of me that easy," Louise said.

"I can't deal with this now!"

"I'm not the enemy, Ruth."

"My fuckin' husband was just murdered! Excuse me if I'm a little impatient here!"

Their attention was quickly diverted to Abigail who stood in the doorway and she finally said "Uncle Albert wants to know where his decaffeinated coffee is that he asked for nearly a half hour ago."

"Don't you know how to knock?" Ruth snapped.

"I'll be right there, honey," Louise intervened. "Just give us a second." Abigail closed the bedroom door and Louise focused on her daughter and said "Jesus, Ruth, you have to get a hold of yourself. You're going to scare Abigail right out of this house."

"Is that a threat?"

"I'll be in the kitchen making decaffeinated coffee," Louise said, calmly. She left the room and closed the door and Ruth resumed playing with her wedding ring. She was still fuming when an instant chill filled the room. She rubbed her arms. The hardwood floor creaked in the corner of the room. Ruth definitely felt a presence. She turned but didn't see anyone and she quickly left the room and the floor stopped creaking.

An hour later, darkness filled the sky as a few guests still lingered in the living room and the stereo played soft jazz music that nobody really liked and Abigail talked to her best friends, Barbara and Janey. All three of them were considered the "gossip queens" at St. Susan Catholic High School. They were the inseparable "chatterboxes" who constantly discussed the latest trendy jeans and shirts and shoes and makeup; and they would excitedly discuss the hottest "movie studs" who had names like Brad and Zach and Leonardo and on and on. Within the gossip queens, Janey Wilcox was the tall stringy blond who usually had a "glazed" look in her eyes. She was usually quieter and more reserved than her "counterpart," Barbara Tilson, who was the outspoken short chunky black haired teenager who avoided shaving her legs on a daily basis; and when she wore skirts, Janey and Abigail began to joke with her and all three of them would laugh and they thought about shopping and watching movies and "checking out" guys and they believed they were always going to be young and happy and friends forever; however now near a brown leather couch Barbara and Janey ate burnt appetizers from red plastic plates.

"You need to eat something, girl," Barbara said.

"I'm not hungry," Abigail said.

"Abby, do the police have any more leads?" Janey asked cautiously.

"There's nothing new, yet."

"I knew the guy that did this would be black," Barbara said, confidently.

"How could you stay that!" Janey snapped. She narrowed her eyes as if she was Chinese.

"Oh, come off it, "Barbara said. "My uncle owns a jewelry store downtown and he was robbed three times in one year. And guess by whom? They were all black. Every single one of them."

"That's just a coincidence," Janey snapped back at her friend. She wanted to be a momentary representative for the black race, but she remembered hearing her mother's "little comments" about the attitude from the black cashier in the supermarket and she remembered hearing her father's response when they got home. "What do you expect!" And Janey would continue to hear the "little comments" about black people throughout the years from her mother and father. Janey didn't want to believe those "little comments," yet she realized she never had any black friends nor did she have any black neighbors nor did she associate with any black people. Also she listened to the nightly news while she ate dinner with her parents; and numerous news segments depicted blacks as savages who committed numerous murders and rapes; and now Abigail's father was a victim of one of those murders. Yes "white people" murdered and raped but that wasn't the situation now; so Barbara and Janey continued to argue about who was more racist.

"Could you please stop!" Abigail finally said. "I already have one bitch to deal with tonight." Abigail turned and walked through the thinning crowd of visitors and exited the back of the house and sat on the steps under a circle of yellow porch light and looked beyond the glow of light and remembered when she was five years old and she helped her father rake gold colored leaves on the grass and they began tossing them at each other; and then Abigail thought about when she was seven years old and it was on a cold day. Francis had just taken the "training wheels" off her pink bike, in front of the house. She was about to pedal when she asked "What about my helmet? Mommy always said to ride the bike with a helmet."

Francis peered up and down the wealthy neighborhood and said "This will be our secret, okay?"

"Okay, daddy," Abigail said. She eventually pedaled and rode the pink bike halfway down the neighborhood.

And now Abigail was seventeen and her father was gone and she was sitting on the steps of the back porch thinking about the memories of her father when her grandmother appeared on the back patio and said "There you are, I was looking all over for you. What are you doing out here?" She sat down next to her granddaughter.

"My friends are acting like jerks," Abigail said.

"Well, that happens," Louise said. She patted Abigail's leg.

"Grandma, do you think the police will find the person that murdered my father?"

The question intimidated Louise since she didn't expect to hear *that* question from her granddaughter. Louise wanted to be optimistic and believe that there was a "probable" chance the suspect would be arrested soon. "I'm sure they'll find him," Louise quickly answered.

"When they do I want to look him in the eyes."

"Let's go inside, Abby." Louise stood and gripped the railing and slowly entered the house.

Yet Abigail continued to sit on the back porch and her anger grew; and this anger felt different. It burned and it stung and it left a "mark" inside of her. She wanted blood. She had an intense feeling of revenge for the black perpetrator.

And an hour later, the remaining family members and friends left the house and Ruth stood outside by her mother's Jaguar, as Louise sat in the driver's seat applying lipstick for some strange reason while peering into the lit vanity mirror in the visor. She finally put the lipstick away and put up the visor and focused on her daughter.

"What were you talking to Abigail about in the backyard?" Ruth asked, suspiciously.

"Oh, nothing, really," Louise said, nonchalantly. "Why do you ask?"

"Just wondering," Ruth said. She became very suspicious since the murder. Ruth kissed her mother on the cheek and told her that she would call her in a few days.

And down the street, Abigail was about to say "goodbye" to Barbara and Janey who were arguing about using the navigation device to find their houses, even though they lived less than two miles away.

"I just want to see how it works," Barbara said, angrily.

"Well, it's my Land Rover," Janey responded. She was determined to protect her sixty-thousand dollar vehicle that her parents purchased for her as an "early graduation gift."

They bought it from a dealership in Santa Monica; and the moment after they arrived, a smiling Middle Eastern salesman approached. He wore tight khaki pants, a tight blue button-up shirt and smelled like "horrible cologne" and he spoke quickly in a thick accent hoping that these "rich white folks" wouldn't hear certain necessary information they needed to know when purchasing the vehicle.

Abigail finally hugged Barbara and Janey and went inside the house and swept the hardwood floor as Ruth wiped the dining room table and tossed plastic plates and half-eaten food into an overstuffed black trash bag. Ruth walked across the hardwood floor to turn off the stereo and her heels clicked loudly on the hardwood floor and she had something on her mind and faced her daughter and said "Abby, I need you to start going to a public school and I need you to get a job after school."

Abigail couldn't believe what she just heard and responded "That's not fair. I have a lot of friends there, and why do I have to get a job? Grandma will help us with money. I know she will."

And those horrible words "Grandma will help us with money" churned in Ruth's head. "There's no way in hell that anyone would help us," Ruth thought. Ironically Ruth didn't need any financial "assistance" considering Francis had a "large" life insurance policy and numerous stocks to "cash in" and Ruth had a two year severance package from her "layoff" at Knopf and Global, the auditing firm, in Beverly Hills.

"Listen, Abby. We don't take handouts. I need you to do this for me. We all need to sacrifice in this situation." Ruth didn't expect her daughter to "roll over" but Ruth was now the "leader" of the household and her words were considered "concrete."

Abigail dropped the broom and stammered to her bedroom and slammed the door. Ruth had to "handle" this situation. She marched into Abigail's bedroom and tightly gripped her daughter's chin and said "There's no slamming doors in this house, you hear me? If you want to go live with Barbara or Janey, that's fine by me!"

Ruth quickly left her daughter's bedroom and softly closed the door and resumed cleaning the living room while Abigail sat on her bed and fought the tears. She finally stood and opened a desk drawer and discovered her "personal" razor and she lifted her shirt and slid the razor across her stomach three times. The "joyful" pain numbed her body and she dropped the razor on the fourth cut and lay on her bed, in a "daze," and stared at the yellow circles of ceiling light above her, and her anger dissipated for the moment although Abigail knew life had changed forever and she knew that her mother was and will always be a "spiteful cunt." Or that's what she thought as she continued to lay on her bed gazing into the circles of yellow ceiling light.

CHAPTER 3

Life was never easy for Tyrone Williams. He was a black man who grew up poor, in South L.A., from the mid-1970s. His parents "Big" Roy and LaRhonda Williams moved from Mississippi to South L.A. It was an area once "dotted" with hope. A place "rooted" with hopeful opportunity for "Southern Blacks" until South L.A. became a treasure trove for murder, rapes, high unemployment, along with having numerous societal issues. Tyrone breathed the world of South L.A., from Slauson to Hoover Street, near the 110 Freeway, North and South. He witnessed the area unfold from "not so great" to fuckin' horrible. He was twenty-seven when he was in the L.A. Riots, which was ominously celebrated on every TV network.

Tyrone became a part of this bleak and dreadful environment and the only time he left South L.A. was to work at Eric's Auto Garage, in West L.A., where he earned nineteen dollars per hour as a mechanic doing oil changes and rotating tires. Tyrone managed to learn a trade after his first stint in prison for "breaking and entering" and "receiving stolen property" at twenty years old; and a few years later, he met his soon-to-be wife, Doris Chestnut, at King's Laundromat. They rented an apartment over a liquor store where they heard screaming and "sporadic" gun fire. It seemed like on Monday, Wednesday, Friday, and Sunday nights were "saved" for brutal and bloody streets fights. And on Tuesday, Thursday, and Saturday nights were saved for gunshots; and it was the "stray bullets" that blew out windows and ripped plaster apart and ended lives.

A few years after getting married, Doris got pregnant and they moved to a small white stucco house, on Prairie Ave., in South L.A. She gave birth to Jamal and a few months later Tyrone was sent back to prison for violating parole and for "assault and battery." One day during a visit from Doris and his son, Jamal, Tyrone realized that he had to get his "shit straight" since another felony could equal "life" in prison. Tyrone was eventually released from prison and Doris got pregnant and gave birth to Keisha. Tyrone tried to "love" his kids the best that he could, but he was constantly consumed by anger; and he was angry for growing up poor and for being a high school dropout; and sometimes Tyrone was angry for being black. He believed at a very young age that "whites" received the "good breaks" in life. "I hate those motherfuckin' white folks," he thought one day while walking to the market and he decided long ago, when his father, "Big" Roy Williams, used to gamble in his house with other ex-cons, that he had a "long fight" in life. So he believed that he needed to hate to survive and now he needed to teach his family that life would be difficult "'cause they were black" and then one day his wife began to die slowly of ovarian cancer.

Tyrone watched his wife evaporate into a barely breathing corpse who spoke incomprehensibly "toward the end" in a "dirty ass" bed at the L.A. County Hospital and her lips were chapped and her eyes bulged from her gaunt face. She was dying and Tyrone knew "death" was near; and Tyrone sat alone one night, in the hospital room and made various promises to Doris and one of the promises was to take care of the kids. After the inevitable death in a dirty hospital bed, Tyrone rode the elevator to the lobby and believed he was receiving a punishment from God, and he completely believed God disliked him. So after his wife's death, Tyrone became angrier. He yelled at Keisha for not finishing the laundry, and he punched Jamal for doing a "half ass" job mowing the grass and he would scream at both of them for not having dinner ready when he came home from work. And the anger dominated Tyrone one evening after receiving a phone call from the administration at Jamal's high school and stating that he "was absent" from school and when Jamal came home Tyrone grabbed Jamal by the throat and slammed him against a wall; and on another evening, Tyrone screamed at Keisha for not cleaning her room "enough." Tyrone became a "ticking" time bomb and during the years of physical and verbal abuse, Jamal began to believe his father "that life would be miserable" because he was black; and he also believed that because he was black that he would also live a poor and angry and frustrated life.

However Keisha believed differently. She knew she was "not" a victim of her circumstances. Keisha was an intellect, but she had to hide it from her parents like some dirty secret. In middle school and in high school, she read about the philosophy of Henry David Thoreau, Ralph Waldo Emerson and read the stories of Booker T. Washington and Harriet Beecher Stowe and Harriet Tubman and Keisha knew she was "different" than her ignorant family. She believed that she was "special" and that God was not punishing her for being black or for being a woman. Yet she discovered that her mother had the same "negative" attitude as her father.

"Girl, don't be gettin' those crazy ass ideas that you goin' to college, 'cause nobody in this family ever did, and there ain't no place for you in politics," Doris said one afternoon after Keisha shared her dreams to her mother; but after that moment, Keisha decided to keep her "dreams and goals" a secret from her family.

Tyrone quickly stripped off his blood stained clothes in his musty and moldy bathroom and stuffed them inside a blue trash bag on the dirty floor. He now stood naked in front of the mirror and studied his image and hoped this moment was a nightmare and he would instantly wake up, but this moment was not a nightmare. He looked at the blue trash bag that was filled with his blood stained clothes.

The moment was real.

And Tyrone carefully opened the bathroom door in the hallway and looked around and knew that Jamal and Keisha were somewhere in the small house and he quickly grabbed the blue trash bag filled with blood stained clothes and dashed inside his bedroom and softly closed the door hoping nobody would see "his black ass."

He tossed the blue trash bag into his closet and began to put on "clean" clothes when a knock on the door punctuated the silence.

"Yeah, whatcha want?" Tyrone asked.

"It's me, daddy. Dinner's ready," Keisha said behind the closed bedroom door.

"I'll be right there," Tyrone said. His heart "raced" for a moment as he peered in the small round mirror that hung haphazardly above the dresser and listened to his daughter back away from the door. He was about to leave when he discovered a moving shadow on the wall behind him as he peered in the mirror. Tyrone froze for a moment. All he could do at that very moment was blink his eyes and he felt a sudden "chill" in the room and the floorboards creaked near his bed. "Somebody is definitely in this motherfuckin' room" he thought and he quickly left the bedroom.

Tyrone entered the kitchen and sat at the table and ate fried chicken, mashed potatoes and vegetables buried in gravy with Jamal and Keisha and after a few minutes of silence he said "Did you talk to that supervisor today at the market, like I told you to do?"

Jamal cleared his throat and wiped his mouth and said

arrogantly "Nah, I didn't."

"What do you mean 'nah'? You know how hard it is for a black man to get a job nowadays? Just 'cause we have one of us in the White House doesn't mean he's gonna do shit for us."

"I ain't gonna get no respect pushin' carts. I got other plans," Jamal said.

"Yeah, like what? What you think you gonna do?"

"I'm gonna be a rapper."

"Shit, Jamal. You know what a black man is without a job? He's a bum. He ain't like them white folks that can 'cruise' through life on a trust fund and shit. We gotta work twice as hard, ya' hear me?" Tyrone said. He tried to be patient with his son but he quickly "lost" his patience and grabbed his son's plate of half eaten food and said "You can eat later. You make me sick."

Jamal didn't move. And why should he? He was tired of his father's brutality.

"What, you got something to say, boy?" Tyrone yelled and Jamal felt his father's anger and he knew that he couldn't over power his father. Tyrone was six feet two inches tall and nearly two hundred and twenty-five pounds of prison muscle. Jamal was five feet ten inches tall and barely one hundred and eighty pounds.

"Daddy, let him eat," Keisha said desperately.

"Girl, don't you be startin' with me," Tyrone said to his daughter. "I don't have time for your mess." Tyrone turned and glared at his son and asked "So what's it gonna be?"

Jamal finally stood and left the kitchen and Tyrone resumed eating as if nothing happened. Keisha looked at her father strangely and noticed that he was much angrier tonight and that he was more aggressive; and then she noticed his shaking hands. "My father is a monster," she thought. Yet she wanted to ask this "monster" some questions although she knew it would be "bad timing" but she didn't care.

"Daddy, how come you got home so late tonight?"

"I had to drop off a friend from work."

"Who did you have to drop off?"

"Girl, stop with the questions and clean up the kitchen. I'm tired of your mess tonight," Tyrone said. He continued to eat his fried chicken.

Keisha wasn't done with her questions. She wanted to know about his shaking hands and then she noticed the "cuts" on his hands. She cleaned the kitchen table before she was next "in line" for her father's wrath. Yet she could not stop looking at her father's shaking hands that had cuts on them.

After Tyrone finished dinner, he sat on his green couch and watched TV; yet he changed the stations until he saw the "top" new story which was the "murder of the white surgeon."

His hands shook more.

He pressed a button on the remote a few times and changed the station to a comedy sitcom with a happy black family who argued about why a dog was being kept in the closet by the "kid" sister and the audience laughed on cue and Tyrone looked at his shaking hands with the cuts on them when Keisha walked by. He told her to sit down. "Maybe this was a trick," she thought. "Maybe he would talk to me and then smack me."

She nervously sat down next to her father and the adjacent circle of yellow lamp light highlighted her beautiful dark skin.

"I didn't mean to snap at you at supper," Tyrone said. "I just miss your momma' and you remind me of her, that's all."

"I know, daddy," Keisha said. She felt uncomfortable next to her father who during that moment wanted to say that he loved her and maybe, just maybe, he wanted to apologize for being an "asshole" father but he didn't say any of the things that he "needed" to say and instead he made excuses in his mind for abusing his two kids. Yeah Tyrone had all of the excuses for being a "cocksuckin' father." He reasoned with himself for a moment and then he told Keisha to finish her homework. She left and

Tyrone sat alone near a circle of yellow lamp light and noticed his shaking hands, again.

He had to do something.

He got up from the couch and grabbed the blue stuffed trash bag from his bedroom closet and left the house from the side door and put the blue stuffed trash bag into the trunk of his Buick Regal and drove five minutes from his house and parked in an alley. Tyrone left the car engine on and stepped out of the Buick Regal and looked up and down the dimly lit alley and opened the trunk and pulled the blue trash bag from the trunk and tossed it inside the dumpster and slowly drove from the alley. He stopped at Izzys', a local "black" bar with a few tables and a fucked up pool table in the back and Tyrone sat at the bar and drank one beer. He was not much of a beer drinker; however tonight he needed one. He looked at his shaking hands again, and he stuffed one of his shaking hands into his pocket and wrapped his other shaking hand around the beer bottle. He peered around the small place and looked at the black folks talking and drinking and a song by a singer named Marvin played from a "shitty ass" stereo; and then Tyrone thought he may know someone in this place since he came here "quite" often. He paid for the beer and looked at the TV monitor in the far corner of the bar and noticed that a boxing match was on and Tyrone felt better, but he left the place anyway and sat in his car for a moment.

He needed to speak to someone.

He drove to his sister's house, in Inglewood, and knocked on a thick security door and the front door opened behind it and his ten year old nephew, Damon, appeared behind the security door and Tyrone said "Git' your momma."

"She's busy," Damon said.

"Hurry up, it's important," Tyrone said.

Damon left for a moment and closed the front door behind the security door and then the front door opened again and Tyrone's sister, Wanda, appeared. She was tall with thick hips and short hair. She glared at him behind the dirty security door and said "It's all over the fuckin' news. How could you be so stupid?"

"What you think I was gonna do, just stand around and let them do that to us," Tyrone explained.

"Don't come here, again. You scarin' my kids," Wanda said. She slammed the door and Tyrone stared at the security door and he wanted to pound on it and scream "git' your motherfuckin' ass out here, bitch. You dumb motherfuckin' bitch! You call your dumbass my sister." But he didn't say any of that "mess" since that would attract attention.

He drove home and for the next two weeks, Tyrone continued his "daily" business of working and trying to take care of his kids, when one night, he desired something. It was a "desire" he couldn't avoid anymore. Tyrone hoped this "desire" would dissipate.

But it didn't.

And this desire only grew and he couldn't resist this "dirty" temptation any longer. He tried his best to "hold off" but he couldn't. He thought about pulling out the Bible from a cluttered drawer in his bedroom, but he couldn't find the Bible since he really didn't look for it; and one night after dinner, he got into his Buick Regal and drove into the streets of South L.A. and noticed the homeless men who drank in front of the corner liquor stores as he dove on Crenshaw Blvd. He searched for his *desire*. He knew he would find "it" since he found "it" many times before. He drove slowly, searching like a hungry predator on Crenshaw Blvd, at night.

And then he found "it" on the sidewalk; and "it" was a black prostitute. And this prostitute was named Candy. Tyrone recognized her from over two weeks ago when he was in the parking lot of a liquor store waiting for his brother, Sal.

Now he drove to the curb and parked and Candy stopped and he lowered his passenger window and "flashed" his smile.

He mentioned that he saw her before and Candy kneeled by his Buick Regal. She smiled and was "ready for business" after a brief session of negotiation and Candy finally got in the car and Tyrone drove her to a motel.

He sensed her nervousness.

As they neared a motel, a song by a singer named Ray played on the radio and Candy thought. "I love this song. I really love this motherfuckin' song."

Now Candy was more nervous than she could ever remember since she started "selling" her body years ago; and now she couldn't "shake" this certain feeling she had. They arrived at the motel, around ten twenty-seven p.m., a few blocks from the 110 Freeway, North and South. Somehow Tyrone convinced Candy to take his money and rent a room while he waited in the hallway in the back. He mentioned that his ex-girlfriend would "check up on his ass" or whatever the "fuck" he said but Candy didn't care. She got paid for her services. She was like a "maid" sent to clean a house who didn't give a "motherfuckin' shit" what she found in the drawers.

Candy grabbed Tyrone's money and rented a room and she met Tyrone in the dimly lit hallway in the back and they walked up an old musty smelling staircase to the room that Candy rented and entered room two-one-seven and Tyrone turned on the lamp, and the circle of yellow light created shadows on the white cracked walls and cheap paintings, and the carpet had cigarette burns and splotches of dried blood.

A few minutes later, Candy slowly undressed by the window and she watched Tyrone as he sat on the edge of the bed and faced the door. She realized that his mood had "severely" changed and the smile he "flashed" twenty minutes ago in his Buick Regal was now gone, and he was quiet until he finally said "I never told anyone this before. My wife, two years ago, she died in a hospital. She had cancer and nobody cared about her. They let her die like some animal out in the desert. And my brother died two weeks ago, at a different hospital; and nobody cared about him either."

Candy glanced at her watch and had to "hurry this shit up" and she approached Tyrone and he stood and faced her and she unbuckled his belt and she said "You know, my auntie died in a hospital. They let her die on the lobby floor and nobody did nothin' about it, 'cause she didn't have no insurance." She pulled off Tyrone's shirt and said "Doesn't that feel better?"

And then it happened.

Tyrone's rage instantly "took" over and he pushed Candy on the bed and he lied on top of her and covered her mouth. Her eyes widened and she struggled under Tyrone's large powerful body and she bit his hand; and he felt the pain and the blood oozed from the cut on his palm and he grabbed her head and "snapped" her neck. Her body went limp and she died with her eyes open within a circle of yellow lamp light.

A minute later after Tyrone realized what happened and what he just did, he stood and walked calmly to the bathroom and grabbed a washcloth and wiped his fingerprints from every place he touched, including the front door knob; and before he left the room, he glanced at Candy's lifeless body on the bed, within a circle of yellow lamp light. Tyrone calmly closed the door with the washcloth and pocketed it and calmly entered the hallway and approached the musty smelling stairway when he sensed a presence behind him and it was the same presence that he felt in his bedroom, two weeks earlier; and then he turned and noticed a moving shadow on the yellow painted wall. He turned and hurried down the narrow staircase and Tyrone left the motel through the dimly lit hallway in the back and away from the broken security cameras. He walked around the motel and dropped the washcloth in the gutter under the sidewalk, which was near his Buick Regal and he got in his car and drove toward his house.

He finally did it!

He killed.

He murdered.

And Tyrone felt a sense of excitement as if he won a trophy for being the fastest runner, or the world's strongest man. Tyrone felt like a different person when he murdered. He had an uncontrollable anger when he murdered. And how on Earth could he blame himself for murdering? He was not mentally responsible or that's what he believed. He already pictured himself one day during a prison interview on TV saying "Shit, how could you blame my ass? It wasn't me. I didn't do nothin'."

Tyrone continued to drive in his Regal and he felt that "chill" again and he sensed the presence again. He adjusted the rear view mirror and peered in the backseat, but nobody was there.

A few weeks before Tyrone murdered Candy on the bed in a motel room, Tyrone had dealt with the "death" of his brother, Sal Williams. He was a fifty-eight year old former auto mechanic who went on permanent disability. He used to work with his brother, Tyrone, at Eric's Auto Garage, in West L.A. and Sal was "much" different than his younger brother. Sal was calm and patient and he was always "well liked" at the auto garage. However Sal was in ill health and underwent a surgery which he died from; and the night he died, Tyrone was lying shirtless on his bed in his dark bedroom and he was staring at the ceiling, listening to the distant sounds of gun shots and police helicopters outside. His bedroom door creaked open and Tyrone noticed a "figure" in his room and he reached under the bed for something and he thought "someone was coming for me."

"Who's there!" He screamed and finally noticed his daughter Keisha as she stepped into a shaft of moonlight and Tyrone noticed she was crying and he asked "What are you doin' in here, girl? Why aren't you in bed?"

"How come you didn't tell us about Uncle Sal?" Keisha asked while wiping her eyes.

"Who told you?"

"Auntie Wanda told us," Keisha said.

Tyrone wasn't ready to explain his brother's death to his seventeen year old daughter or at least not right now. He was much too distraught and so he said "We'll talk tomorrow."

"It's not fair, daddy," Keisha said, as she wiped her eyes again. "He was fine last week. Was he sick?"

Her father never explained to his daughter that his brother had lung cancer, instead he quickly reminded her that life was unfair and said "people are gonna take advantage of you 'cause you're black. Just git' that in your mind."

Keisha knew she wouldn't get any "real" answers; and so she finally said "goodnight" and left the bedroom and tried to sleep but she couldn't stop thinking about what her father just told her about how "people are gonna take advantage of you 'cause you're black."

CHAPTER 4

Francis Stevens was naked and tied to four wooden stakes on the floor of a lit cave and the source of the light came from a fire pit; and Francis squirmed as he saw four large "human-sized" crabs which slowly emerged from the dark shadows of the cave and moved slowly toward him and they looked like they were smiling, as if they were about to eat the chest surgeon "alive." Francis squirmed and yanked at the rope the best that he could and quickly realized that he had been tied and naked in this cave before with the crabs. They never harmed him in the past, but now the four crabs started to pinch at Francis' white skin and he squirmed in pain and blood oozed from the cuts where they pinched him and he opened his mouth to scream but nothing came out and the only noises that were heard came from the "human-sized" crabs; and then Francis awoke in his bed and his shirt was damp from perspiration.

It was six forty-seven a.m. and he noticed that Ruth was not in bed. Francis was breathing hard as he moved the thick comforter from his thin body and emerged from his bedroom; and he was clearly unaware that he had only ten more days to live.

Ruth sat behind her desk in the home office as she was typing her novel that she had originally started in college, over twenty years ago, when she was a junior in college, but her parents wanted her to be an accounting major instead of being an English major so she "stopped writing" and changed majors; and now she looked up from her laptop and noticed her husband in the threshold of the doorway and he looked pale and sweaty and Ruth asked "Are you okay?"

"I think so. You want to take a walk?"

Francis and Ruth walked through the wealthy neighborhood, on Fourth Street, in Santa Monica. February leaves crunched under their footsteps and their morning walks became a routine since they first moved in the house from a small shitty apartment, in West L.A., over eighteen years ago.

"I had that dream, again," Francis said.

"You're kidding," Ruth said.

"I wish I was."

"Don't you think you should see someone about this?"

"What? Talk to a shrink? You know how I feel about them." Francis said.

"Regardless of what you think, Francis, they're not all screwed up people that overcharge to hear your problems," Ruth said. She wanted to smile. She knew her husband despised therapists because he believed problems needed to be solved by the person. "Don't you think you should find out what's going on with these dreams?" Ruth asked. "Maybe they mean something."

"Ruth," Francis said. "I want you to know that you could do anything in life. Don't let anyone tell you that you can't."

"Well, thank you, Dr. Stevens. But where did that come from?" Ruth asked.

"It's just something I wanted to tell you," he said. Francis also wanted to tell her more about his dreams and what he thought they "really" meant; and maybe, just maybe, his dreams of the four "inhuman" crabs were symbolic for something that was about to happen to him, but he didn't want to worry his wife; and so he smiled and they continued to walk within the morning sunlight; and he wanted to enjoy the few "calm" moments with his wife before they began arguing about their daughter.

And so an hour later, during breakfast, Ruth and Francis discussed going to Hawaii after Abigail's high school graduation and Ruth glanced at her watch and asked "Does that girl have any idea how late she is for school?"

Abigail finally entered the dining room half-asleep dressed in her Catholic School uniform. Her hair was still wet from the shower and she sat down and began eating.

"You have to pray first! How many times do I have to tell you this!" Ruth snapped.

"A million," Abigail said, jokingly, but her mother became angrier.

"Look, Ruth, she prays all day in school. How about we give her a reprieve?" Francis said.

"Then you take her!" Ruth said. She marched into her bedroom and slammed the door and Francis and Abigail sat at the dining room table and laughed. Francis wondered how Ruth's mood could alter so quickly and how she could "snap" at her daughter over the "pettiest shit." "Maybe it was her period," Francis thought. Or maybe she needed medication. Could Ruth suffer from a mood disorder? Francis wanted to tell his wife about possibly taking pills and talking to a therapist but he remembered that he disliked "shrinks" and he thought of saying "Listen, you're driving me fuckin' nuts," but he would regret talking to his wife that way.

Francis finished breakfast and brushed his teeth in the bathroom and Ruth stammered inside and Francis sensed an argument. She pointed a finger at him and a large blue vein pulsed in her neck and she said "You know it would be nice if you backed me up once in a while."

"I'm just saying she prays all day. Is that so bad?"

"Well maybe you should be on my side once in a while."

"I know you want an argument, Ruth, but you're not going to get it. Have a good day," he said and kissed her on the cheek.

Francis drove Abigail to St. Susan Catholic High School, in Brentwood; and on the way, Abigail sat in the passenger seat and stared out of the window and asked "You think mom is jealous of us?"

"Of course, not," Francis smiled. "She loves us both very much."

"Are you sure?"

"Am I sure? What kind of question is that? I remember the first time I met your mother."

"Dad, please. You've told me that story a million times. You met her in a basement."

"Actually, it was in a bathroom at a graduation party, in Pasadena. I was twenty-five, and in my third year in medical school." Francis looked at his daughter as she continued to brood in the passenger seat. Francis veered his white Mercedes around a dozen high-end vehicles that were parked in front of St. Susan. He finally parked his white Mercedes and said "You're going to have to play nice with mom. I know it's not always easy."

"You're always protecting her," Abigail said. She grabbed her backpack and was about to leave.

"Don't worry so much, Abby. That's how you get wrinkles," Francis said, smiling.

Abigail finally smiled and Francis kissed her on the forehead and she left the car and Francis watched her daughter mingle with the other teenage girls who also wore the school uniform and he finally drove away and twenty minutes later, Francis arrived at the parking structure, at the Crenshaw District Hospital, and parked and emerged from his white Mercedes and put on his suit jacket and walked through the parking structure and the clicking of his shoes echoed throughout the area. He descended the stairway which smelled like urine and he remembered the "crab people" and then he thought of his sick patients and filling out paper work and ordering X-rays as he kicked crumpled fast food wrappers and Styrofoam cups out of his way on the stairway.

Francis entered the hospital and walked across the heavily waxed floor and thought of the "crab people" again and then he heard the loud comments from the mostly uneducated "ethnic" patients who sat in the lobby chairs or leaned against the government-painted walls waiting to be seen by a physician; and then Francis entered the elevator and stood with sick patients and he could smell the odor from their clothes and from their bodies and Francis got out of the elevator and entered the cardiology department, on the second floor, and he reviewed stacks of paperwork from various patients; and at four fifteen p.m., Sal Williams sat across from Francis in his office and Sal was nervous; and after a few moments, Francis finally said "Sal, I have to be straight with you. I looked at your X-rays and your blood tests." Francis waited another moment and finally said "You have lung cancer."

Sal averted the surgeon's glance and he couldn't think clearly and yes, it was true, Sal did have difficulty breathing, but he believed he couldn't be that sick and Sal was officially devastated as he instantly thought of "chemo" sessions and then Sal became very depressed and asked "Can you talk to my brother?"

Francis said "sure" and Sal and Francis walked through the chaotic lobby and Francis noticed Sal's brother, Tyrone Williams, who was leaning against a wall glaring at various people who walked by and Sal left and sat down on a chair across from the lobby; and Francis instantly sensed an "extreme" negative vibe from Tyrone. Francis introduced himself and Tyrone wouldn't shake his hand and Francis finally said "Your brother has a large tumor in his chest, and it's restricting his blood flow to his heart. That's why he's having difficulty breathing."

"So whatcha you wanna do, operate on him?"

"Yes and I'm hoping to do it soon."

"You ain't just sayin' that 'cause you wanna take advantage of him?"

"Are you kidding?" Francis asked. "Your brother is very sick. Do you understand what I am telling you? If he doesn't have this operation he could die."

"He could die anyway, right!"

"Why don't you let him make that decision?" Francis asked. His face was red from frustration and he believed "this asshole" had an answer for everything. Francis turned and walked through the lobby. Tyrone glared at the white surgeon and envisioned beating the "hell" out of Francis and watching him lay motionless on the ground. Tyrone snapped from his morbid fantasy and tried to "control" his rage. He knew that another felony would put his "black ass" in prison possibly for life.

Twenty minutes later, Tyrone drove Sal from the hospital in his Buick Regal and shadows began to emerge on the street and sunlight glinted on the partially cracked windshield. Tyrone thought that his brother might "really" be sick but he couldn't trust the "white surgeon" and he feared that all doctors "secretly" desired to "kill" his family as the black doctors allowed his wife to die slowly from ovarian cancer; or so he believed.

"All these motherfuckers were bad" he thought; and then he thought about his wife dying in a hospital bed nearly two years ago, as the ovarian cancer "ate her up." Tyrone parked his Regal, at Crown Liquor, on Figueroa and Ninety-Sixth Street and there was trash everywhere and the sun continued to lower in South L.A. and Tyrone waited in the car while Sal entered Crown Liquor and bought a carton of Kools and a six pack of beer or maybe some malt liquor. Tyrone should have stopped his brother from buying cigarettes; yet as long as Tyrone could remember, Sal smoked two packs per day for over three decades. And then Tyrone thought again "there ain't nothin' wrong wit' my motherfuckin' brother" and then he thought about the "dumb white ass" surgeon who was trying to take advantage of his brother and the horrible negative thoughts filled his mind as he continued to wait for his brother in his Buick Regal; and Tyrone listened to a song by a singer whose first name was James and that's when he saw Candy, the black prostitute, for the first time; and she was wearing pink knee-high boots and Tyrone craned his neck to watch her thick thighs framed within her worn black spandex pants. She stopped and noticed Tyrone's "crazed" but friendly look and she "decided" to approach the "brutha'" who sat in the Buick Regal. Tyrone "flashed" his smile and studied her pierced belly button that was embedded in a wave of flab that protruded under her short yellow tube top which constrained her slightly sagging breasts. A thick layer of foundation covered the patches of raw acne on her face. Candy smiled which revealed her front yellow stained teeth that were partially smudged with cheap pink lipstick. Tyrone opened his car door and wanted her. Tyrone felt her sexiness and he desired sex from prostitutes and he liked rough and violent sex and he stifled his fantasies when he "made love" to his wife when she was alive and breathing, and he saved the violent urges for the black prostitutes who wandered the "fucked up" streets of South L.A.

And after the rough and violent sex that Tyrone liked having with the black prostitutes, he would "snap" their necks or choke them or stab them or gouge their eyes out or beat them with his fists or shoot them with his .38 caliber handgun; and when the black prostitutes could no longer survive one of the various atrocities, Tyrone would dispose of their bodies mostly in alleyways or near the side of freeways. After a few days their bodies would be partially eaten by animals and their skin would be rotting and they would smell like "death" and they would become a lingering corpse among garbage and discarded furniture in South L.A. Tyrone loved the feeling of sex and pulling "bitches" weaves and murdering them and he would never feel guilty about murdering black prostitutes "'cause" he was a different person when he murdered them.

Shit.

Tyrone Williams was sick and crazed and a lunatic and he was someone else as he "fucked" and "murdered" them.

Fuck! Fuck!

Tyrone never came inside of his victims and he did his best not to leave "incriminating evidence" inside or around the lifeless black prostitutes; and his wife and kids and his brother, Sal, never knew about his desires and his secret acts of murder.

Now as Candy approached, Tyrone breathed her sex.

He felt it and he waited for it.

Candy believed that Tyrone was "another horny brutha'" until she "felt" his strange vibe.

Yes Tyrone was addicted to rough sex and murder and Candy was addicted to "cheap sex" and a "quick profit" and both addictions were lethal combinations.

Now Tyrone turned and noticed Sal leaving the liquor store; and so Tyrone closed the driver's side door and watched his brother slowly enter the Buick holding a brown bag filled with beer and a carton of cigarettes and Candy realized that the "deal was off." She didn't need an explanation as she built significant "streets smarts" throughout the years to avoid undercover police and Candy walked away and continued down the street in search of "cheap sex" and a "quick profit."

Sal was completely unaware of Candy's presence as he was out of breath and his lower back hurt and he felt like a fuckin' mess. His mind was on the surgery that he needed. Tyrone started the car and drove through dismal sunlight and heavy shadows on Crenshaw Blvd. After a few minutes, Tyrone veered left around a corner of so and so and then turned left around another street and stopped at the King Mason Apartment Complex. The place was filled with thieves, whores, drug dealers and "gangbangers" and they all knew Sal, the slow moving black man who was just another pathetic figure among other pathetic figures, at the King Mason Apartment Complex. Sal lived in the "heart" of gangland;

and now inside the Regal, Tyrone watched his older brother unbuckle his seat belt and grab his brown bag filled with beer and a carton of cigarettes and Tyrone finally asked "So you gonna do it?'

"Do what?"

"Go through with the surgery, that's what?" Tyrone snapped.

"Like I got any choice?"

"We all got choices," Tyrone said. He wanted to "slap the shit" out of his motherfuckin' brother, but he knew that it wouldn't help anything.

"I have to do it and that's it," Sal said. He slowly got out of the Buick.

Tyrone wanted to know if Sal was going to call his oldest son, Malcolm, who moved to Minnesota with his Cuban wife, Belinda, two years ago. Malcolm decided to "cut ties" with his "lazy shit-bag" father, since he believed his father was nothing more than a lethargic waste who spent his life in cheap apartments, smoking cigarettes and "living off the system." Malcolm was a "sensitive" subject for Sal and so Tyrone decided not to mention his name and Sal said "goodbye" to his younger brother and walked slowly to his upstairs apartment and entered the musty smelling place and locked the door since he didn't want any "motherfuckers" walking in on him; and he sat on the couch and pulled out his six pack of beer and carton of cigarettes and turned on the large cheap screen TV that he purchased from a swap meet and he opened a beer and lit a cigarette; and as he lit the cigarette, he knew that he was going to have a life altering surgery soon, and he "knew" that he could "possibly" never smoke or drink beer again; but "it's what keeps me sane," Sal thought. And then Sal realized that he needed to speak to his oldest son, Malcolm. He frequently spoke with his daughter, Laquiesha, and his youngest son, Derrick. Yet he missed Malcolm probably because he was the only person who "stayed" out of trouble in his family and "did something" with his life. Sal hadn't spoken to him for nearly six months and he remembered that he always argued with his oldest son. They even argued about the color of a car one time. "But that 'shit' was in the past," Sal thought, and after his third cigarette, in twenty-five minutes, Sal slowly arose from the couch and walked across the carpet that was strewn with trash and opened a desk drawer and pulled out a phone number and dialed it on his "cheap ass" home phone; and then the line rang a few times and Sal was about to hang up when he heard a soft male voice on the other line who said "Hello."

"Malcolm, it's your father. How you doing?"

"Dad?" Malcolm asked. "What could I do for you?"

"There's something I have to tell you," Sal said, as that would be the beginning of the last conversation that he would have with his son.

CHAPTER 5

Sal awoke early the morning of his surgery and packed his clothes in his suitcase in his bedroom. And while he was packing and pulling clothes from his drawer, he felt "something" inside one of the drawers and he pulled out a small framed picture of himself when he was twenty-one years old sitting on a bench with a beautiful thin black woman; and this beautiful thin black woman was also twenty-one years old and she had a head full of thick brunette curls that framed her youthful face. Her name was Jeanette Turner and Sal had met her in 1975 while he was in Kansas, after returning from the "conflict" in Vietnam. And Sal fell in love with her and convinced Jeanette into moving to Los Angeles where the rest of his family was located and after a few years they eventually had three children but they never married. Jeanette raised her children, Derrick, Laquiesha and Malcolm for over ten years until she met a black tow truck driver named Burt Johnson, who frequented the diner where she was a waitress during the day. He was a "big tipper" who made "frequent" trips to the diner and they started to "fool around" and they fell in love and she decided to leave Sal and her three kids and moved to a duplex, in Riverside, with Burt, the black tow truck driver.

Now Sal stood in the early morning shadows and held that framed picture of the past for a moment and then shoved that "shit" back in the drawer and slammed the drawer shut when Sal heard a knock on the front door. He quickly closed his suitcase and rolled it into the living room where he noticed his open pack of cigarettes on the coffee table. "Maybe I could postpone the surgery," he thought. Yet before he could entertain that "great" idea, someone knocked loudly again on the door. He finally unlocked the door and opened it to see his brother, Tyrone, who already looked pissed off and asked "You sure you wanna' be doin' this?"

"Tyrone, stop asking me that nonsense and take my suitcase. I have to go to the bathroom," Sal said. He left his suitcase in front of Tyrone and Sal walked to the bathroom and Tyrone muttered something and then took his brother's "shit" to the car. And an hour later, Sal was wearing a musty smelling hospital gown and sat in a wheelchair in a room, at The Crenshaw District Hospital, and stared out of the window. Tyrone stood near by and knew his brother was nervous. Tyrone wanted to tell Sal that "everything would be okay" and that he would be "good as new" after the surgery but Tyrone didn't believe in shit like "good" and "new" since he knew life was "fucked up" and "unfair."

Francis finally entered the hospital room in his white medical lab coat and ignored Tyrone who glared at him. The surgeon placed his hand on Sal's shoulder and said "You're doing the right thing, Sal."

Sal felt the warmth of the doctor's hand on his thin brittle shoulder and he realized that he had a "caring" doctor but he never told his younger brother how he "really" felt about Dr. Stevens.

"Thank you," Sal said.

Francis told Sal that the nurse would be in momentarily and they exchanged smiles and he left the room; however Tyrone needed the "last word" with the white surgeon, and so he followed Francis into the hallway and moved close to his face and said "I want you to take good care of my brother."

"I take 'good' care of all my patients," Francis responded.

"I want you to take better care of my brother than any other black folks."

"Do you want someone else to do the surgery?" Francis asked. "I have no problem getting someone else!"

Their faces were inches apartment when an overweight Hispanic nurse named Carmen Espinoza stepped in between them and said "Come on guys, not in here."

She pushed them away from each other. Francis finally turned and walked down the hallway. He needed to calm down before the surgery. Yet Tyrone continued to glare at that white motherfucker and "wished" that he could beat the "holy" hell out of him. Tyrone realized many years ago that he could intimidate white people because of his large arms, his height, his glare, and because he was black; and if any white person looked at him too long, Tyrone would sometimes respond by saying "You gotta problem?" and white people would immediately fear his attitude and his "burning rage." Tyrone enjoyed the "fear" that he could quickly instill on the "white pieces of shit" by uttering a few words or by glaring at them. Ironically Tyrone could not intimidate Francis, and that pissed off Tyrone. Francis constantly dealt with "life and death" at the hospital. Why should he care about this "black motherfucker with a bad attitude?" Wasn't there more "important shit" to worry about? Francis was constantly dealing with malpractice lawsuits and numerous complaints and Tyrone's blind rage was the least of Francis' problems.

Now Tyrone snapped from his violent fantasy of beating the shit out of this "white motherfucker" as Carmen asked "You want me to call security?"

Tyrone focused his rage at Carmen for a moment and then finally turned and entered the hospital room where his brother sat in the wheel chair and who now was very pissed off at Tyrone. He wanted to grab his younger brother by the ear like he used to do when Tyrone was five years old and Sal was fifteen. Unfortunately times have changed.

"What the hell is wrong with you, Tyrone? Why you always startin' stuff with people? He's trying to help," Sal said.

"Fuck him!" Tyrone said. "You think I'm afraid of him?"

"You almost fifty years old and you actin' like a fool. When the hell you gonna grow up!"

Tyrone tried to calm down and minutes later nurses came in the room and moved Sal from the hospital room to the operating room on a gurney, but before Sal was moved into the operating room, he shook hands with Tyrone and said "good bye, brother."

By seven thirty p.m., Francis drove to his house on Fourth Street, in Santa Monica, and leaves drifted across the white beam of the headlights and he tried to relax as he listened to classical music, but the music didn't help him as he finished the most difficult surgery in years. The surgery took nearly seven hours and he "struggled" in getting Sal to stop bleeding. He was able to finally remove the tumor from Sal's body. Now Francis was exhausted and needed food and sleep, but when he arrived home and sat at the dining room table with Ruth, she began to discuss the latest chapter of her novel; and Francis politely listened and helped clean the kitchen counters while Ruth washed dishes in the sink; yet Ruth had something on her mind and she needed to speak to him regardless of his stressful day and Ruth "forgot" to inquire about Francis' surgery. Unfortunately this was a routine process. Francis would come home after operating and then Ruth would sit down and "discuss" or "bitch" about something. Now she said "You know, since I was laid-off, I think Abby should help out a little and get a job, just for a 'little' while." Ruth knew it was a painful topic for her husband but she mentioned it anyway again and again; and she mentioned it now even though her husband endured a very long day in the operating room.

"Ruth, I'm tired. You know how many times we have

talked about this and it's always in the kitchen. She doesn't need a job! You have a two year severance package which is more than most people make in twenty years, so let Abby concentrate on her studies. That's why we pay so much money each semester for her education? Right?" Francis was clearly not in the mood for Ruth's shit.

"Why are you always the one making decisions around here?"

"You're the one that put her in that damn school anyway without my consent. She doesn't need to work and that's it!" Francis tossed a blue sponge on the counter and left the kitchen.

Ruth knew the "privileged brats" from St. Susan never worked. They didn't need to since most of the parents were "filthy" rich, but Ruth wanted life her way.

And that was it.

Ruth was selfish and she knew it and sometimes she wondered what life would be like to live alone and "start over" even though she was "unfaithful" in the past. Yeah Ruth Stevens "toyed" with the idea of "starting over" and then she pulled out a bottle of Scotch from the cabinet and looked at it and then put the Scotch back in the cabinet. She sat at the small kitchen table and brooded and thought about her fantasy life while Francis entered his daughter's bedroom and closed the door behind him. He glanced at the clothes strewn across the hardwood floor. Abigail sat at her desk trying to write her midterm paper on "life and death" as a song played by a band that had the name "black" and "keys" in it, and her father asked "Did the cleaning lady take the day off?"

Abigail smiled and always looked happy and calm around her father. She instantly remembered hearing the sound of her father's footsteps in the hallway when she would awaken in the morning and she always felt "secure," but now she thought about what was on her mind and asked "Dad, do I really have to get a job?"

"Don't worry about it, Abby. You're not going to have to work as long as I'm around and married to you know who," Francis said jokingly and they both smiled and laughed. "How's your paper coming along?"

"Not sure. It's kind of hard."

"You mean difficult," Francis said and smiled again.

She smiled and said "Yeah, difficult."

"Well, just keep at it."

"I have to write about the difference between life and death and talk about Rene Descartes philosophy on death."

"Oh, Rene, I went to school with him," he smiled.

"Goodbye, dad."

"Good night, sweetheart," he walked across the cluttered floor and kissed his daughter on the forehead and left the room.

Francis entered his bedroom and changed into his sweats and his T-shirt and scanned through various stations on cable, hoping that he would eventually fall asleep but he didn't, although Ruth fell asleep quickly. Two hours later, he turned off the TV and stared at the ceiling. He was actually afraid of falling asleep and dreaming of the "crab people" who began to torture him in his last dream; and so Francis stepped from his bed and left the dark bedroom and entered the living room and walked across the hardwood floor and sat on the brown leather couch and turned on the TV with the remote and flipped through the endless cable channels when he noticed a moving shadow within the glow of the TV; and he quickly realized it was Abigail who was covered in a blanket.

"What are you doing up?" Francis asked.

"I couldn't sleep," Abigail said.

"Here, have a seat," he said. He patted the cushion next to him and she sat down and they watched TV.

"Dad," Abigail said.

"Yeah," Francis responded.

"Are you always going to be around?"

Francis focused on her daughter within the glow of the large TV and said “What kind of question is that?”

“It’s just a question, that’s all. I’m just reading about all this life and death stuff and nothing seems to make sense.”

“Unfortunately, life doesn’t always make sense, but like I told you before, I’m always going to be around for you and mom,” he said.

“You promise?”

“I promise,” Francis said.

Abigail smiled and leaned her head on her father’s shoulder and watched TV until she fell asleep.

CHAPTER 6

At one thirty-eight p.m., Tyrone was changing oil on a cheap Chevrolet, at Eric's Auto Garage, in West L.A., when he received "horrible" news on his cell phone. Minutes before that phone call, Don Blue, the manager at Eric's Auto Garage approached Tyrone. Don was a "heavyset" forty-eight year old Boston native who spoke in a thick Boston accent and he never took "shit" from anyone except his customers. He was taught at an early age that "the customer is always right" and the employee is wrong. However Don also believed in being "fair" to his employees especially those that needed a "break" in life regardless of what they had done and that is why he hired Tyrone Williams.

Back in Boston, Don had two uncles who served time for "aggravated assault;" and ironically both uncles told their public defenders that they were "set up" but pleaded "no contest" and served a short stint in prison. However Don's two uncles managed to "straighten out" their life; and then on a hot muggy morning, over eight years ago, Don met Tyrone in his office and learned about his arrest record. Don believed that Mr. Williams deserved a chance, and so Don gave it to him; but now Don could not ignore the growing problem with Tyrone; so when Don approached his employee in the garage he said "Tyrone, you're a good worker. You do solid work, but I have received numerous complaints from customers and even people around here are saying you're always pissed off and taking too long on the jobs."

"Who told you this?" Tyrone said. His anger instantly grew.

"It doesn't matter. Let's forget about it and move forward" Don said. He smacked his thick hand against Tyrone's back and walked to his office.

The anger began to consume Tyrone and he felt that another fuckin' "white man" held a grudge against him because he was black. However Tyrone actually liked Don and didn't consider him "completely white" since he had olive skin. So he dismissed Don's bullshit and resumed working on the oil change on the cheap Chevrolet when his cell phone rang. He wiped his hands on a dirty red rag and answered it and received the devastating news, at one thirty-eight pm. He told his boss, Don Blue, that he had to go to the hospital which had something to do "wit' my brother." And Tyrone quickly changed from his dirty mechanic uniform into his torn jeans, a faded green T-shirt, and "dirty ass" tennis shoes in the garage's small bathroom stall that smelled like piss. And after Tyrone finished changing, he called his sister, Wanda, and picked her up in Inglewood and drove to The Crenshaw District Hospital and they waited in the lobby filled with screaming babies and elderly black and Hispanic patients who sat in orange plastic chairs and after a few minutes, Tyrone heard the horrible news again from an overworked Nigerian staff doctor who said in a thick accent "Your brother died of complications due to surgery."

Wanda instantly cried and Tyrone was stone-faced and responded "I thought he needed the surgery?"

"I have to check the file," the Nigerian staff doctor said.

"Fuck his file! I want to talk to the surgeon!"

"Tyrone, calm down," Wanda said wiping her eyes.

"Don't tell me to calm down," he said. He glared at his sister and then focused his anger at the Nigerian staff doctor.

"Sir, the surgeon will be here tomorrow checking on patients. You could talk to him then," the Nigerian staff doctor said.

"I guess he's too busy to check on my brother," Tyrone said.

The Nigerian staff doctor tried his best to avoid an argument and he told Tyrone and his sister that he could see his brother since he hadn't been moved to the morgue yet. Tyrone and Wanda rode the elevator to the second floor and turned a corner in the hallway and noticed a sign that read "ICU" and they were directed around another corner and they finally discovered their brother on a gurney next to a life support machine that was no longer hooked up; and Tyrone yanked a blue curtain closed and within heavy shadows and under dismal ceiling light, Tyrone and Wanda stood over their lifeless brother. Sal had a long surgery scar in the middle of his chest. Wanda left the room crying and Tyrone continued to stand over his dead brother. The rage filled Tyrone as Sal was the second family member who died in a hospital, in the past two years.

"This has to be a conspiracy," Tyrone thought. He instantly thought of Dr. Stevens and instantly desired cold heartless revenge against the "white surgeon" who had taken advantage of his poor brother "'cause he was black." And those were the four words that he fed his mind as he drove his sister to Inglewood.

Wanda sat in the passenger seat of the Buick Regal, as Tyrone drove. The silence in the car made her feel worse and she listened to the squeaking shocks as the Regal drove over every bump and damn pothole in the street. "Turn on some music," she said and Tyrone turned on the radio and a song played by a singer whose first name was James, and then Wanda said "Don't do anything stupid, Tyrone. You already have two prior felonies."

"Leave me alone, Wanda. I could take care of myself," Tyrone said. He dropped her off in Inglewood, and drove to

South L.A. and turned off the damn radio and he felt the rage in his mind and body, and he tried his best to calm down. He stopped at Izzys', the local "black" bar, in his neighborhood, but he didn't enter. He sat in the Buick for a moment and then drove home. He had dinner with Keisha and Jamal but never mentioned that Sal had died. And then a few hours later, Tyrone laid in bed without a shirt and stared at the ceiling in the dark listening to the "distant" sounds of gun shots and police helicopters outside and he heard his bedroom door creak open and Tyrone noticed a "figure" in his room and he reached under the bed for something and screamed "Who's there!" and then he discovered Keisha as she stepped into a shaft of moonlight, which highlighted the tears sliding down her face and he asked "What are you doin' in here, girl? Why aren't you in bed?"

Keisha asked her father about Uncle Sal's death and Tyrone wanted to know who had told her and she stated that Auntie Wanda told her and Jamal; but Tyrone wasn't ready to explain his brother's death yet and he said "We'll talk tomorrow." And Keisha told her father that it wasn't fair what happened to Uncle Sal and she said that he was "fine" last week and asked if Uncle Sal was sick and Tyrone reminded her that life was unfair and "people are gonna take advantage of you 'cause you're black. Just git' that in your mind."

Keisha said "goodnight" and left the bedroom and tried to sleep but she couldn't stop thinking about what her father had just said about people taking advantage of her because she was black; and she believed that her father was brainwashing her to be a "racist" and to hate white people, like he was brainwashing her brother, Jamal. She knew that all whites weren't "bad" and life wouldn't be "significantly" difficult for "every brutha and sista." Keisha realized that some of "her people" were unjustly punished and the police racially profiled "her people" but she had to stay away from the hatred because she knew that it would corrupt her mind as it corrupted her father's mind.

Tyrone woke up the next morning and realized that he was now on a mission. There was something he had to do and it burned inside of him. Keisha and Jamal awaited an explanation from their father about Sal's death during breakfast. Instead Tyrone bitched about the scrambled eggs being cold and the toast being burnt and stale. He got up and drove to Eric's Auto Garage, in West L.A. and entered Don's office and his boss nearly had a fuckin' heart attack when he noticed his employee wasn't in his uniform and that he was also late; and the one thing that pissed off Don Blue was when employees showed up out of uniform and were late and now he asked "What the fuck is this, Tyrone? Where the hell is your uniform? And do you know what time it is? You're late again!"

"I need a few days off 'cause my brother," Tyrone said.

"What do you mean? What's wrong with your brother?"

"He died last night,' Tyrone said. He momentarily struggled with the words.

"I'll give you a few days off but I need you back here on the weekend," Don said. He tried not to be the "biggest" asshole boss. "Just remember Saturday is our busiest day."

Tyrone wanted to beat the shit out of his boss but then he realized he was on a mission, so he left and got inside his Buick Regal and drove to a church, on Central Avenue and Flower Street but he didn't go inside. He continued to sit in his Buick Regal and listened to the traffic that raced by; and it was at that very moment that Tyrone thought about how his family might not be able to afford a "proper" burial for his brother. His frustrations grew and he felt the tension in his shoulders and neck; and he thought he couldn't breathe; and then he thought about finding another black prostitute and murdering her and then stealing her money from her purse, since he was running lowing on cash.

However he was still on a mission. He reached under his car seat and pulled out a knife with a six inch blade that he usually kept under his bed; but today was a "special" day and it became clear what Tyrone must do.

The day evolved into evening and sunlight diminished outside of The Crenshaw District Hospital and Carmen Espinoza walked through the crowd of people in the lobby and she could smell their body odor and their rancid breath as they passed by talking and Carmen looked at some of the weaves on the black women who walked by. Carmen was relieved to leave the hospital and she thought about what she would eat for dinner and then she thought about sitting in her bathtub and soaking her feet and possibly pleasuring herself in the warm water and she could already feel the cold porcelain on her back as she sat in the warm water. Now she walked across growing shadows on the cracked gum-stained pavement and noticed the crowd of patients and nurses waiting for the elevator. She couldn't "handle that crap now" so she entered the stairway of the parking structure and ascended the stairs which was scattered with trash; and she could smell the urine that wafted from the corner of the dimly lit stairway. She finally reached the landing of the fourth floor, of the parking structure, when the door smashed open, nearly hitting her in the face; and in that moment, she saw the face of a black stranger in a green hoodie who bumped into her and knocked her against a wall and she yelled "Hey!" but the black stranger was gone and she couldn't forget the large angry eyes and the large nostrils of the black man in the green hoodie and she was slightly dazed as she continued through the doorway of the employee parking area, on the fourth floor of the parking structure; and she walked toward her car when she discovered a trail of blood that extended from a white Mercedes. She inched cautiously around the car and couldn't believe what she just discovered under a circle of yellow parking lot light. She instantly felt nauseous and she dropped her purse and ran screaming toward the stairway.

In Santa Monica, Abigail and Ruth finished dinner and Ruth continued to stare at the empty chair at the table and they had already prayed to the Lord and Ruth had called Francis' cell phone twice during dinner and left two "slightly" calm voicemails; and after dinner, Ruth quietly washed the dishes. Abigail offered to help after she cleared the table and Ruth responded "Why don't you put the milk away like I told you to?"

Abigail was too concerned about her father to argue with Ruth and she placed the milk in the Sub-Zero refrigerator and left the kitchen and Abigail sat on her bed studying for her midterm on "life and death" when the phone rang and Abigail kept reading until her mother entered pale and distraught and said frantically "It's Francis, he's gone!"

In South L.A., Tyrone snuck into his house and grabbed a blue trash bag from the kitchen cabinet and hurried into the bathroom and stripped off his blood stained clothes and stuffed them into the blue trash bag on the dirty floor and he peered in the mirror and stared at his naked body and studied his image hoping this was all a "bad motherfuckin' dream" and he quickly grabbed the blue trash bag stuffed with blood stained clothes and he opened the bathroom door and looked around and rushed into his bedroom and "softly closed the door" and tossed the blue trash bag inside his closet and quickly put on "clean" clothes when a knock on the door "punctuated the silence" and Tyrone asked "Yeah, whatcha want?" and Keisha responded on the other side of the door and said "It's me, daddy. Dinners' ready" and he said "I'll be right there." Tyrone was "freaked out" for a moment and then he looked at a "small round mirror" that hung "haphazardly" above the dresser and he heard his daughter back away from the door and Tyrone discovered a "moving shadow" on the wall behind him as he continued to look in that "small round mirror" above the dresser. He felt the "chill" and heard the floorboards "creak" near his bed and he thought that somebody was "definitely in this motherfuckin' room."

He finally left his bedroom and ate dinner with Keisha and Jamal. They ate fried chicken, mashed potatoes and vegetables buried in gravy, and Tyrone asked Jamal if he talked to the supervisor "today" at the market and Jamal said he didn't do it and Tyrone mentioned how hard it is "for a black man to get a job nowadays" and then he mentioned that just because there's a black man "in the White House" doesn't mean "he's gonna do shit for us" and then his son responded that he wouldn't "get no respect pushin' carts" and he told his father that he wanted to be a "rapper" and Tyrone asked his son if he knew "what a black man is without a job" and so on and so on.

Jamal eventually left the kitchen after his father took his "plate of half eaten food" but Jamal wanted to stand up to his father but he didn't, so he eventually left the kitchen; and Keisha noticed his father's shaking hands and she asked her father why he "got home so late tonight" and then she finally noticed the "cuts" on his hands but she didn't say anything about that, nor did she say anything about his shaking hands.

CHAPTER 7

After the murder of Francis Stevens, several media vans parked along Fourth Street, in Santa Monica, hoping to get a "glimpse" or interview of the "perfect white family" who were coping with their "butchered" family member and then reality was distorted into fiction. One tabloid newspaper featured a story about the "white surgeon" who had sexual relations with "big foot" weeks before being slaughtered. Another tabloid newspaper featured a story that the "white surgeon" had a "homosexual" relationship with an elderly actor whose first name was Jack. The stories became more bizarre as the "black man in a green hoodie" was still "on the loose" and the only "concrete" evidence that homicide detectives had were Carmen's statement and a grainy footage of a black man in a green hoodie running by a vending machine, near the parking structure, which was repeatedly televised and narrated by various TV anchors, over and over and so on and so on.

And the days of "loss" turned into weeks and that is when Abigail began to experience life of an "average" teenager. She lived with a single parent, attended a public school and got a "shitty" job after school. Her misery began in Grant High School, where she was a white innocent face among minorities and shrewd jealous "bitches" and "asshole guys."

"They're all bitches," Abigail thought and "the dudes are a bunch of lame wannabe gangbangers."

Abigail was changing. The hatred was spreading inside of her like cancer; and now the cancer was plaguing her veins. She never disliked anyone until her father was murdered; and then the hatred slowly morphed in her cells and gradually multiplied until it filled her total existence. She hated just about everyone in the public school. "Fuck them. Fuck all of them. Those disgusting cocksuckers. Those pieces of shit!" She thought day after day. Abigail tried to avoid the glares from the jealous "bitches" and female gangbangers with hickeys on their necks. A month earlier, Abigail was a sweet "good white Catholic girl" who hung out with other "good white Catholic girls."

It was over.

She was now seen as the "white bitch with perfect white teeth and the perfect ass" in tight jeans and only if the entire student body, at Grant High School, knew the dreary "truth" about her father's murder, which became the main topic of conversation throughout the city. "Who killed the white surgeon in the parking structure of the city's largest HMO Hospital?" was the common question asked among the city's residents; and during the sensationalism of the story, Abigail managed to stay out of the media, and so students in that shitty public high school were unaware of Abigail's unfortunate situation.

During lunch, Abigail sat alone in the school library and thought about her pervious life, a life with Barbara and Janey and laughter and white happiness with her white father and she thought about the walks through the white park with her white father eating at white restaurants with her white father, "but now life was bleak and dreary." It was filled with color and not the color she liked but disliked; and then a month passed and then two months passed and she was shoved into a change of "shit" and "crap" dealing with her "cunt" mother who drank Scotch like soda; it was her mother who ordered and bossed her around like an indentured servant.

"Fuck her," Abigail thought. "That cunt could burn in living hell." Life was bitter for Abigail Stevens. She tasted murder and it stung and tore her "white" little world apart. And the misery grew each day for Abigail as she sat in Trigonometry class, English class and Art Class. The shit was all the same day after day. She detested everything about Grant High School, the "cunts" and the "bitches" and the "asshole guys" who stared at her ass and she hated the musty smelling hallways and the overcrowded classrooms and the incompetent teachers who mumbled for fifty-five minutes until the school bell rang. The monotony and hopelessness of the public school system nauseated Abigail day after day; and her misery grew and so did her anger and she was forced to get a "shitty ass" job after school due to the request of her "cunt of a mother."

And on a Saturday afternoon, Abigail finally got a "shitty ass" job.

* * * * * * * * * * *

Lester Jackson prayed at the foot of his king size bed, at his home, in Westchester. Lester was a sixty year old black man with high cholesterol, who wore large rimmed glasses and thick sweaters. Before leaving every night before work at Rite-Aide, he prayed intensely, in his khaki colored pants and in his thick green sweater; and his hands were tightly interlaced and his eyes were focused on the large cross above his bed and during those few intense minutes, Lester Jackson would pray for help with a "problem" that nobody really knew that he had. Lester was addicted to gambling. He would drive to any casino, in California, and sometimes he would drive to Reno or to Las Vegas over the weekend and return to work by Monday night. He loved the "real" casinos, unlike the ones in the California desert. He loved the smell of stale cigarette smoke and he loved the dice, the chips and the "stakes" involved. Yet during his numerous drives to the various casinos in California and Nevada, Lester realized that he needed to "break the gambling habit" and attend church every Sunday. So one day he followed the path of the Lord and became a "good Christian." He read his Bible in the small office, at Rite-Aide, where he was the night manager. But the "gambling" feeling returned, so he joined Gambling Anonymous hoping that would be more effective in combating his addiction, but the desire for playing 21 and Black Jack and Craps would not leave him and he thought of renting an apartment so he wouldn't have to pay his mortgage every month and so he would have more money to gamble, but the thought of living in an apartment at sixty years old was "way too depressing," so he decided to stay in his house, in Westchester; and although Lester Jackson was a gambling addict, he never missed a day of work nor did he call in sick for his job as the night manager, at Rite-Aide. His younger brother, Clarence, owned the store and was originally hesitant to hire his brother; yet one night, over ribs and stir-fried noodles with his Chinese wife, Sonia Lee-Jackson, Clarence decided to hire his brother since Lester had previous managerial experience. Clarence knew that Lester managed employees and ordered supplies at his previous jobs; and Clarence asked Lester how he would manage employees and how he would deal with employees who had "conflicts" with each other and then Clarence realized that his older brother might be a "good" manager; so Clarence decided to hire his brother as a "temporary" night manager; yet Clarence didn't know that his older brother had a gambling problem. And months later, after Clarence hired Lester as the night manager, a short Mexican cashier named Betty Rodriguez "witnessed" Lester taking cash from the company safe and stuffing it inside his black satchel, as he forgot to close the office door. And at the end of his shift, when the store was closed for business, he would set the alarm and lock the store and calmly walk to his blue Prius, in the empty parking lot holding his black satchel and Betty never told Clarence about what she had witnessed, but she told the other employees who never informed Clarence. However Lester's habits continued, until Clarence realized that "someone" was stealing money from the company safe, so he spoke to his day manager who had access to the safe and the guy said "I have no idea. I count the 'shit' three or four times before Lester comes in" and so Clarence spoke to his older brother, Lester; and Clarence had a "feeling" that his brother had something to do with the "missing" cash. He reviewed security cameras and finally discovered that Lester was leaving every night with a black satchel. Clarence decided to personally speak to his brother alone, so he drove to his house on Lester's day off, on a Thursday night. During the drive to Westchester, Clarence realized that his brother never drank, never smoked, and rarely ate fast food. He graduated from Arizona State University, with a degree in Economics, and he never even received a moving traffic violation.

However Lester failed at everything in his life. He was either fired or "laid-off" from numerous jobs and was divorced after being married for six years to a white woman named Maggie Freeman, who was a mortgage lender at a private bank, in Beverly Hills. She was thirty-two and Lester was forty years old. She realized one day that Lester was always going to be "unsuccessful in life" and "lifeless in bed" and so one afternoon, she "hooked up" with her yoga instructor, and filed for divorce, stating "irreconcilable differences," and so the story goes.

Now on this Thursday night, Clarence arrived at Lester's house, in Westchester, around nine-thirty p.m. They sat at his kitchen table for twenty minutes drinking Brandy when Clarence finally asked "Are you stealing money from the company safe?" And when Clarence didn't receive a "satisfactory" response, Clarence lost his temper and threaten to "beat the shit" out of him if he didn't get the truth; so for the next thirty-five minutes,

Lester explained that he had a gambling problem and that he attended Gambling Anonymous meetings and attended church on Sunday, and that he read "passages" from the Bible every night; and Lester explained that he was "desperately" trying to quit gambling. Clarence finally stood from the kitchen table and said "You better pray harder, brother; and if you steal from me again, I'm going to beat the shit out of you and then I'm gonna call the police" and then he instructed Lester to return that "damn money" right away.

And then as Clarence was leaving, Lester said "Look, I'm a thief and a wreck and I'm very sorry, but I'm the best damn night manager you ever had in that store."

"You get one more chance, Lester! That's it, and then I'm calling the police."

Clarence left and drove home to his Chinese wife, in his leased Lexus, and he realized that Lester was indeed the "best" night manager that he ever had. In the past six months, revenue significantly increased and not one employee quit and very few employees called in sick and stopped "bitching" about their low wages and lack of wage increases; and at the end of the Lester's shift, every aisle was neatly organized and the floor was immaculate. Customers deposited numerous comments in the "comment box" mentioning how employees were "helpful" and "courteous" and some customers even wrote that the reason they kept shopping at the store was because of the "smiling night manager" who was always "well dressed" and "respectful." So Clarence realized that he made the "right" choice in hiring that "cocksuckin' thief." However Clarence hoped his brother would never steal from his safe again; and Lester did his best not to gamble, again. Lester attended two church services, on Sunday, and volunteered to clean the church parking lot and assist in the church bookstore. And Lester followed his brother's advice and prayed harder. And slowly his urge to gamble slowly dissipated.

Throughout the next few months, Lester received awards

from "corporate headquarters" for being the best manager of Rite-Aide in Southern California and Lester was proud of his accomplishments and of his employees; and suddenly one day a Mexican cashier named Esmeralda Hernandez submitted her "two week notice" so she can focus on starting her avocado store with her husband, Hector. So Lester had to find another employee who would "fit in" with the "Rite-Aide Team." He was seeking a "team player." He needed someone that would work efficiently without any supervision. Lester leafed through countless applications and interviewed over a dozen candidates, and discovered people who were too old, too slow, too stupid or too bitter; and then on a Saturday afternoon, Lester interviewed Abigail in his windowless office and he instantly realized that she was intelligent and could be a "team player" and he liked that she didn't seem desperate for a job.

Ironically Abigail hoped that she wouldn't get the position. She hoped Lester would tell her that they were "seeking" someone with experience. However the more Abigail detested the interview the more Lester wanted Abigail to be part of the Rite-Aide Team. So after a twenty-five minute interview, he offered her a job "on the spot" and she received her Rite-Aide uniform which consisted of a red and blue-checkered vest and a white button up shirt and navy blue slacks; and now Abigail Stevens had a "shitty ass" job after school.

A few months after Lester hired Abigail, he was in bed trying to sleep when he started to get a "strange" feeling; it was a feeling that he couldn't forget; and it was a feeling that he hadn't encountered in quite "some time." He finally felt the "urge" to gamble. He could feel the chips in his hands and the touch of the cards; and he imagined himself tossing the dice across the gambling tables, in Reno. He couldn't shake this horrible feeling and he knew it would be a matter of weeks or days before he "fucked up" again. Yet he had a problem. Lester needed money to gamble. He could barely pay his mortgage along with the phone bill and electric bill and cable bill and the monthly payments on his blue Prius. So as he carried his black satchel into Rite-Aide every night, Lester Jackson thought of taking just a "few bucks" and putting them into his black satchel. But Lester remembered that his brother told him to "pray harder" but this time Lester couldn't "resist" that horrible ugly feeling to gamble, again.

CHAPTER 8

Carmen Espinoza became extremely paranoid weeks after she discovered Francis' bloody and mutilated body, in the parking structure, of The Crenshaw District Hospital. And moments before she discovered the "mutilated" body, Carmen could not forget the face of the black man, in the green hoodie, on the landing in the stairway, of the parking structure; and during the night of the murder, Carmen spoke with two veteran homicide detectives named Johnson and Preston; but at first, she wasn't sure what their names were and they urged Carmen to make a "statement" so they drove her to the nearby police station and she sat in a small room and faced Johnson and Preston and she attempted to answer the questions about the black man wearing a green hoodie that knocked her against a wall and continued to run down the stairway. And she thought about the questions "How tall was he?" and "What did he look like, specifically?" and "How black was he?" and "Would you recognize him if you saw him again?" And then Carmen answered the questions the best she could but she was shaken, distraught, distressed and a fuckin' emotional wreck. She remembered receiving Johnson's business card; and then she remembered sitting on her brown couch, in her townhouse, in Marina Del Rey, holding her Siamese Cat, the night of the murder, while shaking and crying as she watched the nightly news and she cried harder when she noticed herself, in the background of a news report, on the TV, and she was too distraught to speak on camera. And as she sat on her brown couch with her Siamese Cat, she wondered if the "black man wearing a green hoodie" was watching her. "Of course he was watching," she thought. Maybe he noticed her near the yellow "Do Not Cross" tape on the news. Maybe he remembered her from the stairway, of the parking structure. "Yeah, I'm sure he knows who I am," she thought to herself. Carmen locked her doors and windows and checked them repeatedly; and then she set her alarm system and "jumped" at every sound outside and then her Siamese Cat got scared which caused the cat to hiss at every sound; and Carmen became a "prisoner" in her townhouse, in the marina. She took a temporary leave of absence from the hospital. She could barely sleep and eat. All she could think about was the surgeon's bloody and mutilated body and she imagined the black perpetrator stabbing the white surgeon like a crazed animal. Everyday she peered through the newspaper and looked at the sketches of the black suspect in a green hoodie in which she assisted a sketch artist at the police station and the images became infamous within the media; and the Latino mayor "attempted" to take advantage of the fear and created a website to help assist in the "capture" of the black perpetrator. Residents could log into the website of so and so and anonymously leave any information, which may lead to the arrest of the "black man in the green hoodie." And the Latino mayor believed that the website would "help" him in securing more votes for the upcoming election, in L.A.; but ironically during the massive man hunt for the black suspect who murdered the white surgeon from Santa Monica and while the Latino mayor was hoping to increase his votes for the upcoming election, there was "very little" media attention on Candy, the black prostitute who was murdered in a "shitty ass" motel in South L.A. Unless it was a "slow" news day, Candy was never mentioned; and as the coverage of the "dead white surgeon" continued, Carmen's anxiety intensified. She would lie in her bed, at night, wondering if the black stranger would break into her security gated townhouse, in Marina Del Rey, and "mutilate" her as he did to the "white surgeon." Carmen lost weight and stopped showering and continued to sit on her brown couch every day with her Siamese Cat watching Spanish novellas in her townhouse. Then one morning, Carmen decided to gain control of her life and went back to work at The Crenshaw District Hospital and began eating and showering and decided to start exercising in the community recreation room; and Carmen saw a therapist who smelled like garlic; and Carmen eventually made progress with the therapist and realized that the incident wasn't her fault and she realized that murder was sometimes an unfortunate part of life; but how come she didn't know murder was a part of life since she was a nurse? Probably because it was different to see a stab victim being carted inside the hospital instead of "noticing" a warm bloody body in a parking structure; or that's how she reasoned it in her mind. And her therapist who smelled like garlic told Carmen that "it was pure bad timing" for her discovering the body of the dead white surgeon. And Carmen eventually fell asleep without prescription pills and believed that the black man in the green hoodie was not trying to find her and stab her and kill her; and so Carmen eventually returned to online dating, and after experiencing more "bad dates" with "horny ass" men, she decided to continue her therapy.

Once Carmen returned to work, she parked her four-door Saab on another floor, in the parking structure of the hospital. She tried her "best" to resume her life as if "nothing" ever happened and she went out with her friends after her shift, at the hospital, and they had drinks and they planned a cruise and discussed trying to fit in a bikini that "originally" fit them a few years ago. Carmen started to live her "normal" life until two months after the murder, as she was trying to fall asleep. Carmen instantly remembered something and she quickly turned on the lamp; and within a frame of yellow lamp light, she found Johnson's business card, on the night stand, as she finally remembered where she originally saw the black man in the green hoodie. She called Johnson and left him a voicemail around midnight. Since authorities did not have a "lead" in the case, residents of L.A. were still awaiting a name, a mug shot, or something. People "needed" to know who stabbed the white surgeon twenty-five times, two months ago, in the parking structure of The Crenshaw District Hospital.

And the next morning, Detective Johnson arrived at Carmen's townhouse, around eight thirty a.m., and he had a sleepy look on his face; and as he sipped the decaffeinated tea that Carmen had offered him, she told Johnson that she "possibly" met the black suspect a few days before the murder, in the hospital hallway. She mentioned that she was "breaking up" a near physical altercation between the black man and the white surgeon. Johnson scribbled notes as Carmen told him that this black stranger entered a hospital room after the near altercation, but she wasn't sure who it was that he was visiting and Johnson said "I'll take care of it from here. We'll be in touch." They shook hands and Johnson didn't want to get too excited or hopeful since he and his partner chased false leads for two months. They received numerous e-mails and phone calls that had nothing to do with the murder. A special team of "high-level" homicide detectives were assigned to find the "White Surgeon Killer." Johnson and Preston led the team of "high-level" detectives and began reviewing footage from security cameras in the hospital from the last six months; and then the news "broke" that the "black suspect" had nearly gotten into a "verbal altercation" two days before the "butchering" of the white surgeon in the parking structure. The media retuned to The Crenshaw District Hospital and interviewed black elderly patients again about the "White Surgeon Killer;" and once again viewers were morbidly entertained by the sad unfortunate story.

Two weeks after the murder, Tyrone drove down Crenshaw Blvd, at night, thirsting for violent sex which resulted in a horrible "neck snapping" end for Candy; and when Detectives Johnson and Preston arrived at Tyrone's white stucco house, on Prairie Avenue, in South L.A., on a cold gray evening, Tyrone just finished dumping a body of a black prostitute who was wrapped in plastic, in an alley, a few miles from his place, and he had already scrubbed the blood from his car with supplies that he kept in his trunk. He returned to his driveway, around six forty-seven p.m., where the detectives greeted him and flashed their badges and Tyrone turned and noticed Jamal and Keisha in the doorway and they waited and wondered what was happening. Johnson requested Tyrone to come down to the station to answer a few questions. Tyrone was calm and the detectives escorted Tyrone into an unmarked car and Tyrone did not realize this would be the last time that he would ever see his house again, nor would he ever see South L.A., except for pictures of it; and during the drive to the police station, in South L.A., in the backseat of the unmarked vehicle, Tyrone realized that he could "probably" continue murdering black prostitutes in motels and other places and continue to dump their bodies in alleyways probably for a few more years until the "body count" reached twenty or so. However once he murdered a white man, Tyrone had "crossed the line" and he didn't just murder any "ordinary" white man, it was a white surgeon from Santa Monica; and that incident dominated the media with the common caption "White Surgeon Murdered; Black Male Sought."

Now Tyrone sat in a small chair in the interrogation room and faced Johnson and Preston who had to be careful in "handling" this suspect since they were dealing with a "high profile" case and they didn't want to appear as if they were two "white racist" cops bullying a "poor black man" who hadn't been arrested yet. The detectives instantly knew they were interrogating a "seasoned" thug who breathed self-loathing and hatred and

Tyrone answered most of the detective's questions with "Fuck if I know" or "Fuck that shit" or "Fuck that" and on and on. Yes Tyrone was an experienced criminal. He had the criminal attitude, the way he walked, the way he sat in his chair, the way he made eye contact with Johnson and Preston; and the detectives knew "one" more felony could put Tyrone away for "life." They reminded him of his past criminal record but Tyrone still didn't care. He didn't give a fuck about anything and he actually believed that he was going home after they "held" him for twenty-four hours; and then the detectives had Tyrone's Buick Regal impounded and investigators discovered "hairs" and remnants of dried blood in his trunk and "semen stains" in the backseat and the evidence did not link him to the murder of Francis Stevens, yet; but the detectives had "new leads" on other cold cases and now Tyrone was officially arrested the next day for "murder."

Yet Tyrone still thought he was still going home since they couldn't find a weapon, but then the detectives "eventually" linked his DNA with the DNA that was found on Francis' body, but before all of that occurred, his public attorney visited him in jail and warned Tyrone that the evidence was "gowing" due to Carmen's testimony and that another witness came forward; and then another. One pedestrian witnessed someone in a "green hoodie" who gotten into a Buick Regal, a few blocks away from the hospital, the evening of the murder, who "eventually" identified Tyrone in a police lineup.

A few days after detectives "officially" arrested Tyrone, Keisha visited him in L.A County Jail and she was crying and said "The police came by with all these people."

Tyrone was slightly confused since his public attorney never mentioned that event to him. "What people? What are you talking about, Keisha?"

"They found things. They found things at the house, in the garage."

"What, what did they find? What are you talking about,

girl? Speak up!"

"They dug up the garage and found clothes, women's clothes, and some had blood on it and they found pictures, hundred of pictures of all these women and now me and Jamal can't go back in the house 'cause it's treated like a crime scene, or that's what one of the detectives said to us," Keisha said. She wiped her tears. "Did you do something wrong, daddy? What did you do? What'd you have all these things for?"

"What pictures did they find?" Tyrone asked his daughter. He acted as if he had no idea about women's pictures or anything that the "search team" had discovered in his garage. It was one big surprise to him. He thought it was all a joke and he even wondered how women's blood stained clothes were found inside his garage. Yet Tyrone still believed that he wasn't a "horrible" person. He thought of himself as a "good person" living in an unfair world. Tyrone Williams was clearly a misunderstood person until anger seized control of his central nervous system and he became a "horrible person" who murdered until the anger subsided.

Now Keisha continued to cry as a sheriff escorted Tyrone back to his jail cell in his blue jump suit; and it was then, and, only then, that Tyrone realized that he had fucked up. He knew that he was never going home. "That nigga' was gonna rot in prison until he dies" someone said after the bail hearing for one of the black prostitutes. And before detectives linked Tyrone's "DNA" to Francis' Stevens, there was "overwhelming" evidence that "tied" him to seven of the ten dead black prostitutes, in South L.A. Yet it would take six months of legal battles, before the District Attorney, Brad Dirkson, a white Republican, charged Tyrone with the dead black prostitutes; and he said one day during a "private" luncheon with other white Republicans "I need to take care of this surgeon thing first and then take care of the other shit. It 'all' just piles up like trash." Brad was clearly a politician and if he could get another "fucked up high profile criminal case" off the streets, he felt better. And once Tyrone was "linked" to all of the ten dead black prostitutes, images of their faces were released to the media and they finally gained the media attention they deserved; and Brad, the District Attorney, stood in his thousand dollar suit, in front of a police station, in South L.A., next to an easel filled with pictures of the ten black prostitutes when they were alive; and he stated to the media that he was very concerned "that there may be more 'victims' out there."

The media discovered that some of the murdered black prostitutes were mothers who had "disappeared" over twenty years ago. Once their identity and their names were officially released, hatred in the black community grew and Tyrone was safer in county jail than on the streets of South L.A. Yet his family wasn't as fortunate. The media gathered around Auntie Wanda's place in Inglewood; and Jamal and Keisha had to move to their cousin's house in Chino Hills, until the media discovered them there; and so they moved to another cousin's house in Apple Valley, over one hundred miles from Inglewood and Jamal and Keisha no longer had to wake up and find media vans parked outside. They didn't have to be "subjected" to the constant chatter of camera men setting up camera shots and news anchors talking outside.

However Jamal decided that he wasn't going to live in fear from anyone and after several conversations with Keisha, he persuaded her into moving back to their "auntie's house" in Inglewood. And once they returned back to Inglewood, they decided to drive to their "old" house in South L.A. and the house was boarded-up and the walls were covered in massive amounts of multi-colored graffiti; and then the bank repossessed the piece of shit. So Jamal and Keisha realized they were going to stay in Inglewood and live with their Auntie Wanda.

One night in a "makeshift" bedroom at her auntie's house, Keisha cried as she believed her father was punishing them for his own mistakes and his desire to murder. She also believed that her father murdered for pure enjoyment and then she wondered if her future would be "marked" with court appearances and being "forced" to endure her father's mistakes. Keisha finally quit college and watched "daytime soaps" and wished that she could have the life of an actress, a white actress who only had to memorize "lines" from a script and collect a "large ass" paycheck and drive home to her white house and enjoy a candle lit dinner with her white spouse and enjoy a white bubble bath; everything was "white" and nice in Keisha's unknown fantasy. She snapped from the bleak future and remembered when she told her mother years ago that she was going to graduate college and pursue politics. Now Keisha looked in the mirror and she was proud that she had "goals" and "dreams" but she was also proud to be black and she was "not" going to allow racism or prejudice to corrupt her mind. She resumed college and avoided the media vans that parked on her auntie's street and she avoided watching the news. Keisha eventually changed her last name to Waters, graduated Northwestern University, and married Gerald Green, a black physician and she became the first black District Attorney, in Los Angeles. Her past struggles eventually dissolved but she never forgot about that moment when she stood in her auntie's "makeshift" bedroom and looked in the mirror and was proud of who she was, and that was in 2012. She also would never forgot about her father's criminal trial and the moment Tyrone was "charged" for murdering the "white surgeon" and for the murder of ten black prostitutes. Yes Keisha's life was temporarily fucked up due to her father's mistakes. Yet there would be one family that would forever be changed due to Tyrone's anger.

More than sixty days after Francis Stevens was murdered, Ruth answered the phone in the kitchen, on a Tuesday night, at eight thirty-four p.m., while drinking her favorite cheap ass Scotch; and that is when Detective Preston notified Ruth that an arrest was made, in South L.A. The information came fast and she remembered the words "we need you to come down to the station tomorrow" and the conversation was over; yet she was still holding the receiver when the detective hung up the phone and she finally hung up the receiver and Ruth was instantly overcome with pain and grief. She was "enduring" life without Francis. She was sinking into a pit of hell and then she heard "Who was that?" and she looked up from her glass of Scotch and noticed Abigail in the doorway of the kitchen.

"It was nothing, nobody. Just go back to your room."

"I'm not going back to my room. I want to know who called," Abigail said. She realized something and asked "They found him didn't they? They found that piece of shit! How could you just sit there and not feel anything!"

"You have no idea what he meant to me, do you? You think I don't care what happened? How could you talk to me like that?" Ruth asked.

"And do you have any idea what he meant to me!" Abigail demanded. And Ruth really had no idea how much Francis meant to her daughter, nor did she completely realize how angry Abigail had become in the past two months. Abigail wanted justice. She could taste it and feel it. She finally left the room, disgusted.

Ruth continued to sit and drink her cheap ass Scotch and then she remembered that she needed to eat. She had already lost ten pounds since her husband's murder. She drank throughout the day, only to return to her bed lying alone within the moonlit shadows; and during those moments in her bed, alone, she sometimes imagined her husband entering the bedroom, smiling, and then she would feel the chill in the room. And in her home office, while writing her novel, *The After Life*, papers would mysteriously fall from the desk and onto the floor. And sometimes when Ruth would walk across the living room floor, she would hear the floor creak behind her. She felt the presence and sometimes heard the distant soft voice that called out her name. Regardless of the unexplained disturbances in the house, Francis was dead and gone; and now more than sixty days later, Ruth would finally see the "black suspect" who may have been responsible for murdering her husband and "fucking up her life." And Ruth entered the police station the next day after receiving the phone call from Detective Preston. She entered a small dark room and looked through a two-way mirror and saw Tyrone Williams; and she instantly recognized his face from the "heavy" media coverage after he was "first" arrested for the murder of three black prostitutes; and she thought "Oh, that's a fuckin' surprise. It had to be a 'Tyrone' who killed my husband." And a few days later, Abigail saw Tyrone Williams, at the downtown courthouse, during his bail hearing. He was shackled in a blue jumpsuit, in the holding area.

"He looks mean," Abigail thought.

And in the holding area, Tyrone spoke to his public attorney and pleaded "not guilty." The judge denied Tyrone's bail due to the "severity" of the crime and before Tyrone was escorted from the holding area, he made eye contact with Abigail who sat across the court room. She stared at the black man who may have murdered her father, in the parking structure of the hospital; and it would be several months before jury selection would begin and Abigail wanted to believe Tyrone murdered her father and she hoped law enforcement arrested the "right" person. She heard about innocent people being "locked up" for twenty years until another piece of evidence coincidentally "showed up" and the innocent person was released. But in Abigail's mind, she didn't care who was locked up, she wanted the right person to die a painful death in hell for what that piece of shit did to her father.

Although Abigail realized that she needed to put "closure" on this part of her life, she had to *believe* that Tyrone Williams murdered "her best friend." Yet she barely could restrain her desire to get revenge on that fuckin' black man in the dirty ass blue jumpsuit. Regardless somebody was going to pay the price for her father's murder.

Back in the courtroom, the mood quickly shifted as two sheriffs escorted Tyrone from the holding area and back to his cell. People were leaving and Abigail and Keisha noticed each other. They both had an instant "connection" as if they had already known each other. Abigail was known as the daughter of the white surgeon who was viciously murdered. Ironically Keisha wanted to apologize for her father. "What would I say to her?" she thought. She was actually embarrassed for her father but Jamal couldn't "give a fuck" about anyone's daughter. But Keisha was different and she was genuinely sorry about Abigail's father. She wanted to talk to Abigail and get an e-mail address or a phone number and have discussions about how they could move forward "black and white." But Keisha knew that her entire family and her friends would see her as a "traitor" for what would be seen as "kissing up" to the "white folks." Although she knew her brother and her Auntie Wanda didn't hate white people "per se" but they never had anything to do with them.

Now Keisha watched Abigail as she turned and they both got one last glance at each other; and then Abigail left the courtroom which "officially" ended the "black and white" relationship before it started.

The weeks painfully "dragged on" for Ruth and her daughter; and Ruth continued to write and drink Scotch during the day; and at night, Ruth would religiously watch the "late breaking" news on Tyrone Williams, and Ruth stayed up late to watch hour long profiles on the "White Surgeon Killer" and on a Thursday night, Abigail had the "night off" from working at her shitty job and she entered the living room, where Ruth sat near a circle of yellow lamp light on the brown leather couch, holding a glass of Scotch and another news report on the "White Surgeon Killer" was on TV, which showed Tyrone in the courtroom shackled in his "dirty ass" blue jumpsuit pleading the words "Not Guilty" to the judge and Abigail heard the words from the TV and asked her mother "Why did this happen?" Abigail didn't want to speak to her mother anymore about the murder, but it happened.

"I wish I knew, Abby," Ruth said. She was clearly buzzed and drunk and screwed up. "Every night I think about this, and how could this have possibly happen to us. We're just bad people, you and I. We're bad white people."

"Don't say that!" Abigail snapped.

"It's true. I know it. I make you pray. I made everyone in this damn house pray and look what happened. I made you go to that Catholic School, and what did you learn? You learned that innocent white people are murdered. Your father, my husband, is now gone. Dead like a nail."

"Stop it! Why are you saying this?" Abigail pleaded with her mother. Yet Ruth was too "fuckin" drunk to care about anything. She had to say what she was thinking after a few glasses of Scotch. She couldn't give a "rat's ass" if she was scaring her daughter. She was drunk and she didn't give a shit about anything right now.

"He was my husband, your fuckin' father, murdered, in a parking lot. How could this all happen?" Ruth tried to stand but she fell back down on the brown leather couch nearly spilling her glass of Scotch.

"Look at you! What's a matter with you? You're just a drunk," Abigail yelled. "You're just a miserable drunk."

Ruth didn't care and said "You're right, Abby. I'm a bad person, a bad white person, just like you, just like all of us. We're bad white people."

"We're not bad people! We didn't do anything!"

"Yes we did," Ruth said. "We hung them from trees like animals. We made them slaves. And now were paying our penitence. All of us. We have to suffer our penitence."

"I can't fuckin' believe you!" Abigail said and stammered into her bedroom and slammed the door. She hated her "cunt of a mother." Abigail didn't care what her mother thought about her anymore and Abigail didn't care about anything. She sat on her bed, crying, looking at pictures of herself with Barbara and Janey, while her mother sat on the brown leather couch in the living room drunk constantly watching news updates and hour-long profiles on the "White Surgeon Killer." Now Abigail raced to her desk and opened the drawer and found her razor and lifted up her shirt and was about to "subdue" her pain with another episode of "cutting" but she saw that her other "cuts" were healing so she decided to put the razor back in the drawer and laid back on the bed and thought about the "past life" with her father. His name was now only a reminder of what occurs to "good" innocent people, good ol' white people who "minded" their business. These were the white people who tried to have a loving family; and now life was over for her white father. Abigail experienced the murder of a family member. At this moment in time, Abigail knew that she had to eventually get the fuck out of this house before she became crazy and started to drink. So the next night, Abigail was "slightly" relieved that she was working at the shitty ass job which gave her time away from her drunken "cunt of a mother."

Within the past few weeks of working at Rite-Aide, Abigail became proficient as a cashier. Lester taught her how to scan items, operate the cash register, and return the correct change to customers with a "smile" and how to quickly bag items. Sometimes Lester would watch Abigail work and smile proudly as she worked at the cash register, while other cashiers fumbled with the buttons and were easily distracted. Lester began to notice Abigail's work ethic. She was always punctual for her shift and her uniform was always clean and she always completed every task with diligence and without any complaints.

On a certain night, Lester attempted to make "small talk" with Abigail when she was mopping the floor. Lester wasn't aware that his "star employee" was the daughter of the "white surgeon" from Santa Monica. Abigail usually answered Lester with a "yes" or a "no." And she usually averted eye contact with the black man when he spoke to her. Abigail didn't want to hate Lester. She knew he was a "nice" person but her anger made her hate; so she disliked him because he was black and sometimes she wondered at night, in her bed, if Lester Jackson was the real "White Surgeon Killer" who had eluded police and kept a "low profile" as a night manager, at Rite-Aide. She was willing to believe anything since anger distorted the truth; and it was her "growing" anger that made her hate life including the shitty ass public school that she attended; and one day while sitting in English class, Abigail listened to the teacher's instructions for the midterm which consisted of writing about the theme of isolation in the short story, The Open Boat, written by an author whose last name was Crane; and Abigail and the rest of the class had to write about a time in their life when they felt isolated and compare it to the main character's isolation in the short story. The students had forty-five minutes to write in their blue test booklet; but Abigail didn't care about the story. Yeah the main character was isolated. "Big fuckin' deal," Abigail thought. So Abigail decided to write what she really believed in her heart about her own isolation, in her blue test booklet, in the shitty ass English class.

At home during the day, Ruth sat in her office and continued to write her novel, *The After Life*. She thought about giving up on writing the novel since the death of her husband, but she had the "burning desire" to write a novel since she was a junior in college. She could still remember when her parents told her not to bother writing a novel. "You're no Hemingway," her mother once told her. "What good will come out of this, anyway?" her mother, Louise asked. Ruth was twenty-one years old when she heard the bullshit; and so she listened to her mother and focused on her accounting classes. Yet after the death of her husband, all she did was write and drink Scotch. She had to finish her novel and show herself that she could fulfill her goals regardless of what was happening to her. And she remembered how Francis sometimes told her during their morning walks that she could do anything. So every day Ruth worked on her "new" career despite the pressure of not having an agent and "losing" her husband and possibly her mind.

However one morning after vomiting in the toilet from a bout of nighttime drinking, Ruth decided to do something different; and so she ate breakfast and showered and brushed her teeth and drove to church. She entered the church and dipped her finger in holy water and made a cross with her finger across her chest and kneeled at a pew and prayed silently for a few moments; and she finally stood and noticed Father Harris at the end of the pew.

"I thought that was you," Father Harris said. He was in his mid-sixties and had a "warm" smile and his gray hair was combed back.

"Hi, Father," Ruth said. She forced a smile and approached him.

"I'm very sorry to hear about Francis," he said and gently took her hand. "I believe that God has a new plan for you and your daughter."

Ruth didn't want to hear about a "new plan." She was absolutely devastated and she wanted her husband next to her and she finally said "Thank you, Father." Ruth was about to leave but Father Harris felt something was bothering her.

"Ruth, is there something else on your mind?"

"What, what do you mean?" Ruth asked.

"I feel there is something else troubling you."

Ruth was much too exhausted to make excuses and asked "Why did this happen, Father? Why did this happen to us?"

"I, I don't know, Ruth," Father Harris said. He wanted to tell her that God would "fix" all of her problems and her daughter's problems if she only had a little bit of "faith" and believed that something "great" would happen in her life. Yet Father Harris knew that Ruth probably didn't want to hear about "faith" and so she pulled her hand from his grasp and walked toward the door and before she dipped her finger in holy water again, Father Harris asked "Will I see you and Abigail this Sunday for service?"

"I don't know, Father."

Ruth left the church and sat in her Lexus SUV for a moment and felt the heat from the sun that filled the car and she wiped her tears and started the car. And on the drive to her house, Ruth realized she was out of Scotch. She drove to a liquor store and picked up another bottle of "cheap shit."

CHAPTER 9

Danny Ruiz sat in his green 1973 Pontiac Trans Am, in the parking lot of Hong Li's Chinese Restaurant, in Hollywood, near Gower and Vine Street. He was listening to Motorhead's 1980 Album, Ace of Spades. Life was all about Lemmy and his fuckin' singing and Eddie's fast guitar riffs and Phil's pounding drums; and Danny knew every song on the cassette and memorized the lyrics. He thought about the time when he had sex with Becky or Laura during the song Love Me Like a Reptile; and Danny snapped from his daydream when the passenger door opened and his drug pusher, Rocky, entered and slammed the passenger door and smiled at Danny; and when he smiled he revealed his yellow rotten teeth. Rocky had long brown tangled hair and wore a faded Saxon T-shirt which had the words, Wheels of Steel on it, and Rocky finally said "What's up, bitch?"

"You're late," Danny said, irritated. He had to start his work shift soon and he was tired of waiting for this loser. Danny put his hair into a ponytail and dug into his pocket and pulled out cash and exchanged it for a vile of Rocky's "good shit." Rocky counted the cash and Danny pocketed the vile of coke and said "It's all there."

"I can't be too careful. You know what happened last time, right?" Rocky smiled again revealing his yellow rotten teeth. "And if you ever wanna do that thing again, let me know."

"I don't do that shit anymore," Danny interjected.

"Sure, only when you're 'hard' on your luck, right?" Rocky smiled and patted Danny on the head with the cash and said "See you around." He left and calmly entered his fucked up Mazda and drove away and Danny grabbed his white collar shirt from the backseat and stepped outside and looked around the parking lot for a moment. He was uneasy about making a "deal" so close to work, but he did it anyway.

Danny "clocked" into the restaurant holding his white collar shirt and entered the bathroom and put on his white collar shirt over his white T-shirt and entered the stall and locked it and pulled out his vile and snorted coke into each nostril and he loved this shit. It was like he was making instant love to himself. He didn't really care about much right now as he stood in the stall nor did he think about being nearly broke.

He officially began his afternoon shift "high as shit" and took orders from the customers who sat in booths and at tables; and during his break, he snorted coke again from the vile in the bathroom stall and he finished his shift a few hours later and "clocked" out and drove to theatre row, on Santa Monica Blvd. and he was "slightly" high. Danny parked at the curb and took off his white collar shirt which was now sweaty from work and put on a Motorhead T-shirt over his sweaty white T-shirt and entered a dimly lit musty smelling hallway of a building and checked the roster of actors for the upcoming play of Jack and Jane, which was located on a bulletin board on a wall, and he didn't see his name on the roster and he got "pissed off" and he entered the theatre. Actors were practicing their lines on stage and Danny noticed the heavyset director, Jim Bloomberg, sitting in the front row. Jim was in his mid-forties and he was a "no nonsense" director with twenty years of experience directing plays and he looked up from reading a scene and noticed Danny who asked "Can I talk to you for a second?"

Jim knew what Danny wanted but he also knew Danny was a burnout "druggie" who still believed that he had a career in theatre. Jim was used to dealing with "druggies" in theatre; and Danny wasn't any different than the "others" since they all believed they could handle their drug use.

"So what's up?" Jim asked.

"I checked the roster and I'm not on it."

"And?"

"And what?" Danny asked. His face turned red and his voice got louder.

"Listen," Jim said. "You're a talented actor but you have to clean yourself up. There's no place for a drug addict in theatre, at least not in my productions."

"I don't do drugs!" Danny said. He was about to explode with anger.

"Look, I'm not saying it, you are." Jim was clearly not intimidated by Danny and said "You want to stop doing what ever you're doing and then we'll talk about putting you in a play; but until then, I can't deal with this shit."

"What shit? What are you talking about?"

Jim stood and moved closer to Danny and said "Excuse me, but I have a play to direct."

"This is bullshit. I'm ready, just give me another chance."

"I'm tired of repeating myself. See me when you're 'clean' and then we'll talk."

Danny clenched his fists; and in that moment, he wanted to beat the "shit" out of this small chubby man. "Well, fuck you!" he said and those two words echoed throughout the theatre. The actors were instantly silenced on stage. Danny expected Jim to punch him or grab him by the shirt, but nothing happened. It was quiet, all too quiet. Actors and "stage hands" stared at the "whacked-out druggie." Danny finally left and passed actors practicing their lines in the dimly lit and musty smelling hallway. Danny was "hurt" since he wanted desperately to be a theatre actor. "I don't have a drug problem," he thought. "No fuckin' way" as he left the building.

Darkness filled the sky when Danny drove to his apartment, in West L.A. He parked his green 1973 Pontiac Trans Am in front of a garage that was part of the apartment complex and turned off his car and he suddenly thought about his childhood; and he remembered his white father, Steve Dixon, and his Mexican mother, Maribel Ruiz, who divorced the white "piece of shit" when Danny was a teenager; and Danny began to remember when his father would come home exhausted from working nearly twelve hours a day, in a cold meat packing plant, and when he came home he would hear music coming from Danny's bedroom and he entered to discover Danny doing homework while listening to music, and so his father beat Danny with his fists and yelled "I told you not to have that shit on when you're doing your homework!" and sometimes another beating would follow with the question "Why isn't dinner ready?" and then another beating occurred one night when his father found dirty dishes in the sink when he came home and he would scream "I thought I told you to clean the dishes!" Over and over Danny recalled his father screaming which would usually follow with a barrage of punches to Danny's arms and back; and Danny then thought about when his father whacked his leg with a garden tool, in his bedroom; and he thought about how his father slammed him against a wall in the kitchen and choked him and threatened to kill him for any bullshit that he could think of at the moment; and in retaliation, Danny would toss things in his bedroom and his father would enter his son's bedroom and discover numerous stuff on the floor and furniture turned over, and Steve would resume punching and choking his son until he thought he might kill him; and Danny endured the abuse as this scenario happened again and again; and his mother, Maribel, would come home late from the bar and smell like alcohol and she hated motherhood and marriage so she decided not to come home one night when Danny was fourteen; and Danny finally ran away from home and his grandmother, Josephina, eventually gained "custody" of her grandson and raised Danny in West L.A. and he went to a new junior high school and then went to a high school and he made "white" friends who introduced him to Motorhead and Iron Maiden and Overkill and Slayer, and he grew his hair long and hung out with "white metal heads" who invited him to a party one night. And at this party, in a white area, a wealthy white student introduced Danny to cocaine and to girls and he fell in love with both. He dropped out of high school but decided to attend community college "for the fuck of it." He was still unsure what he wanted to do with his life until he "accidently" stepped inside a theatre class, and looked on stage and discovered two actors practicing a scene. And something "happened" inside of Danny and he thought "I could fuckin' do this!" So Danny sat in a squeaky chair and watched how people could be a different person on stage. He knew at this very moment that he was "born" to be the best damn theatre actor in L.A. His name would be synonymous with the great theatre actors like so and so. Danny enrolled in acting classes and read books on theatre acting. And one day he shared his dreams with his grandmother who said "Is that like an actor in the movies?" And then one day he decided to share his "goals and dreams" with his cousin, Gerald, during a funeral and he asked "Are you kidding? Are you a fag or something?" So Danny decided to keep his "goals and dreams" to himself.

Danny didn't care what "bullshit" his family had to say about his theatre acting. The moment Danny walked on stage he felt the "rush" and delivered his "words" with intense emotions. Students believed he was a "natural." Yet unfortunately the "rush" he experienced on stage did not compare to the "rush" of snorting cocaine. He loved the feeling of "blow" in his nose. Cocaine became his friend and his enemy and Danny worked two jobs so he could buy more coke and one day while working at a

Hollywood pizza place as a delivery person, he delivered pizza to a guy named Rocky who heard from another guy that this was the guy "looking" for coke. Rocky got Danny the best "shit" and if Danny ran out of money, Rocky worked out a "payment plan" where Danny would suck Rocky's dick and a few of his friend's dicks and sometimes the guys would come in his mouth and he would spit it out or vomit in the toilet. Danny finally realized that he needed to get himself "clean" so he quit snorting coke and focused on acting. He studied his roles and practiced and delivered his best performances in "local" plays. Students and teachers discussed his acting abilities and he became known as a great theatre actor, in community college; and he began dating an actress named Claire; and unfortunately Claire offered Danny cocaine at a house party, in Venice; and within a few weeks he was hooked on coke again; and when he ran out of money, he sucked Rocky's dick and sometimes he would suck Rocky's friend's dicks for more cocaine in a shitty Hollywood apartment. Rocky was attracted to Danny so he offered to give Danny a thousand dollars worth of some "good shit" if he allowed him to fuck Danny in the ass, but Danny said "no fuckin' way," but Danny realized that he needed to quit cocaine "for good" so he decided to change his entire life and move out of his grandmother's house and work in a Chinese Restaurant, in Hollywood; and his grandmother offered to help him with "some" of the bills and part of the rent while Danny was in search of his "big" break as a theatre actor.

And as Danny continued to act in local plays and continued to audition, the days turned into weeks and the weeks turned into months which turned into years, and his acting gigs were "off and on" and his paychecks were small; and then his grandmother died and left him a "medium-size" trust fund which he spent most of it on his green 1973 Pontiac Trans Am and on rent and of course on coke.

Now Danny was twenty-eight years old sitting in his dark car after not getting the role of Larson in Jack and Jane, and he wondered how life moved so fast and he finally got out of his car and walked to his apartment on the bottom floor and entered and turned on the light and turned on the stereo and cranked Motorhead's 1986 album, Orgasmatron; and he sat on his green couch and emptied some of his newly purchased cocaine on the glass table and began to cut a "massive" thick line of coke with an expired credit card. After quickly snorting the "massive" thick line with a twenty dollar bill, Danny was hungry. He checked his refrigerator and couldn't find much to eat except a few slices of stale pizza and a smelly chicken burrito. He needed food and he drove to the closest place and parked in the mostly empty parking lot of Rite-Aide and bought orange juice, frozen pizza and a few other "things" and stood in line and he noticed the most beautiful cashier with a great "rack." And then Abigail noticed Danny at the far end of the line. They exchanged eye contact and there was an instant connection. She kept looking at him and his long brown shoulder-length hair and she liked his slight arrogance and the "I don't give a shit" attitude.

Danny finally placed his items on the conveyer belt and realized how young she appeared and he thought "She must be in high school, but what a fuckin' rack and a cute face. I would definitely fuck her."

Abigail scanned the items on the conveyer belt and she pushed a few buttons on the cash register and said "That'll be twenty-four dollars and twenty-seven cents."

Danny checked his wallet and realized that he was short a "few bucks" and asked "Um, how much is it, again?"

Abigail looked around for her boss and said "Give me what you have." He handed her the money and she quickly counted it and opened the register drawer and put the money inside and closed the drawer and bagged his items and said "So how are you going to make this up to me?"

They smiled.

"What do you have in mind?" Danny asked.

"You know, my mother tells me never to talk to strangers."

"Do you always do what your mother tells you to do?"

"Usually, never," Abigail said.

They smiled again.

Abigail scribbled her phone number on the back of his receipt and handed it to him along with his bag of groceries and she said "This is from a good Catholic girl."

Danny finally drove home with his partially paid groceries and a phone number from a posssibly "underage" girl. "Maybe something will turn around for me once and for all," Danny thought. He finished another line of coke on the glass table, in his apartment. "Fuck yeah," he thought, as he remembered getting a hot chick's phone number.

And an hour after Abigail met Danny, Ruth picked her up at Rite-Aide and she expected her daughter to "bitch" about how she hated her job and the public high school that she attended and everything else in her life. Yet Ruth couldn't believe that her daughter was silent on the way home. And when they arrived home, Ruth went into her bedroom and drank more Scotch and Abigail went into her bedroom and hoped Danny would call, but she didn't want him to call too soon. Abigail had limited access to guys, especially "hot" guys like Danny and as she undressed in her bedroom, Abigail decided to call her friends Barbara and Janey and tell them about her "dream guy" but when she spoke to them they both sounded bored and they only asked a few questions. Abigail realized that their friendship stopped the moment she left St. Susan. She only had seen her friends a few times since she began attending public high school and so Abigail thought that maybe, just maybe, Barbara and Janey only liked her because she was the same as her, a rich white girl who attended an all girls private Catholic high school, in Brentwood. Yet Abigail tried her best not to be "hurt" by Barbara and Janey's attitude; and as Abigail got into bed and turned off her lamp, she realized there was another reason why she was excited about meeting her "dream guy." She knew that her mother would hate Danny which would make Abigail feel better since her mother forced her into a shitty ass public school and made her get a shitty ass job after school. And two days later, Abigail came home from public school and discovered a note on the dining room table with the scribbled words "Danny called" with his phone number below; and when Ruth heard her daughter enter the house, she marched into the living room and an argument ensued and Abigail smelled the alcohol on her mother's breath.

"Who the hell was that? He sounds much older than you," Ruth said.

"Well, you're not going to stop me from seeing him," Abigail said and walked into her bedroom and called Danny and made a date; and the next evening, Danny arrived at the Stevens' driveway, in his green 1973 Pontiac Trans Am and knocked on the door and Ruth answered it. "This guy is probably thirty years old. And look at that hair and that car, and is that the best shirt he has?" She thought to herself.

"Can I help you?" Ruth asked.

Danny smiled and said "Hi, I'm looking for Abigail. Is she here?" Yet his "politeness" was seen as condescending to Ruth and she thought he was smug and he was really trying to say "I'm going to have sex with your daughter tonight and there's nothing you could do about it, bitch!"

Ruth fumbled with her words as anger and frustration stopped her from formulating a complete sentence. Luckily Abigail appeared in the doorway, a moment later, smiling. She was wearing tight jeans and a semi-nice shirt that outlined her large chest. She finally promised her mother that she would be home by ten p.m. as Danny escorted her to his green 1973 Pontiac Trans Am and he opened the passenger door for her.

A minute later, Danny slowly backed out of the Stevens' driveway and he drove Abigail to a diner and once they arrived the conversation was exciting and they fell "in love" in a booth, under a circle of yellow light. They wondered where they were for each other in the past and Danny had enough cash to pay the bill; although Abigail brought "enough" cash in case he did not have "sufficient" funds to cover the twenty-two dollar bill and the tip; and a few days later they went on another date and a few days after that they went on another date; and Abigail was "correct" in believing that her dating an "older man" would piss off her mother; and so they began to argue incessantly.

Abigail continued to date Danny and the relationship eventually became "physical" and it started with "touching" one night, when Danny brought Abigail home and he parked in the driveway. They began kissing in his green 1973 Pontiac Trans Am; and he was surprised how "well" Abigail could use her adolescent tongue in his mouth, and they were both aroused. He moved his hand over her shirt and felt her hard nipples; and then he slid his hand under her shirt. Abigail was still a "minor" and at first Danny "felt" strange to feel her breasts. Yet Abigail didn't mind. She had experimented with her virgin body before, at night, in her bed. However this was the first time that a "stranger's hand" moved under her bra and felt her hard nipples. She moaned by the soft touches of this older man as he cusped her C-cup breasts and she felt the "wetness" between her legs. She loved the moment but once she left the car and entered the house, Abigail felt "dirty" like a whore. She showered and laid in bed and vowed never to allow another guy touch her until she got married; and then she fell asleep and woke the next morning and thought of Danny's soft hands on her breasts and the wetness between her legs from the previous night and she shook off the "Catholic guilt" and decided to fool around with Danny again; and then a few weeks later, Danny "made love" to Abigail in his apartment and the entire experience was strange to her. She was completely naked in front of a man; a Mexican-American put himself "inside" of her white body, and she bit into her bottom lip trying to endure the pain as he moved "in and out" of her tight fitting body, in his bed.

And then it was over. He came inside of a "rubber" and she was shaking slightly. She was scared and excited and embarrassed and horny and she realized that she hadn't "come" but that was okay. It was her first time and now her virginity melted away; and later that night, Abigail noticed small splotches of blood in her panties and that was a "normal" reminder that her "virginity" was gone and she felt like a "whore" again and she showered and laid in bed and told herself that she would never have sex until she got married; and then she awoke the next morning slightly in pain but she had this strange urge to have sex again with Danny. She wanted more of Danny and he wanted more of her seventeen year old body and they continued to have sex over and over; and then one day Abigail "ditched" a few afternoon classes and sat on Danny's green couch and Danny put on Motorhead's 1979 album, Bomber, and then he made Abigail swear to a secrecy pact. She put up her hand and "swore" that she would never tell anyone about what he does in his apartment and he asked "You promise?" and she said "Yes" and she got tired of the interrogation and said "Just tell me, Danny," but he wanted to make sure that Abigail wasn't a "narc" even though he was having sex with her. Danny finally pulled out a vile of cocaine and emptied a clump of white powder on his glass table and Abigail watched her boyfriend as he carved a line of coke with his expired credit card.

"Is that cocaine?" Abigail asked. She was slightly nervous. She wanted to run from his apartment, for the moment. She should have told him to take her the fuck home. She had never seen cocaine except in a few movies and one of them being Scarface. Yet she had seen "pot" before and tried it and coughed out the smoke and she never felt the "buzz." But this was different.

This was cocaine.

Danny finally looked at his underage girlfriend and asked

"Do you mind if I do a line?"

"Isn't it bad for you?"

"Not if it's used in moderation," he said. "It's all about moderation, but if this is making you feel uncomfortable just let me know. We could leave. I swear. I just want you to be comfortable."

"It's, it's okay," she said. "I just never knew anyone that did this before."

He smiled and snorted a line of coke from a twenty dollar bill and he was instantly high; and after a minute of watching him get high, she asked "Can I try?"

"Sure, but you don't have to do this. I'm not pressuring you to do it. I hope you know that."

"I know," Abigail said and nodded her head.

Danny prepared a line of coke for his guest and said "It's probably gonna taste like aspirin, and it's gonna burn for a minute." Danny instructed her to close one nostril with her finger and she did so and then she leaned over the glass table while Motorhead was heard from the stereo and she grabbed the twenty dollar bill and snorted her first line of cocaine. She instantly leaned back and touched her nose and said "Fuck, that does burn."

"I told you."

"It tastes like shit," Abigail said.

"You'll get used to it," Danny said and smiled. "I'll get you some water." At this moment, Danny was turned on to see a "hot young blond" on his green couch. He gave Abigail some water and then she asked for another line and he asked "Are you sure you're okay?" and she said "Yes" and Danny cut a second line of coke for Abigail with his expired credit card.

She closed her nostril again and she snorted her "second" line of coke through the twenty dollar bill and she began to feel "different."

Danny drove Abigail home an hour later; and on the way

home, she stared out of the window and she felt "dirty" again. She was having sex and now she was snorting cocaine. What would her father think?

She didn't know what he was thinking because he was dead and gone because an angry black man murdered him. She felt the anger grow inside of her all over again. She wanted to go back to her "old" life of being an innocent Catholic girl. But those days were gone and she entered the house and had dinner with her mother at the dining room table and Ruth drank her Scotch and she slurred her words and Abigail smelled her harsh stinging breath across the table.

Abigail realized the "old days" were definitely over as she tried to focus on her homework after dinner; and then she sat back in her chair and thought "If my cunt of a mother is going to get fucked up, well, so am I."

The next week, Abigail ditched her last class of the day which was art or geography or some "shit" since she really couldn't remember. All she could think about was Danny picking her up, and then he arrived and he drove her to his apartment which smelled like sour trash, but she didn't care. He snorted a line of coke and then cut a line for his underage girlfriend. She snorted it quickly and was still surprised how the coke still burned her nostrils and how much it tasted like aspirin. However after a few times, Abigail began to enjoy the drug and during the "high" she forget about her "cunt of a mother" and her dead father who was murdered by a black man and she forget about the horrible public high school that she attended and she forget about her shitty ass job, at Rite-Aide. It was all about getting "high" and having sex with Danny; and before Abigail realized it, she was snorting coke every day with her boyfriend and they began mixing cocaine with sex and that was the "best high" she thought. They would both "come" together within a self-made heaven. And those great feelings ended once she entered her mother's house. Ruth would wobble to a chair, in the dining room, and accuse her daughter of "being cheap." And on a warm evening, when Danny dropped Abigail off at home, Ruth wanted to call Abigail a "slut" and yell at her and say "I'm sorry I had you." Instead Ruth said "I don't like that guy you're seeing,"

"Don't you want me to be happy!" Abigail pleaded.

"How could you say that! You're such a spoiled brat!"

"Would you rather me come home and watch you get drunk," Abigail said as she glared at her mother. Ruth approached her daughter and raised her hand. "Are you going to hit me?" Abigail asked.

And it was all true, Ruth wanted to hit the shit out of her daughter, but she could only scream and berate her daughter so she lowered her hand and Abigail realized she was "wasting" her time and entered her own room and slammed the bedroom door.

Ruth was too drunk to chase her daughter and grab her chin and tell her "there's no slamming doors in this house," again.

Ruth stumbled into the kitchen and thought of sending that "brat" to boarding school in Oregon or Washington or Hawaii. And as Ruth opened a new bottle of Scotch and poured herself another drink, she wondered if she kept Abigail in a Catholic School and didn't "force" her to get a job after school, would her daughter be happier and not become involved with that "human sludge" who dropped her off almost every night after work.

"Maybe I did fuck up," she thought for a moment; but then Ruth would be admitting a "wrong doing" and Ruth believed that she didn't make mistakes with her daughter, nor did she believe she was selfish. How could Ruth Stevens admit to herself that she had fucked up?

Sometimes at night, Ruth would sit in her home office and drink a glass of Scotch near a circle of yellow lamp light and try to erase the horrible fact that her husband was never coming back. She wrote for a few hours and stumbled to her bedroom and passed out on the bed; and one night, Ruth had a dream about another man. This man was quiet and reserved and "genuinely" nice; and in this dream, she floated through the clouds and danced with this "dream man." She was calm and there was no more guilt about how she treated her husband when he was alive; nor did she have guilt about how she was currently treating her daughter. She was now dancing with this man, in the clouds, and she was happy and she loved the moment; and then her home phone rang and Ruth instantly awoke from her dream and she was instantly sick from drinking and sick from guilt and sick of being a single parent. She looked at the clock and noticed it was eleven-thirty four a.m. She finally answered the home phone and listened to an "unfamiliar" voice from the administration office of Grant High School; and Ruth only comprehended the words "behavior" and "suspension."

"I'll be right there," Ruth said and she hung up the phone and rushed into the bathroom and vomited in the toilet; and when she was done vomiting she walked to the sink and splashed water on her face. She was barely able to stand and she leaned on the sink and her head pounded and she said "Why did you leave me, you bastard!"

Ruth heard a noise and turned and noticed the bathroom door opening wider. She was too exhausted to worry about "weird shit" happening in her house again, so she wiped her face and finally showered and her head continued to pound and her back was stiff; and once she finished showering, she dried her body and her private area with a large blue towel; and she remembered that this was the second time that Abigail was in trouble at school, in six months, and realized that Abigail "never used to get in trouble."

Forty-five minutes later, Ruth entered the administration office after parking in a reserved space, in the parking lot of the high school, and she saw her daughter brooding on a wooden bench in the administration office and Ruth was going to "ball her out" until a Chinese administrator appeared and brought her through the office area that smelled like Pine-Sol and mothballs; and Ruth spoke with the vice principal and then the principal and then the Chinese administrator directed her into the high school counselor's office because this was the second time that Abigail was in trouble and so Ruth met Norm Jacobs. He sat behind his clean desk as he rested his hands on Abigail's blue test booklet.

"What's the problem?" Ruth asked. She was defiant and pissed off like her daughter. She was tired and hungover and she hated everybody and everything and how his office smelled like stale paint.

"Have you spoken with the principal?" Norm asked.

"Well, kind of. What's this about anyway? Something about what she wrote in English class?"

"Do you mind if I read you something that she wrote?"

"Please," Ruth said.

Norm picked up Abigail's blue test booklet and opened it to page one and read "I can't believe I'm sitting in this shitty ass school. All I think about every day and every night is killing that black piece of shit who murdered my father and I think about strangling that black cocksucker before I go to bed every night," Norm stopped and glanced at Ruth who appeared lost and he believed that she probably wasn't listening, but Norm continued to read anyway. "And I think about him being dead as dirt, and until that happens, I won't live in peace until that black cocksucker is dead and gone. I'm sure if the writer of The Open Boat was still alive today, he would feel the same way." Norm put the blue test booklet down and said "It goes on like that for several pages."

Ruth continued to fidget with her wedding ring that she never removed after the death of her husband and she mentioned that there was a "recent death in the family" and she averted eye contact with Norm; and Norm asked Ruth if "Mr. Newmark" suspended Abigail for three days, and Ruth slightly raised her voice and said something like "Yes he did." And Norm said that he would try to reduce Abigail's suspension to "two days" and then Ruth said "I think my daughter needs professional help" and she continued to "fidget" with her wedding ring and still "averted" eye contact; and Norm replied "Why would you say that?" And they momentarily continued their conversation and Norm said something like "If you have anymore questions, please don't 'hesitate' to call anytime" and he handed Ruth his business card and she took it and stood up and put the card "carefully" in her purse; and then Norm stood up and they shook hands and Ruth finally looked at Norm and told him that he was a nice man or something like that and he said "Thank you" and then she averted eye contact once again and she left his office and drove Abigail home; and a few hours later, Ruth prepared dinner at home and sat across from her angry daughter at the dining room table and it was evening, and the lights were off but there was still some daylight outside, but there was heavy shadow that filled most of the room and Abigail began to eat without praying. Ruth pleaded with her "horrible daughter" to pray first but she didn't listen and Ruth pulled the plate of food away from her daughter.

"I thought we stopped praying in this house," Abigail said.

"You know the rules," Ruth said. She glared at her rotten ass daughter.

Abigail stood up and finally said "A fuckin' black man killed my father, and you sit there and you drink and you judge me! Who are you to tell me what to do!"

Ruth sat calmly at the table and wiped her hands on a napkin as if she expected the blame. She realized that her daughter was on drugs since she was thinner and angrier and ditching school and she believed Danny was supplying her with drugs and filling her mind with more hatred. Ruth stood and faced her daughter and said: "I want you out of this house. Take your things and don't come back. I don't care what you do or where you go. I just can't do this anymore, you hear me! People stare and they point and I have to come home to you, to this place; and it's not right, not at all."

Ruth left the dining room and sat on the edge of her bed and cried; and a few minutes later, she heard her daughter slam the front door. Ruth wasn't sure if she made the "right" decision but it was the only one she could think of at that moment. All she knew that she was lost like her daughter.

And on the corner of Fourth Street, in "white" Santa Monica, Abigail stood next to her suitcase. The yellow circles of street lights glowed above her as night evolved; and then she heard the roaring engine of Danny's green 1973 Pontiac Trans Am in the distance. She was excited that she was going to live with Danny and not having to deal with her "cunt of a mother." Abigail should have been depressed and felt a sense of rejection that her mother kicked her out of the house; but instead she felt "free" to do whatever the fuck she wanted; and Abigail was "free" from being subjected to watching her mother stumble into the living room when she returned from work or from her boyfriend's apartment; and so when Danny finally arrived in his green 1973 Pontiac Trans Am, Abigail tossed the suitcase in the backseat and she sat in the passenger seat and they kissed passionately for a moment. He floored the gas pedal, turned up the Motorhead song, Love Me Like a Reptile, and he drove his underage girlfriend to his one bedroom apartment, in West L.A.

CHAPTER 10

Six months after Francis Stevens died, Ruth nearly completed the first draft of her novel, *The After Life* and during the day, she continued to write and drink; and sometimes at night, when she couldn't sleep, Ruth would lie awake in the moonlit bedroom listening to the floors creaking and doors closing in other parts of the house; and she really didn't care about that "ghost stuff." She really only cared when she was out of Scotch; and on a certain evening when Ruth completed the last chapter of her first draft, she discovered that she was completely out of Scotch. She brushed her teeth and got into her Lexus SUV and drove to the market; and during the drive she knew she was a "miserable" drunk of a mother, and she hurried to the liquor section, in the market, and placed two bottles of Scotch in her shopping cart and Ruth was suddenly "overcome" with depression and loneliness; and it was during those "bouts" of depression and loneliness that she needed to speak to someone so she can bitch about her life and her daughter. She tried her best to "shake off" this feeling as she stopped in the frozen food section and pulled out two overpriced frozen pizzas and two cartons of mint chip ice cream and put them in her shopping cart. She paid for her items and watched as one of the brown hairy "baggers" placed her items inside the shopping cart. She rolled the cart to her Lexus

SUV and opened the hatchback and placed the groceries in the back and closed the hatchback and pushed the cart into some unknown direction of the parking lot and got into her Lexus SUV and sat in her driver's seat. She listened to the silence and forgot what it was like to be kissed and to make love. She sometimes thought about being "touched" when she was lying alone in bed. She was almost forty-five years old and she still desired someone to be inside of her and to kiss her neck and gently suck on her breasts. The fantasy momentarily filled her mind and then she became depressed again. She found it quite strange that she could be "fine" one moment and "shitty" the next. Yes Ruth could have obtained pills from a "quack" doctor since she was still trying get over a "death in the family." However she relied on her two new bottles of Scotch to take care of her problems.

Now in the driver's seat, Ruth searched through her purse and finally discovered Norm's business card, which she received the same day that she kicked her "bratty ass" daughter out of the house. Ruth dialed Norm's office number and left a voicemail stating that she needed to discuss her daughter. She was sure that Norm would call her in a few days. She drove home depressed and lonely and wanting another glass of Scotch.

Ruth filled her glass when she arrived home and she wanted to stay busy and she was tired of writing for the day. She began folding clothes that were in the dryer and that is when she heard the floor creak behind her and she shivered from the sudden chill; and then she heard the distinct sound of footsteps behind her. She instantly turned behind her but she didn't see anything. She was now "freaked out" for a second. She resumed folding her clothes when she discovered some of Abigail's T-shirts and socks and wondered how they ended up in the dryer since she hadn't been home for a few weeks.

Ruth entered Abigail's dark bedroom with the folded clothes and turned on the light. She instantly felt the cold air in the bedroom. She put away Abigail's clothes in the mostly empty drawers. She walked to the bedroom window and opened the curtains and looked out in the dark backyard and she remembered looking through this same window, on a Sunday morning, when Abigail was five years old and watched Abigail and Francis toss gold colored leaves at each other on the grass in the backyard. Now Ruth yanked the curtains closed and wanted to forget about her daughter and her dead husband. She was about to leave the bedroom when she noticed a framed picture of Francis and Abigail on the wall. Abigail was eight years old blowing out the lit candles on the birthday cake and her father was sitting next to her, in the picture. The year was 2003 and Abigail Stevens was the happiest girl in the world with her father. Ruth had seen this picture on the wall many times before, but now this picture had a new meaning. As Ruth continued to study the picture, she noticed a moving shadow on the reflection of the glass. She turned around but nobody was there, again.

Ruth turned off the light and left Abigail's bedroom and entered her bedroom and turned on a lamp, on her night stand, and put her folded clothes on the dresser and studied her image in the mirror which was partially highlighted by the circle of yellow lamp light across the room.

She pulled at the lumbering bags under her eyes. Ruth felt old inside and defeated. She realized that her life had "officially" fallen apart. She secretly wondered if her life would become any worse. Yet that was a question that she was afraid to ask. She started to believe that she was dying inside. Maybe "death" had found her and was allowing her to die slowly. She lost her husband and a job that she had for over twenty years and now her daughter was doing drugs and having sex with an older man. "Why couldn't she date an Ivy League scholar?" she thought. "Shame on her."

Ruth felt like she had lost everything and her life had been reduced to living alone and listening to mysterious noises in her house while she was writing a manuscript that may never get published. Her life was sinking to the very bottom of hell, as her teenage daughter was living with an "older man."

And then her cell phone rang.

Ruth grabbed her cell phone from the bed without looking at the incoming phone number since she "assumed" that it was her daughter wanting to come home and beg for forgiveness. And instead when she answered the phone, she heard the voice of Norm Jacobs, the high school counselor.

Fifteen minutes later, Ruth hung up the phone, applied lipstick, put on a sweater, and drove to Denny's on Lincoln and Colorado Blvd., in Santa Monica. She knew meeting Norm was "strictly" for "emergency purposes."

Ruth met Norm in the front lobby area and they shook hands and sat in a corner booth and ate cheap diner food. And then Ruth finally said after an intermittent conversation "I think this is all my fault."

"What do you mean?" Norm asked.

"You don't know me, Norm. I cheated on my husband. I was thirty years old. What did I know? I thought I knew every damn thing. Abigail was only five when it happened."

"Ruth, that was in the past," Norm said. "That's all that matters now."

"No, no, it's not. It's right in front of me," Ruth said.

"You made the family work."

"I kicked Abigail out of my house, Norm. I know, I know. What kind of mother kicks her own fuckin' flesh and blood out of the house!"

"What?" Norm asked. "You have to get her back! She needs you."

"I understand," Ruth said.

"You need to call the police!"

"That'll just make things worse," Ruth said.

They continued to speak for a few more minutes about the situation and then Norm paid for the bill and they walked out of the diner; yet before they exited the booth, Ruth felt a chill and it was the same feeling that she had felt in her house for the past six months but she had to ignore it now. Norm walked Ruth to her Lexus SUV and there was an awkward moment. It was a moment they both hadn't felt in many years.

"I'm sorry for bothering you with my problems," Ruth said.

"I'm glad you called," Norm said.

They kissed softly and said "good night."

Ruth sat in the driver's seat of her dark car and felt that same chill again and then she felt a "presence." But now there was something on her mind. She started her car and noticed it was nine twenty-nine p.m. on the dashboard and drove from the parking lot of the diner and ten minutes later she arrived at the Rite-Aide parking lot and instantly discovered Danny's green 1973 Pontiac Trans Am. She parked and turned off her headlights and noticed Abigail walking out of Rite-Aide, in her uniform. She got inside Danny's car and he sped from the mostly empty parking lot. Ruth followed Danny to his apartment a few miles away from the store. Ruth parked across the street and watched as Danny and Abigail emerged from the Trans Am, in front of a set of apartment garages. They held hands as they entered the downstairs apartment and Ruth "officially" knew where her daughter was residing and there was nothing stopping Ruth from banging on the front door and demanding her daughter to come home and finish her education at the shitty ass public high school; and at this very moment, Ruth thought about how she forced her daughter to change schools in the middle of the school year and to get a part time job. Now everything backfired. She wondered if she would be in this situation if she had to get her fuckin' way all the time. Ruth had to focus on the current situation. Could she just barge into Danny's apartment? Who knows? She may get shot. And what would intruding on their "space" accomplish, but "piss off" her daughter? So Ruth drove home and laid awake in her bed. She realized that she had to deal with the "source" of the problem.

In the morning, Ruth drove to Danny's apartment and waited in her car for a few hours until Danny appeared holding his white collar shirt and got into his car. Ruth started her Lexus SUV and followed Danny to the Chinese restaurant, in Hollywood. She parked at the far end of the parking lot and noticed Rocky entering the Trans Am. And a few minutes later, Rocky left and drove from the parking lot in his "fucked up" Mazda. Ruth finally knew that Danny was buying or selling drugs. Danny emerged from his Trans Am holding his white collar shirt and approached the restaurant. Ruth watched him and waited. She needed an element of surprise.

Ruth waited for a few minutes and then finally entered the musty smelling Chinese Restaurant and looked around and noticed Danny who was now wearing the white collar shirt and he was taking an order from a table of Japanese businessmen. He finished writing the order and walked toward the kitchen when he discovered Ruth. She quickly approached him and said "I want my daughter back, asshole!"

"You kicked her out. Remember that?" Danny asked. He was nervous and worst of all this "bitch" was ruining his coke high.

"Do you want me to notify the police that you're having sex with a minor? How would that look when the police pull you out of this shit hole in handcuffs? You think you'll get another job, again?"

"You think you can come in here and threaten me!" Danny knew customers and other waiters were starting to look at them, but he needed to put this "bitch" in her place.

"Look motor mouth, I know you deal in drugs. I saw that piece of shit leave your car and I bet I know what you're doing with my daughter in your place. I just want her back, that's all. You can go back to your cave and 'fuck' up your own life, but I want her back. That's it!"

"I guess you're getting dementia in your old age. You kicked her out! What kind of mother would do something like that?"

Danny walked away and entered the kitchen and customers and employees were staring at Ruth. She finally turned and left the "shitty ass" place and got in her Lexus SUV and realized that she had one more thing to do before she returned to her house, in Santa Monica.

Now at this moment, hazy afternoon sunlight glowed within the dirty white curtains that hung above the green couch, where Abigail sat and snorted another line of coke, on Danny's glass table, as she listened to Motorhead's 1980 album, Ace of Spades; and she was high and enjoyed the "fucked up" and rebellious life of ditching class, living with her older boyfriend and having sex and snorting coke; and then she heard a knock on the front door.

Somebody was after her.

Abigail stood up quickly and nearly knocked the cocaine on the floor. She freaked out. "Maybe it's the cops ready to bash in the door," she thought. She quickly scooped the cocaine into a small secure envelope that was constructed with magazine paper and hid it under the couch. She checked the peephole in the door, but she couldn't really see who it was except that it was some old "bitch" outside. She opened the door to discover her mother. They were both clearly lost without each other but that didn't matter right now.

"What are you doing here!" Abigail snapped.

"I need you back, Abby. I do, I swear," Ruth said.

"You got rid of me, remember that?"

"I'm sorry, I swear. I was just overwhelmed and you weren't behaving."

"I'm not leaving,' Abigail said. She was sickened by her mother, but she was also confused.

"If you don't leave this guy, he's going to do something terrible. I feel it in my bones, Abby. He's not a good person. You have to trust me."

"I couldn't trust you since I was five years old. I remember what you did to dad!"

"Please don't say that Abby. It's not fair," Ruth said.

Abigail slammed the door in her mother's face; and for the next forty or so minutes, Ruth sat in her Lexus SUV and cried within afternoon shadows. She officially felt abandoned. Ruth realized that she made life worse by kicking her daughter out of the house. Now she wanted her daughter back and she did everything she possibly could to get her daughter back without making things worse. Yes Ruth Stevens begged and pleaded with her daughter and she could have called the police and reported that her daughter was "possibly" doing drugs and "possibly" having sex with an older man, but she couldn't get herself to call the police on her daughter.

A few hours later, Danny finished his shift at the Chinese Restaurant, in Hollywood. He pulled his hair out of his ponytail and clocked out of the "shit hole" and it was dark outside and Danny drove home from work and had to decide what to do about Ruth. He could hire Rocky to find some people to murder that "bitch" but he didn't want to create more problems, but he had to do something quickly. His Chinese-American boss spoke to him before he left about the incident that occurred in the dining room during "peak" business hours. "Listen, Danny, I don't care what you do on your free time, but make sure you don't bring it to work. It's not good for business." As Danny drove to his place, he constantly heard his boss's words echo in his mind.

Danny arrived at his apartment about thirty-five minutes later to find Abigail snorting more of "Rocky's shit" on his bed, within a circle of yellow lamp light. He wondered "how in the hell" could she not overdose on this stuff, but he joined Abigail on the bed and he snorted a line of coke and said "We have to leave L.A."

"What do you mean? What's going on?" Abigail said. She was definitely "coked up" and Danny had never seen her fucked up like this but he had business to discuss.

"It's your fuckin' mom! She came by the restaurant today. She totally embarrassed me."

"What! How did she know where you worked?"

"Fuck if I know!"

"She didn't mention anything when she came by."

"What!" Danny said. "She was here? That bitch was here, at my place? Why didn't you say anything?"

"What was I going to say, Danny? I didn't think it was important."

"How the fuck could you not think that was important! What are you, stupid?"

"Fuck you," Abigail said. She was exhausted. Her mind was fried from snorting cocaine all day and every day.

Danny inhaled deeply and he slid his hand through his hair and said "Look, I'm sorry." He needed to calm the fuck down. He was stressed beyond anything he had felt before in his life. "We just need some cash so we can get out of here."

Abigail snorted another line of cocaine from a small compact mirror and she touched her nose and paced the room and said "I know where we can get some cash!"

"Where!"

"I know where this black dude keeps his money?"

"What fuckin' black dude? What are you talking about?"

"It's, it's the black dude, the night manager at my work. His name is Lester Jackson, and get this," Abigail spoke as if she was talking to herself "He steals cash from the safe. He's all fucked up from gambling."

"How do you know he steals cash from the safe?"

"I just know," Abigail said. She continued to pace the small room, away from the circle of yellow lamp light. "Some

Mexican chick at work, her name is Maria or Betty – or some shit. She told me one night that she saw Lester pulling cash from the company safe and sticking it inside his satchel a few times. Or some shit like that. He probably does it every night."

"How the fuck does she know?"

"You wanna interview her or some shit? I told you, she told me she saw him take it a few times. I guess he forgot to close the office door."

"What if she's fuckin' lying?" Danny asked Abigail. He had so many questions about this situation. Danny paced the small bedroom as Abigail continued to talk, but he wasn't listening anymore. He was thinking about this "Mexican chick" and the "black dude" that Abigail just had mentioned; and he instantly realized that this story barely made any sense to him, but he desperately needed "cash" so he pulled out his 9mm Smith & Wesson, from a drawer, and told Abigail how they were going to take the black dude's money.

CHAPTER 11

Ruth tried to compose herself after visiting Abigail that afternoon at Danny's apartment; and she hoped that Abigail would return back home. However Ruth had to move "forward" in her life; so she attempted to have a "normal" relationship with Norm Jacobs. Yet during an afternoon of shopping at the mall with Norm, she "believed" that she saw her dead husband in the mirror, in an expensive clothing store. She was trying on the most "beautiful" brown suede jacket when she thought she saw her dead husband in the mirror behind her. She said "I can't do this" and peeled off the most "beautiful" brown suede jacket and tossed it at Norm and she left the store and Norm said "Wait, Ruth!" He quickly hung up the jacket and caught up with her outside of another store in the mall and she was pale and shaken and Norm said partially out of breath "Talk to me, Ruth. Is it Abigail?" And Ruth stopped and faced Norm and explained that it was her husband and that he was following her and he was "everywhere" and so on, and Norm said "Maybe he is trying to tell you something and that everything will be okay" and Ruth and Norm hugged within the thick crowd of strangers and some of them stopped and stared. And within that very moment, Norm could have instantly discontinued this "normal" relationship but there was something about Ruth that he liked. "She's a great woman, just a little troubled," he thought. "Her husband was murdered. What should I expect?" He continued to reason with himself later that evening, as he drove Ruth to an upscale Italian Restaurant, on La Cienega, near Beverly Boulevard. The primary reason that Norm wasn't "freaked out" by Ruth's explanation of seeing her "dead husband" in the mirror of the "high-end" clothing store was due to his numerous experiences of dealing with "fucked up" teenagers and parents within the past fifteen years or so. And being a high school counselor prepared him for this day.

Or so he thought.

Now at this upscale Italian restaurant, Norm and Ruth sat by a window and they glanced at the strangers who walked by outside; and inside this dimly lit place every table had lit candles. And within the glow of white light, Ruth began to calm down and "color" returned to her face as she sipped from a large glass of Chablis. Norm noticed Ruth's smudged lipstick on the rim of her wine glass; and for some reason, he was slightly "turned on" by it, and maybe he had a fetish that made him excited by smudged lipstick marks on the rims of wine glasses. And he was turned on as Ruth ate lasagna while he ate chicken primavera. Then as they continued to eat, Norm and Ruth discussed their hobbies, their goals and where they dreamed of taking vacations in foreign countries. And during their romantic dinner, Ruth and Norm purposely avoided the subject of "death" and runaway teenagers. Lately Ruth mostly thought about death and murder and she was tired of it. She needed something "new" in her life."

And so after dinner, Norm drove Ruth home. It was nine forty-five p.m. and Ruth stood under a circle of yellow porch light in front of her front door and looked at Norm who believed that it was the "end" of the night. Ironically Ruth invited Norm inside for a "drink" and Ruth had a glass of Scotch and Norm had a glass of cheap red wine. And they danced awkwardly to The Rolling Stones' song, Angie, from 1973; and the song made her think of her dead husband, but Ruth continued to dance with

Norm and they finally held hands and kissed softly during the song. The kissing became intense and they moved to the bedroom as the music continued and they resumed "making out" on her bed, near a circle of yellow lamp light and they softly caressed each other and Norm slowly moved his hand up her dress, feeling her soft skin on her inner thighs.

Ruth closed her eyes and began to moan. She had been waiting for this moment; and now she moaned and pressed her fingernails into Norm's back; and Norm gently slid the strap of her dress down and moved Ruth on her back and he "gently" sucked on her nipples and they were bright pink and Ruth was "extremely" turned on; and Ruth continued to moan and continued to press her fingernails into his back. She wanted Norm inside of her.

And she wanted it now.

However Ruth knew she was an emotional wreck and wondered why she should be having sex with this stranger while her daughter could be "dismembered and stuffed neatly into a designer suitcase," Ruth thought. "Or, maybe she's selling drugs or her body."

The horrible thoughts began to flood Ruth's mind and the thoughts eventually "turned her off" and she heard Norm unbuckle his pants during this very moment. She opened her eyes and stood up and said "I can't do this" and pulled up the straps of her dress.

Norm stood and buckled his pants. Ruth wanted to say "It's all my fault" and she wanted to apologize to this very "nice man," in her bedroom. She was embarrassed. Ruth believed that she could handle a "new" relationship, but in her mind and in her heart, she was severely "outmatched" by the troubling thoughts that stopped her from enjoying a "new" life with a man.

And there was also the guilt.

It was the guilt she felt about her daughter and her husband and how she mistreated them both.

"Will I see you again?" Norm asked at the front door.

"I don't think so," Ruth said. "I have so many problems." She attempted to wipe the smeared lipstick from his face. She noticed the "hurt" in his eyes from being rejected. "How could this be?" Norm thought. "I did everything right." Norm truly cared about Ruth and she knew it. And Ruth had an opportunity to stop Norm from leaving her house, but she was confused and angry and felt betrayed by life; and no matter how much she prayed or drank, she could not forget that a black man murdered her husband; and now "death" had taken over her life and she could not erase that fact.

And so Norm finally left the house and Ruth leaned against the door and listened to Norm getting into his car, slamming the car door and driving slowly down the street. She wanted to cry, again; but she was tired of doing so and she was tired of being depressed; and Ruth Stevens was tired of drinking Scotch. Yet she started to cry; and yet within the bullshit of her life, she knew deep down, in her heart, that she had to be strong.

Ruth entered her daughter's bedroom and turned on the light and instantly felt the cold draft in the room. She looked around and thought about Father's Harris' sermon "months ago" about being positive during life's tragedies. So Ruth began to "believe" that Abigail wasn't doing any drugs and her boyfriend, Danny, was a good influence on her life and he was "ultimately" convincing Abigail to stay in high school and graduate and attend college and major in something that would yield a lucrative career like architecture, and Ruth would gladly pay for her education. And at this moment, Ruth became hopeful that maybe her life and her daughter's life would "slowly" improve. She turned off the bedroom light and left Abigail's room and thought about a hopeful future with her daughter; and Ruth only had "hope" at this moment, and she cherished it the best she could.

CHAPTER 12

Danny and Abigail waited patiently in his green 1973 Pontiac Trans Am, in the mostly empty parking lot of Rite-Aide. It was a cold night and this would be the night they would "carry out" their plan. Danny was going to follow Lester to his house, or to his apartment, or to his townhouse, or to where ever the fuck he lived. Abigail was going to put on a black ski mask and black leather gloves that Danny had purchased and she was going to point the loaded 9mm Smith & Wesson, at Lester, when he got out of the car, in the neighborhood where Lester lived; and Abigail was going to grab the black satchel from Lester and get back in Danny's car, which would be parked down the street, with the headlights off, and the engine would be "running," and Lester wouldn't have a fuckin' clue what just happened to him and he would be "too shocked" to chase after Abigail who would be wearing a black ski mask and Lester would be unable to get an "accurate" description of the car or of the license plate or of Abigail; and Danny and Abigail would drive off with the satchel and begin their "new" life with the stolen money, or so they believed.

Consequently the plan that the young "cokeheads" created was clearly fucked up, and they had no way of determining where Lester actually lived. What if he drove somewhere else after work?

Danny and Abigail didn't even know if Lester lived alone or where he actually lived. He could have driven over ninety miles to Riverside County. And one fact that was severely overlooked during the planning stage of the robbery was that Abigail never fired a handgun. Yes she held the 9mm and reviewed handgun safety rules with Danny. "Never put your finger on the trigger unless you're going to shoot" and "always point the gun at the ground unless you plan to shoot someone." Danny reviewed the gun rules in his bedroom one night with Abigail and she nodded her head as if she was listening, but all she could think about was robbing the black man; and another issue in the robbery plan was that Danny was sending Abigail out of the car and she was going to point a loaded gun at a stranger while she was wearing a black ski mask, which may increase the chances of Abigail accidently pulling the trigger. And aside from the numerous issues in planning the robbery, Danny and Abigail never discussed if Lester didn't steal money from the company safe the night they plan to rob him. Danny thought about this issue and "hoped" that money was in the black satchel, but he never mentioned it; all he really cared about was getting high and having sex with his underage girlfriend and leaving Los Angeles for good; and now they sat in the darkness in his green 1973 Pontiac Trans Am waiting for Lester Jackson, as Abigail snorted more coke from a small compact mirror that was on the console; and now she was very high, so fuckin' high. She put the compact mirror into the glove compartment and she put on her leather gloves and asked "Are you ready to do this shit?"

"Yeah, of course," Danny said.

Now there was an underlying problem that Danny didn't know about at this very moment. Abigail had a "secret" plan of her own. During the past few months of snorting cocaine and drinking beer, Abigail started to "really" believe that Lester Jackson murdered her father and thought that Tyrone Williams had nothing to do with the "actual" murder, and it started when she shared this belief with Danny one night, in his bedroom, which led to an argument and it started when she said "I think Lester Jackson killed my father."

"What, what do you mean?" Danny asked. "I thought you said that motherfucker was in jail!"

"He was or is, but I don't think that was him that did it. I think he was an imposter or something. You know how these black guys are falsely arrested all the time and how they look alike. I saw it on TV about this black dude that committed this crime, but this other black dude was arrested instead, for like twenty years."

"What are you now, a fuckin' attorney?" Danny asked. He was losing his patience with his underage girlfriend. He wanted to believe that Abigail was another "bitch" that he was tired of fucking, but he really did "care" for Abigail.

"I don't think that guy in jail killed my father," Abigail continued. "I think Lester Jackson did it. He killed him"

"Then who is that piece of shit in jail!'

"I told you, he's an imposter. The police have the wrong guy. I know it!"

Danny really didn't care what Abigail really said anymore. It all sounded like bullshit and he knew that her boss, Lester Jackson, at Rite-Aide, didn't murder her father or anyone else. He knew the real "murderer" was in jail awaiting trial. "Everything she is saying was so fuckin' stupid," Danny thought. And when Danny told her that she was "crazy" they started to argue, again; and Abigail cried and Danny consoled her on the bed near a circle of yellow lamp light; and for weeks, they continued to argue about who the real murderer was as they continued to plan to rob Lester Jackson. And during one night, Danny Ruiz began to realize that he was fucking up Abigail's life. Yes he gave her cocaine; and yes he took her virginity and she bled and she "officially" quit high school; and now she planned to rob her night manager. In addition to the mess that Danny brought to

Abigail's life, there was a possibility that she could overdose from snorting so much coke. "Fuck it," he thought. "It's her life." He tried to rationalize the situation. Yet Danny knew it was his responsibility to take care of her because she was underage and she was living with him, but Danny could barely take care of himself and that became his excuse for allowing Abigail to snort so much coke. Now after so many months of snorting cocaine, she was on "edge" and she lost a "significant" amount of weight and she had thick pink bags under her eyes and she appeared "bug-eyed" and she stopped taking daily showers. And one night, when Danny was taking out the trash to the dumpster, he thought of cancelling the robbery. "This is stupid," he thought. "We still have more shit to think about."

However Abigail knew that Danny was starting to feel "backwards" about the robbery and she urged Danny to "carry out" the plan and she began calling him a "pussy" and accused him of being a phony and a liar and then she would lock herself in the bathroom and Danny threatened to call her mother and Abigail eventually unlocked the door and they would "make up" and they would have sex on the bathroom floor; and then they fought the next night; and then Abigail would lock herself in the bathroom and Danny would threaten to call her mother, again and again and they would "make up" and they would have sex on the bathroom floor, again and again.

Their relationship was "officially" turbulent, but what kept them together were Rocky's cocaine and the sex, so Danny decided to proceed with robbing Lester regardless of the numerous deficiencies in their planning. And as the date of the robbery neared closer, Abigail "truly" believed that Lester Jackson murdered her father. "Fuck, Tyrone," she thought. "It was all about killing Lester Jackson." And although Danny was clueless about Abigail's plan, they both decided to risk their lives together because they also believed that they were in love and they disregarded the numerous problems in their robbery plan, as they hoped the "flaws" would miraculously work themselves out someway.

And now they waited for Lester to leave Rite-Aide and it was eleven fifty-six p.m., and then Danny and Abigail noticed Lester leaving with the black satchel.

"There he is," Abigail said as she pointed at Lester. She pulled the 9mm from under the seat and quickly opened the passenger door.

"Where the fuck are you doing!"

"Just follow me," Abigail said. "I have a plan."

Danny grabbed her arm but she snatched it away and exited his car wearing the black leather gloves and holding the loaded 9mm. Danny cussed but she left to carry out her own plan. At that moment, Danny should have left her ass in the parking lot with a loaded 9mm but he was in love, so he decided to wait and watch as Abigail approached Lester near his blue Prius; and before Lester noticed Abigail, he accidently dropped his keys on the ground and picked them up; and that is when he discovered Abigail pointing a gun at his stomach. He thought he was dreaming, but it was all "real" and very scary and she said "Put your fuckin' hands up!"

It took Lester a moment or two to realize that he was being robbed by this "white bitch;" and then he dropped the black satchel, on the ground, and kept the car keys in his hands as he raised them and he stared at Abigail and never believed that an "employee of the month" would rob him.

"What, what is this?" He asked.

"You do anything stupid and I'll blow your fuckin' head off. Open both doors, slowly," Abigail said.

Lester unlocked both doors and opened them and Abigail carefully pulled the black satchel from the ground and she got in the backseat and Lester got in the driver's seat and they both closed the doors and Lester finally asked "What do you want?" His voice broke, as he was having difficulty speaking.

Abigail searched through the satchel and instantly found a stack of cash. She pointed the gun to his head and said "Drive, asshole."

"Where?"

"Just drive. I'll tell you where to go." Lester started his car and was about to drive when Abigail said "Turn on your headlights, asshole." He turned on his headlights and they drove to the community park, in Mar Vista, and this was the same park where Abigail had numerous meaningful conversations with her father, and this was the park where she learned how to walk, and this was the park where Abigail started to learn how to ride a bike without "training" wheels. Now this was the park where Abigail marched an innocent black man across the dark wet grass. She ordered him down within the middle of the moonlit darkness. Lester got on his knees on the wet grass and faced his possible death sentence. He looked up at the "white bitch" who pointed the weapon at his head and she couldn't hold the gun still.

"What did I do?" Lester pleaded. He began to cry and he was sick with fear.

"You killed my father. I know you did it! Just admit it!" The rage filled Abigail's body. She waited months for this moment, and now she was beyond angry and "coked up." But for some reason, she couldn't shoot the crying black man who was on his knees on the dark wet grass. She had to "carry out" her own plan, but she still couldn't hold the gun still.

Lester finally stood and he tried his best to talk her out of killing him and he said "Look, you don't want to do this. It's all a mistake. I swear. Let me go, and we'll forget about it. I'll forget about it. I know you're angry. I see that."

Abigail lowered the gun and Lester felt slightly hopeful. Yet he didn't notice the dark figure behind Abigail, which turned out to be Danny, who grabbed the gun from Abigail and shot Lester four times in the chest. Lester collapsed on the wet grass and died instantly. His eyes clamped shut forever, but not before he got one last look at Abigail and the gun shots were deafening and time moved slowly just for a second.

"Get the fuckin' satchel and meet me in the car now," Danny said. He glared at Abigail and he had a "look" in his eyes that she had never seen before, and he walked away toward the parking lot as if nothing happened. Abigail peered at the black dead corpse on the wet grass. Her ears still rang from the guns shots.

BLAM! BLAM! BLAM! BLAM!

She barely heard what Danny had just said to her, but she knew she had to get the money from the blue Prius and leave. She finally turned and walked away from Lester and stopped and vomited by a tree and she heard sirens in the distance. She eventually reached Lester's blue Prius and took his black satchel from the backseat. When she entered Danny's green 1973 Pontiac Trans Am, she was pale and mentally and emotionally exhausted. She thought she was going to vomit again, as Danny sped onto the freeway and then onto the highway; but she didn't vomit, and within less than two hours they arrived in Palm Springs, at the Desert Lodge Motel, which was located off Highway 111. It was nearly two a.m. and the air was still warm when Danny parked his car and turned off the engine and they both listened to the dark desert silence for a moment. They were "officially" sober; and it was the most sober they had been since they met each other six months earlier.

"How much do we have?" Danny asked.

"I already told you. It's in the fuckin' suitcase."

"Well tell me again!"

"Two thousand," Abigail said. She wiped her tears.

"That should get us around in Arizona for a while," Danny said. He looked at Abigail and said calmly "I'm going to get a room. Just wait here for a second."

"Why did you do it?"

"Why do you think?" Danny asked. "Do you have any

idea what the fuck you did? We were supposed to follow him to his fuckin' house!" Abigail cried and wiped the tears but she kept crying. "Look" Danny said. "You didn't kill him. It was me. I did it!'

"Do you think that matters now! Who is going to believe it!"

"This is what you wanted, right? He killed your father! Now you have justice. Isn't that what you wanted?"

"Shut up! Just get out of here!" Abigail said and cried loudly.

Danny grabbed the car keys and stepped out of the car and slammed the car door behind him; and Abigail looked down at the leather gloves in her hands and started to realize what had happened and she "felt" equally responsible for someone's "death."

A few minutes later, Danny entered the lobby of the Desert Lodge Motel and rented a room from a white motel clerk named Roy; and Roy didn't like Danny "probably" because Danny was Mexican and he "appeared" suspicious and he had shoulder-length hair and he wore a faded Motorhead T-shirt and showed up at two a.m. in a loud rumbling car.

"Where you coming from?" Roy asked.

"San Diego," Danny said.

"Oh, yeah."

"Yeah," Danny said.

"My brother lives there. What part?" Roy asked.

"Near the ocean"

"Huh? You mean, Oceanside?"

"Yeah."

"Anybody with you?" Roy asked.

"No."

"How many days you staying?"

"Just one night."

"That's not very long," Roy said. "Where you headed after this?"

"Should I get a room somewhere else?" Danny snapped.

Roy smirked and he rang up a total on the cash register and Danny gave him cash and Roy took the cash and gave him a motel card key for his room. Danny grabbed it and left. And Roy continued to watch Danny because he was Mexican and he had long shoulder-length hair and wore a faded Motorhead T-shirt and showed up at two a.m., in a loud rumbling car. And those were "probably" the reasons why the white motel clerk named Roy didn't like Danny Ruiz.

And a few minutes later, Danny reached into the trunk of his car and grabbed his suitcase and Abigail grabbed her suitcase from the backseat and her suitcase had Lester's cash inside of it. She followed Danny upstairs to the motel room. She could barely pull her suitcase up the stairs toward the small motel room. Once they entered, Danny locked the door and turned on the lamp and looked around the small room with cheap furniture and the place smelled like stale cigar smoke. "Maybe the place has cameras," Danny thought. He knew the police would be searching for them soon. He stood by the window behind the dusty drapes and stared at the parking lot. He knew the sun would rise in a few hours and he was exhausted and he needed more "coke" and he was about to get some from his suitcase and then he noticed Abigail near the bathroom.

"Where are you going?" Danny asked.

"I have to pee. Is that okay?"

"Well, hurry the fuck up," Danny said. He watched her for a moment until she entered the bathroom and locked the bathroom door. Danny was delirious. He needed "coke" and he realized that in a few hours he would become the most "wanted man" in L.A. County for robbery and murdering an innocent black man. Danny had to do something quickly. He peered at the cheap clock on the wall and it was nearly three a.m.; or maybe it was four a.m. Danny was unsure anymore about anything. He just murdered someone and he realized that he couldn't just stand by the dusty drapes waiting for the cops to find him and handcuff him and toss him in prison for the rest of his life where he would get butt raped by large white and black and Hispanic men, in the shower area, and in his cell, until his rectum bled or until he contracted HIV; and he would spend the rest of his life sucking men's penises until they came into his mouth. He could "suck" dicks for drugs but he couldn't do it to be someone's "bitch." And once Danny was apprehended, he wouldn't be able to afford a "competent" attorney and he would be "stuck" with some dumb fuckin' public attorney, in a cheap suit, who couldn't give a "rat's ass" about another Mexican who fucked up and murdered some black man.

Danny was beginning to panic.

The motel walls were closing in on him and the room was getting small and he thought the sunlight was glowing outside along the ridges of the mountains. Danny grabbed the 9mm from his suitcase and tucked it in his waistband and left the motel.

Now in the bathroom, Abigail finished peeing and she wiped herself and flushed the toilet and washed her hands; and she was about to leave when she stopped and peered into the mirror, within a circle of dim yellow motel light. And in that moment, it was all very true. She didn't "look good." She was seventeen but her beauty had faded into "shit." She had those large pink puffy bags under her eyes and she had stress lines on her forehead and her cheeks were gaunt and she was officially a "cokehead."

However that was the least of her problems. She had allowed hatred to control her life. For a moment, she remembered the beautiful afternoon, at the community park, in Mar Vista, with her father, when she was almost thirteen years old and the leaves that blew across their feet and she told her father that she wished that he'll always be around and he said "Listen, Abby, I'm not going anywhere" and that was a "special" moment that she cherished in her life and she would do anything to have it back.

Now she put her hand on the door knob, in the motel bathroom, and felt a chill. She thought she was getting sick and then she felt a presence like she never had felt before.

Abigail finally opened the bathroom door and quickly realized Danny was gone! She opened her suitcase and found the money stuffed inside. She rushed outside and noticed Danny had left in his green 1973 Pontiac Trans Am. Now she was "officially" alone and the love she felt for Danny was gone and the "high" she felt from the coke was gone. Her father was gone. Her mother was in the city, unaware of her whereabouts.

Abigail had nothing.

She rushed back inside and closed the door and locked it and slid to the floor and cried. Yet she had to do something because she didn't want the cops to bust through the door and see her crying like a "fuckin' baby."

She had to be tough.

Two hours later, Danny was speeding near the Arizona border in his green 1973 Pontiac Trans Am and the sun was rising behind him in the far distance. Maybe he could escape the authorities, in California, and maybe he believed that he would be "safe" in Arizona and then he would try to communicate with Abigail. Now he could not take his foot from the gas pedal. He sped by cars, trucks and campers.

He couldn't stop!

Maybe he was possessed as he drove faster and faster as Motorhead blared from the cheap speakers. The raspy vocals, fast guitar riffs, and the pounding drums filled the car and may have possessed him to drive faster; and then Danny noticed siren lights in the rear view mirror. Danny pulled over on a dusty road and turned off his car and the dust trailed in the sunlight, as the sheriff parked behind him. The sheriff got out of his car and approached slowly and placed his hand on his holster, as Danny sat in the driver's seat of his car and peered at the 9mm in his lap and then peered in the left hand mirror and noticed the sheriff approaching with his hand still on his holster. Danny finally opened his car door and quickly stepped outside and pointed his 9mm at the sheriff who instantly pulled out his weapon and fired two shots into Danny's stomach and chest. Danny fell against the open car door of his green 1973 Pontiac Trans Am. Danny slid to the ground and his eyes slowly closed and his body went limp with the 9mm in his hand.

The sheriff called for "back up" on his portable radio and he continued to approach the Trans Am. He pointed his weapon at the vehicle and said "If someone's in there you better put your hands up now, or you will get shot!" The sheriff moved closer and didn't see anyone and it was during a certain moment that he discovered five bullets on the passenger seat. The sheriff realized that the "Hispanic male" may have been pointing a gun without any bullets; and so the sheriff instantly "wondered" how he would write this "situation" in his report; or he could "hide" the bullets. "Fuck," he thought. "Maybe I should include the 'truth' in the report."

At the Desert Lodge Motel, the white motel clerk named Roy stood behind the counter watching the morning news. The top story was about a possible "murder/robbery situation" in Mar Vista, in West L.A. and Roy heard the words "motive" and "two suspects" in a "greenish colored Pontiac" and "white female teenager" and a "Hispanic male, in his late twenties to early thirties."

Roy peered out of the dirty office window and noticed Abigail walking across the hotel parking lot with a suitcase. He dialed nine-one-one on the phone and told the operator that a "Mexican dude" and a "white chick" came into the motel this morning around two a.m. and said "The "Mexican dude drove off a few hours ago but the white chick is leaving right now. I think they have guns and knives. How do I know?" he asked in the phone. "I just know," and Roy listened to the police operator and said "Okay, will do" and then he hung up the phone.

Twenty minutes later, within the early morning heat of Palm Springs, Abigail walked down a populated street barely able to carry her suitcase. She was lost and finally heard a short burst of a police siren behind her. She stopped and turned and noticed a Palm Springs Police Car. She didn't run. She stood still. The officers emerged from the police car with their guns drawn and ordered her to the ground. Abigail was quickly apprehended on the hot sidewalk and handcuffed, and people watched and pointed as she was unsure what was happening. All she remembered was hearing a siren and then remembered officers on top of her on the hot sidewalk cussing and yelling and punching her, or that's what she told her attorney after being transported to a police station, in Los Angeles.

CHAPTER 13

Various police operators received numerous phone calls about a shooting at the community park, in Mar Vista, and by dawn, officers located Lester's blue Prius; and as sunlight filled the skies, police tape surrounded the parking lot, at the community park; and Lester's blue Prius was carefully examined for "prints" and other "incriminating evidence" and during the search, a few strands of long blond hair were pulled from the backseat and "sealed for evidence." Ruth would quickly learn that these "long blond hairs" belonged to her daughter; and Ruth thought she was "dreaming" or had to be dreaming when she opened the front door after hearing the doorbell while she was writing in her home office. She was rewriting the subplot between the mother and the son, in her novel, *The After Life*, when the door bell rang.

She answered the door to discover detectives Preston and Johnson and they flashed their badges and the detectives politely invited themselves inside and Ruth sat on the brown leather couch as she heard the words "your daughter" and "accomplice" and "first degree murder" and "robbery" and then she was told that "Danny Ruiz was shot and killed by a sheriff deputy, near the Arizona border" a few hours ago. And that's about all she remembered hearing from Preston and Johnson. She was nauseous and she couldn't believe that life was actually getting worse after her husband's murder.

But it was happening.

"All of this shit must be a dream," she thought as she sat in a daze on her brown leather couch. She was barely unable to recover from the "mental" punch to her head and the "mental" kick to her stomach. And it was a beating that life gave her which never seemed to end. She didn't know how much more "bullshit" she could endure. She barely had the strength to do anything but cry.

A few days passed days before Ruth could visit Abigail at a juvenile detention center. Once the day arrived, Ruth waited for her daughter in the visiting room as other female teenagers spoke to their parents, or their boyfriends, or their guardians. Finally a guard escorted Abigail inside the room. She was handcuffed and shackled and moved slowly in her blue jumpsuit. She appeared thinner than the last time that her mother had seen her and her hair was a tangled mess. Abigail sat down at the table and avoided eye contact with her mother. Ruth knew she only had a few minutes to speak to her daughter but she was unsure how to begin the conversation; and so she said what she thought.

"What the hell were you thinking? Do you have any idea what you're being charged with? Do you, dammit!" Ruth waited for a response but Abigail was quiet. "Tell me something," Ruth continued. "Please say something! Tell me that I'm dreaming and that I'll wake up and that this never happened." But Ruth knew that she was not dreaming; however she "felt" like she was indeed trapped in a nightmare. All she really knew that life was getting worse than she had ever expected. She used to believe that all the "crap" that people encountered in life was their fault. Ruth discovered that was a falsehood. In the past twelve months, Ruth was laid-off and her husband was murdered and now her daughter was being "charged" for first degree murder and robbery.

Life only got worse for Ruth Stevens, but Ruth needed to hear her daughter speak so she said once again "Please say something."

Abigail finally pushed the tangled hair from her face and said "I'm pregnant."

The white District Attorney, Brad Dirkson, who was a Republican, decided not to charge Abigail as an adult making her "possibly" eligible for parole in three years. However once the media began to "publicize" the incident, the case became "high profile" and Brad, the white District Attorney, was called a "racist" so he decided to charge Abigail as an adult. She was now facing over twenty-five years in prison for the murder and robbery of Lester Jackson, yet Abigail was refusing to plead guilty.

In the media, Abigail was the white innocent teenager with blue eyes and sandy blond hair who may have brutally shot and "gunned down" an innocent black man for "cash" and then the story gained more attention when "traces of cocaine" were found in her blood and in her boyfriend's blood. TV executives were now "desperate" to create an updated version of "The Long Island Lolita" set in Los Angeles, in 2012, which would include elements of "murder for passion" and "drug use" and "hatred."

It was sensationalism and the story was sensational.

And for the second time in over six months, Abigail Stevens was caught in a "high profile" case which revolved around a black man. On screen, Abigail was the white teenage girl who previously attended an all girls private Catholic high school, in Brentwood; and then a black man murders her white father so she "seeks justice" and guns down a "random" black man and steals his money and leaves the city with her "cokehead" boyfriend. Numerous periodicals featured a cover story on Abigail and Danny's life which suggested that Lester Jackson's murder was nothing more than an "act of revenge" and Abigail was the coke addicted teenage girl who shacked up with her long-haired Mexican boyfriend.

A month after Lester's murder, the public continued to speculate what "really happened" the night at the community park, in Mar Vista, since Abigail was very "tight lipped" about that unfortunate night. There was a rumor that Abigail was trying to buy drugs from Lester after heroin was discovered, in his house, after his murder. The media merged "lies" and "truth" together for ratings.

The public wanted more sensationalism. They were obsessed with Abigail and it was the "horrible" obsession that would make it very difficult for the pristine white girl to receive a "fair trial" in L.A., so the "defense" requested to have the trial moved to Northern California. The entire case was a mess "in the eyes of the media." And as the media continued to "probe" the murder of Lester Jackson, Abigail never revealed that Lester Jackson stole money from the company safe, so investigators had to figure out how "two thousand dollars" ended up in Lester's black satchel. They spoke to Lester's younger brother, Clarence, about Lester "possibly" stealing money from the company safe; and then the media hounded Clarence and he would peer directly into the TV cameras and say "jus' mind your own damn business!"

New pieces of the murder and robbery unraveled almost everyday and L.A. residents "thirsted" for more soap opera details about Abigail Stevens, the white teenage prima donna and her deceased Mexican boyfriend. However as black residents demanded for "rapid justice" and white residents demanded a "fair trial," it would be another year before Abigail's trial began for the shooting death and robbery of Lester Jackson.

More than five months after Abigail's arrest, Ruth stopped writing the first draft of her novel and eventually stopped bathing. She avoided calls and stopped peering out of the window to look at the "media circus" outside her house. She sat on her brown leather couch and drank Scotch and vomited throughout most of the days. She probably should have driven herself to the hospital but secretly she was hoping that she would suffer a massive heart attack on the hardwood floor, in her living room, next to a bottle of Scotch. She thought the only way to "escape" her painful life was suicide. She didn't want to take pills and all she had was a few aspirin in the house. She thought of slitting her wrists, but she didn't want to look at blood seeping from her wrists as she waited for "death." So she thought of drinking herself to death since "death" would be easier than living in a world of shit; however ironic events usually occur during tragedies; so during a morning of Ruth's attempted suicide as she continued to drink Scotch on her brown leather couch and heard the voices of the media outside her window, she "suddenly" realized that today was the one year anniversary of her husband's death. She finally had a reason to live, at least for today. She got off the brown leather couch and showered. And in the shower she realized that she couldn't let her husband know that she was "too weak" to continue living regardless of the unfolding tragedies in her life, so she washed her body for over twenty minutes, and then stepped from the shower and dried herself and shaved her armpits, her legs, and trimmed her private area with a device she purchased from a beauty supply store downtown, a few months earlier; and she applied deodorant and dressed and combed her hair and ate breakfast which consisted of cereal and stale toast and after breakfast she "felt" better. And she tossed out the empty bottles of Scotch that were on the kitchen counter.

Ruth got in her Lexus SUV and backed out of the driveway and she secretly hoped that she would hit a member of the media, or at least run over their fuckin' feet but that didn't happen. She finally drove out of the neighborhood and to a nearby florist and picked up flowers and drove to the cemetery, in Westwood, and placed the flowers on her husband's plot. She was going to cry again but she couldn't. She was actually bored of crying. She sat for a few hours near his headstone and thought about her life with Francis; and the sun began to lower in the sky and shadows extended across the cemetery. She finally got back into her Lexus SUV. She drove to the church she used to attend with her family and quietly prayed on her knees. She finally arrived home thirty minutes later; and it was dark and most of the media had left for the night. She entered the house and poured herself another glass of Scotch from an "emergency supply" that she kept under the sink; and then she stood at the doorway of her daughter's dark bedroom and immediately felt the cold still air. And as she looked around the dark room, Ruth wanted to "blame" herself for everything until she remembered that she was tired of doing that also, so she left her daughter's bedroom and Ruth entered her bedroom and turned on the lamp and placed her glass of Scotch on the night stand and sat on the edge of her bed away from the circle of yellow lamp light. She looked at her wedding ring and inhaled deeply and realized that she needed to make a change in her life. She finally removed the wedding ring from her finger and said "I love you, Francis Stevens."

Ruth stood up and kissed her wedding ring and walked to the dresser and placed her ring inside a drawer. She suddenly felt a presence behind her; and this time, it was a very strong presence. She heard the floor creak behind her and she felt a strong chill; but for some strange reason, Ruth closed her eyes and smiled.

BIRTH

CHAPTER 14

It happened around nine forty-five p.m. and he didn't expect it to happen. But it did. He was done with love and he didn't want anything to do with love, but it still happened. Francis Stevens was twenty-five years old, in 1992, and he had a thick mustache. He was about to start his third year in medical school and he was living in a "shit hole" apartment with his college friend, Omar Morales, in West L.A. And now Francis was talking to his "so-called" girlfriend, Jennifer Singleton, at a college graduation party, in Pasadena. And at this moment, he was bored with this tall white brunette woman who was a "junior" in UCLA and majored in anthropology. There was nothing "striking" or "intriguing" about Jennifer. She was someone that could go undetected in a cramped room like this room which was now packed with numerous college students who were about to graduate in a few weeks after finals. People chatted about their numerous "dreams" and "goals" and now this boring woman, named Jennifer Singleton, spoke about her father's corporation, and about her mother who was a third grade teacher, and about her younger sister who wanted to travel to Bosnia for some strange reason and so on and so on; but Francis didn't care about this useless shit.

Francis and Jennifer had been dating for nearly two

months and she rarely asked him questions, but Francis was "done" with love for right now; so he didn't care about being bored with Jennifer Singleton. He recently just ended a two year relationship with Tanya Clancy. They were about to move in together with her four cats and Francis knew that he wasn't ready for a commitment with her since she had obsessive compulsive disorders like checking the oven, the heater, and the front door while Francis tried to study for a stressful medical exam. He decided to study at the library but she would visit him there and after Francis believed that she was nothing more than a distraction, so he decided to call it quits; and at this moment, Francis stood listening to Jennifer who changed her subject from her sister's quest to Bosnia to her aunt's increasing glaucoma problem.

And it was during this moment of useless chatter that Francis discovered the most beautiful woman in this cramped room. And this woman was Ruth Gordon. She was twenty-two years old. "She is gorgeous," Francis thought. He was going to marry her and his mind was "made up" and the feeling of "having her" burned inside of him; and Francis was instantly in love and infatuated and obsessed in a matter of a few seconds. Yet his excitement was slightly "deflated" due to her large bulky overweight boyfriend, Conrad Miller, who stood next to her. His chunky fingers were wrapped around a glass of red wine. Conrad was thirty-four years old and was an "average" salesman for his parent's wineries. Nobody at the party knew much about him except that his parents were extremely wealthy from their wine business and Ruth's friends at the party knew that Conrad treated Ruth like royalty. He bought her diamond studded necklaces and brought her to sporting events where they sat next to celebrities. She was brought backstage after music concerts to "briefly" meet the band and get an occasional autograph. Ruth and Conrad flew in his father's private jet to Santa Barbara for a quick oyster trip and to San Francisco for an art gallery. She was the queen and

Conrad Miller was the king. However Ruth and Francis already had something in common. They were both bored with their relationships. Ruth was bored with the "royal" treatment and Francis was bored with Jennifer's personality. Ruth and Francis were already "perfect" for each other. They just didn't know it, yet.

Francis looked at Ruth numerous times and that's when Ruth noticed him. They both smiled. "He's kind of cute, but I hate his mustache," she thought. Across the crowded room, Ruth sensed that Francis was kind and honest which were a set of traits that Ruth had "rarely" seen in guys, including her boyfriend, Conrad. "Where are the nice men?" Ruth thought to herself one day. Yes Ruth actually disliked being pampered. She really just wanted "substance" from a guy. And now Francis watched Ruth leave the living room. And as he watched Ruth, he knew that he had to follow her and he excused himself and followed Ruth as he held his half-filled glass of Chablis and moved slowly through the thick crowd. Francis couldn't find Ruth in the hallway. "Fuck, I hope she didn't leave," he thought. Francis had to use the bathroom so he waited in front of the closed bathroom door hoping that his "dream girl" was inside. His heart beat quickly as Ruth finally opened the door; but at that moment, she accidently bumped into his wine glass which caused wine to spill onto his one hundred dollar shirt.

"Oh, my God! I'm so sorry," Ruth said.

"It's, it's fine," he said. His smile quickly dissolved.

"Are you sure? Follow me," Ruth said. She innocently grabbed his hand and pulled him inside the bathroom and Francis inconspicuously locked the door behind him. Ruth dabbed his shirt with a damp washcloth and attempted to "rid" the stain but Francis didn't care about the shirt anymore. He smelled the scent of her perfume and noticed how "clean" she appeared. He grew increasingly nervous with her touch and he glanced at her perfectly painted fingernails. He was in love but he had to "move" quickly before someone fidgeted with the door knob and banged on the locked bathroom door.

"I'm really sorry. My boyfriend says I'm so clumsy. You should see me when I'm drunk," Ruth said while continuing to dab at the stain with the damp washcloth.

"That's your boyfriend out there?"

"I'm sure you could hear him across the room."

"Actually, I can," Francis said.

They both laughed.

"Who are you here with?" Ruth asked.

Francis hesitated for a moment and then said "Well, I'm here with a woman named Jennifer, and if I hear about her cats or her sister again I'll probably go insane." Francis said. "I'm actually sure of it."

"I hear ya'," Ruth said. "I think I memorized how many stocks Conrad has and when to buy and when to sell." She continued to dab the damp washcloth at the stain.

"Look at us. We're standing here, talking about my date and your boyfriend. That's not good," Francis said.

An awkward moment evolved between them.

"Well this is the best that I could do with the shirt," Ruth said. She put the damp washcloth down on the counter and was ready to leave.

"You certainly have a gift. I barely see the stain anymore," Francis said, lying.

"I'm sorry, again. Well, have a great night. If your girlfriend wants to know what happened just have her come see me," Ruth said. She smiled but for some strange reason she was becoming increasingly nervous.

"I'm sure she won't even notice." Francis said, quickly. "Can I see you one time?'

"I'm sorry, but I've got a boyfriend, and it wouldn't be fair to him.

"You're right," Francis said.

Ruth didn't have much time to decide what was "right" or

"wrong." She finally said "I probably shouldn't be doing this." She grabbed a piece of toilet paper and scribbled her phone number on it with lipstick that she found in a drawer and gave him the phone number. They smiled and shook hands and they "officially" introduced themselves; and Ruth left the bathroom and Francis was the happiest person in Pasadena that night, in 1992.

An hour later, Conrad drove Ruth back to Sherman Oaks and she stared out of the window; and while Conrad spoke about his father's new winery, in Santa Barbara, Ruth felt "slightly" ashamed about giving her phone number to Francis. Although she felt like she made the "right" choice. She also knew that she could never marry Conrad, although her parents wanted her to marry him due to his parent's wealth. They didn't want Ruth to struggle to pay the mortgage and bills every month. "And what about kids?" her mother asked one night over dried-out lasagna. "Children are very expensive. You need someone with money, and lots of it." Ruth knew that Conrad could support a family, but she wanted a man who didn't "live off" his parent's wealth. Conrad wasn't a "bad person" but just boring and self absorbed; and always discussing his parent's money. Yes Conrad was "good" to Ruth, but he rarely inquired about her life. How was she doing in college? Was she close to finding a job after college? What did she want to do with her life? Did Conrad know that Ruth wanted to become a novelist instead of some corporate zombie? She pondered those questions. She knew Conrad didn't even notice that Ruth was unusually quiet on the drive home, as he navigated on the empty lanes of the 101 north freeway, in his newly purchased Jaguar.

Ruth arrived home around eleven forty-five p.m. and before she stepped out of his newly purchased Jaguar, she mechanically kissed Conrad on the lips. And Ruth did feel guilty. Yet she didn't feel guilty for giving her phone number to a male stranger, in the bathroom of a party. Rather she felt guilty because she continued a relationship that she should have ended "months" ago. It was Ruth's parents who pressured her to try the make the situation work, but the more she tried to make "it" work, the more she began to despise Conrad. She thought about the way he always ate with his mouth open, the way he snorted and farted harmoniously when he slept; and Ruth despised that Conrad never exercised, and during sex he would lay his large body on top of her, nearly suffocating her. And now when she walked inside her parents' house, on Del Rey Avenue, in Sherman Oaks, in 1992, she had to do something to change her current situation with Conrad.

Now Ruth quietly ascended the dark staircase hoping that she wouldn't wake her parents, especially her mother, Louise, but it happened anyway; and Louise emerged from the master bedroom when Ruth reached the moonlit landing. At this moment in time, Louise was forty-five years old and she had thick graying shoulder-length curls and she wore a robe from 1977 and she appeared exactly the way she would twenty years later, frumpy and slightly wrinkled and Ruth said "hello" to her mother who followed Ruth inside her bedroom and Ruth wasn't in the mood for her mother's inquiries.

"How was the party?" her mother asked quickly. "How is Conrad? Are you two 'love birds' getting along?"

"Mom, we're not lovebirds and we're not getting along," Ruth said as she turned on a light switch and turned on her lamp, on her night stand, and changed into her pajamas.

"What? Is he acting up?" Louise was instantly alarmed.

"No. I'm just tired of him!"

Louise was clearly unhappy with her daughter's response since she wanted her daughter to marry someone "wealthy" instead of waiting for a man to accumulate riches in his fifties and sixties. And she wondered how anyone pays bills when someone is trying to accumulate wealth. And then Louise said "Look, Ruth, he'll grow on you."

"Jesus, mom, he's not fungus."

"You know, you are impossible, and please don't use the Lord's name in vain!"

"Well, I can't get used to him," Ruth said.

Louise grabbed her daughter's hand and Ruth knew that "touch" meant that her mother was going to try to say something meaningful. "Ruth, you're twenty-two years old. You're just too young to understand what I'm talking about, but your father and I want the best for you."

Her mother continued to lecture Ruth on love and finances. Twenty minutes later, Louise left her daughter's bedroom and Ruth finally turned off the light and got into her bed, near a circle of yellow lamp light. She thought about the stranger that she had met a few hours ago which caused her to smile. She finally turned off the lamp and slid her hand under her pajama bottom and pleasured herself and closed her eyes. She stifled her moans as she came. A few minutes later, Ruth fell asleep.

Now in West L.A. near the 405 Freeway, Francis lay on a faded brown couch, in a small crowded apartment that he shared with his college buddy, Omar; and this was the week that Francis had to sleep on the couch while Omar slept in the bedroom; and this was the week that Francis had to listen to Omar having sex with a blond hair woman, or a brunette, in the bedroom; and Francis hated hearing the sounds of the mattress squeaking, the sexual moans from Omar and from his "sleepover" guest. Francis would usually pound his fist on the bedroom door or the wall to signal for them to "shut the fuck up" and that would work for a moment; but then the mattress would squeak again and the moans were heard again and again. However this night was very different for Francis who continued to lie on the faded brown couch, near a circle of yellow lamp light. He couldn't sleep. He pulled out the piece of toilet paper from his pocket and looked at Ruth's scribbled phone number and he continued to stare at it until he eventually fell asleep.

In the morning, in the San Fernando Valley, Ruth

woke up and smiled after remembering meeting Francis. She showered and had to leave to finish studying for her final exams. She dressed quickly and tried to rush by her parents with her backpack when her father, Ben Gordon, stopped her. He was a large fifty-four year old man with high cholesterol who sold "advertising space" to corporations; and as his daughter rushed by he said "Hey, little lady, come and eat. We need to talk. I have a few questions for you."

Ruth turned and put her backpack on the floor and sat at the breakfast table with her parents and said "I have to get going soon." Ruth began nibbling on a short stack of pancakes.

"Ruth, could you please pray before you eat!" Her mother demanded. "How many times do I have to tell you?"

She quickly prayed and resumed eating.

"So what's this nonsense about you not wanting to date Conrad anymore?" Ben asked.

"I just don't like him," Ruth said.

"What do you mean you don't like him? Did you ever like him?"

"Yeah, I suppose," Ruth said.

"You know his father is a 'good' man. I've known him for over twenty years."

"I'm not dating his father," Ruth said. 'You only like Conrad because his parents have money, and money usually makes people into jerks."

"Please watch the way you talk to your father," Louise snapped. "And what is so wrong with being wealthy? God forbid we can have a little piece of it."

For the next fifteen minutes, Ruth attempted to explain to her parents that she was "no longer" interested in dating Conrad Miller. She also told them that Conrad was dull and all he did was talk about himself and his father's wineries.

"That's what guys do, Ruth. You have to learn that. They talk about themselves and money," her father said proudly and smiled as he ate another strip of bacon.

Yet Ruth didn't care what men were supposed to do or not do. She excused herself and put her plate in the sink and was nearly outside when the yellow colored phone on the kitchen wall rang. And she didn't pay attention until after her mother answered the phone and said "Ruth, it's for you. It's a guy."

Ruth raced to the phone and grabbed the receiver. A large smile evolved on her face as she heard Francis' voice. She didn't care that he didn't wait the "traditional" three days to call a woman. He called now and she liked that. He was assertive and that was a "great quality" to have. Her parents stared at her in disapproval. Louise and Ben "wished" it was Conrad on the phone but they knew it wasn't; and an hour later, Ruth met Francis at a café, in Westwood. They sat by a sunlit window and discussed her life's goals, which included writing her novel, which was something that she never discussed with Conrad and rarely with her parents; and her parents only wanted her to focus on obtaining an accounting degree so she could make "real" money.

Now Ruth told Francis about the plot of her novel, which revolved around Corrine Dolans, a housewife in the Midwest, who lived with her husband, Steven Dolans, and her two children, and she has an affair with Dale Hartmen, a ten year veteran of the towns sheriff's department; and one day, Dale is gunned down during the "line of duty" by a "cokehead" and he watches Corrine from the after life and how she deals with her two children and her husband after his death. Ruth mentioned that she didn't have a title yet and Francis smiled at her and she said "I know I shouldn't have told anyone. I knew it was stupid."

"No, not at all," Francis said. "You should pursue it. You *must* pursue it."

"I would love to but my parents really don't want me to write for a living. They think most writers are broke and live in apartments."

"Well what makes Ruth happy?"

Ruth didn't have a quick response to an easy question since she was unsure what "happiness" really meant. She knew her parents weren't really happy with each other. She always felt the "coldness" between them and she wanted more than what they had emotionally and financially.

"I guess happiness is graduating college, getting a 'good' job and buying a nice house and having a family."

"Is that what happiness is to you?" Francis asked.

"I think so. Well what is your idea of happiness?" Ruth asked.

"Happiness is when you found the love of your life and you never let go," Francis said.

Ruth smiled and she wanted to laugh but she didn't want to embarrass him and she finally said "Now you sound like a writer." She knew what he said was "corny ass shit" but they both smiled and she "actually" loved what he said; and she loved the fact that Francis knew what to say to her as Conrad was 'clueless" about saying the "right" thing at the "right" time.

Sunlight began to diminish and Francis walked Ruth to her "beat up" 1987 Toyota Corolla, in the college parking structure, a few blocks from the café. Ruth finally realized that she didn't study for her exams, but it didn't matter. They stopped within long shadows near her car and they kissed for the very first time; and when Ruth arrived home it was dark outside and her parents were waiting for her at the dinner table. Ruth prayed and they discussed the "new guy" who called earlier. Ruth explained that she met the "new guy" in the bathroom of the graduation party that she went to last night.

Ben and Louise finally realized that Conrad wasn't going to satisfy Ruth, and it would only make them happy if she married Conrad. Ben and Louise tried not to be selfish parents but they couldn't help it since "selfishness" was in the family tree and would "stay" in the family tree for many years; and now Conrad drove from Encino to Sherman Oaks to pick up Ruth to go to a jazz club. Strangely Conrad never thought his relationship with Ruth felt "strained" until Ruth entered his car that night and said that she wanted to "end the relationship." Conrad was confused since he was never "dumped" in his life; and at thirty-four years old, he was finally discarded from a relationship and left to rot in the emotional winds of life.

"What are you talking about?" Conrad asked. "I thought everything was great between us. I bought you jewelry and necklaces and we flew in my father's private jet and stayed at the best hotels."

"It has nothing to do with that," Ruth said. "A relationship is about getting to know each other. I feel like I don't know anything about you."

"Well, what do you want to know?"

"See, you just don't get it, Conrad!" Ruth noticed the anger in Conrad's eyes and it was something that she hadn't seen since she had started dating him a year ago.

"You're making a big mistake, Ruth, a big fuckin' mistake!"

"Time will tell," Ruth said. She left the car and stammered toward the house, and Conrad started up his newly purchased Jaguar and sped from the driveway and down the street away from the Gordon's house, on Del Rey Avenue, in Sherman Oaks.

Ruth didn't look back.

CHAPTER 15

Francis "officially" began dating Ruth in the summer of 1992. They were usually together and they always talked; and they talked in his pre-owned silver Mercedes. They talked in her driveway, on Del Rey Avenue, in Sherman Oaks, and they talked on the phone, at night, until sunlight filled the skies. Francis sometimes brought Ruth to his one bedroom apartment that he shared with Omar, in West L.A., near the 405 freeway; and one night, Ruth witnessed Francis arguing with his roommate, Omar, about how he was "supposed" to get the bedroom that week. A tall blond haired woman waited impatiently while checking her nails in the living room, until Francis finally allowed Omar to have the room with the clean sheets. And it was that night when Francis slowed danced with Ruth, in the cluttered living room, to The Rolling Stones' song, Angie, from 1973; and during that song, Francis said "I love your story and it's going to be a great novel one day." Ruth was excited and she finally experienced this feeling called "love" and people began to know that Ruth was in love and her parents even noticed the she looked "great" and "happy." And during The Rolling Stones' song, Angie, from 1973, Francis asked "You know what I've been thinking about?"

"What?"

"I'm thinking that you and I should move in together,"

Francis said. He held her tight during the song. She would love to "move in" with him but she knew it would be difficult to get her mother's consent to move in with another man. Yes Ruth was twenty-two and she could do what she wanted, but Ruth wanted her mother's consent to move in with her "new" boyfriend, so she had to choose a time to approach her mother about the situation.

A few weeks later, Ruth spoke to her mother when she was in the backyard trimming her rose bushes on a warm August afternoon. Louise loved spending hours in the backyard "tending" to flowers. Ruth approached slowly and had a quick conversation with her mother and she started it by saying "Francis asked me to move in with him."

"And what did you say?" Louise asked.

"I said I would," Ruth said, slightly nervous. "I love him."

"What do you know about love?" Louise scoffed. She finally turned and looked at Ruth. "You're twenty-two years old."

"You always do that to me, mom! Every time something great happens in my life you want to dismiss it."

"Don't get that tone with me, Ruth!" Louise snapped. She tried her best to remain calm. "Listen, Ruth, do you know how much responsibility there is in a committed relationship?"

"You would have never said that if I was going to move in with Conrad," Ruth said. She was frustrated and she wanted to cry, but she didn't want to do it in front of her mother; and she knew she had to be tough during this moment. She was about to leave when Louise thought about her own mother, Jean, who despised Ben. And Jean thought Ben was lazy. Louise felt the pain "now" as she did over twenty-five years ago, and Louise didn't want to be like her mother.

"Hold it, Ruth," her mother said. "If you want to move in with him, your father and I want to talk to him. I want to find out what he's about instead of a casual 'hello' and 'goodbye'."

Ruth smiled and wanted to hug her mother but she couldn't remember the last time she did so. Ruth didn't even hug her mother after graduating high school or when she graduated college a few months ago, and she wasn't going to begin now; and so Ruth thanked her and walked upstairs to call Francis. She walked by her parent's bedroom and noticed her father sitting on his side of the bed, in his white T-shirt and wrinkled slacks. He was slumped over and tired from work. Ruth stopped in the doorway of her parent's bedroom and looked at her father who appeared defeated within afternoon shadows. She quickly thought about when she was seven years old and she sat on her father's lap and he said "Be happy, Ruth. Misery is overrated." Ruth never realized what her father meant for many years; and now she entered her parent's hot and stuffy bedroom and noticed her father was pale and she asked "Is everything okay, dad?"

"You know, I will always love you, right?"

"Of course, why?" Ruth said as she continued to approach her father.

"I just want you to know that I'm proud of you. I'm not always going to be around to tell you that."

"I know, dad, but do we need to talk about this now?"

"Just remember life is tough and not always fair," Ben said. "You have to be tough like I always taught you. It's hard to tell what's around each corner."

Ruth knew that her father was mentally drained from life and from being married to an unhappy woman for so many years; and now something inside of Ben was "burning out" at fifty-four years old. Ruth asked her father several times if he was okay and he had the same response every time on that warm August afternoon, in Sherman Oaks. "I'm fine, Ruth. Stop worrying."

Ruth finally left the room and thought about Francis coming to dinner and a few days later, Francis had dinner at the Gordon's house, in the dining room; and they used their "fine" dishes and silverware. Ruth knew that her parents were going to "test" Francis and his patience; and strangely that plan back fired. Francis loved the attention although he never really enjoyed family dinners with his own parents, Robert and Josephine.

Now Louise started the dinner with a lengthy prayer and she quoted passages from the Book of James. They finally began eating the dried-out prime rib, the tasteless string beans and the watery mashed potatoes. During the dinner, Louise needed to know if Francis could actually take care of Ruth; and Francis mentioned that he was attending medical school, at UCLA, and he was going into his third year and that he would eventually become a chest surgeon; and Ben appeared surprised. "Ruth never mentioned anything about Francis becoming a surgeon," he thought.

Yet Louise wasn't satisfied with Francis' responses and she wanted blood so she asked "What if things don't work out as a surgeon?"

"Mom, he's not trying to be an actor," Ruth said.

"Well what if things don't work out between you two?" Louise continued and Ruth was officially embarrassed.

Francis calmly answered each question as he looked at Louise and Ben. Ironically Louise knew that Ruth found a "great guy." And this was a guy who would never run from his problems or his spouse. She realized that fact during dinner. She also knew that Francis adored Ruth. However Louise didn't want anyone to know that she actually liked Francis. Her conversations with her husband about Francis consisted of "He's okay" or "He's fine," but deep down she felt that Francis had much more "substance" and "character" than Conrad.

Ben also liked Francis but he was vocal about his feelings. "I really think they're going to do well together," Ben said one morning while patting aftershave lotion on his face, while looking in the bathroom mirror. Although Ben was not surprised that Louise was cynical and jealous about Ruth and Francis. He knew that his wife, Louise, desired to be young and attractive again, like her twenty-two year old daughter; but at forty-five years old, Louise appeared much older than her age and she became increasingly jealous of her daughter's youth and beauty.

And so a month after the dinner with Francis, Ruth was carrying boxes from her room and setting them on the hardwood floor, in the living room, as she was officially moving out; yet she detected her mother's bad mood as she swept the floor. Louise stared at the stacked boxes near the staircase. She disliked that her "only" child was moving away and so she asked Ruth "Are you sure you want to be doing this?"

"Mom, please. Don't start. Everything is going to be fine. I promise," Ruth said and ascended the stairs.

Louise wasn't actually sure if she was angry because her "only" child was moving away or because she was "flat out" jealous of Ruth's life and her youthful love. It was the beginning of an exciting time for her daughter. Louise wanted to be "happy" for Ruth, but she wasn't and she heard a knock on the screen door. Louise focused her anger on Francis who stood behind the screen door. "This is the asshole who is stealing my lovely Ruth away from me," she thought.

"Hi, Mrs. Gordon," Francis said. He entered and she noticed his black shirt that outlined his thin "lean" body. He wore jeans and his hair was black and thick and combed back. There was a large smile on his young handsome face. He was a specimen of happiness and youth, even with his thick mustache.

Louise scowled at Francis. She felt "old" around him and "wished" her husband was still thin and muscular and eager for a great career, as when they dated over twenty-five years ago. "We all change," she thought one night as she examined her sagging breasts and her thick spider veins on her pasty white calves in the full length mirror that hung on the back of her bathroom door.

Francis peered at the stack of boxes and was about to start "small talk" with Louise until she said "You better not do anything to my daughter, or I'll come after you." She tried to stop her emotions, but she couldn't. She finally said what was on her mind and Francis finally "witnessed" the real Louise Gordon; and this was the "bitch" that Ruth would talk about periodically. Now the angry sad soul appeared in front of him.

"I'll take great care of her," Francis said. "I promise." He smiled and that only pissed off Louise even more and he instantly realized it. He turned and ascended the stairs, and he was glad that Ruth was finally moving away. "I know Ruth will never become bitter and resentful like her mother" he thought to himself. Francis entered Ruth's mostly empty bedroom and he wanted to tell Ruth about what her mother had said to him but he decided to keep it a secret.

Ruth and Francis moved into a small one bedroom apartment, in West L.A. They were nearly inseparable. Francis and Ruth held hands everywhere and had sex on the kitchen floor and in the living room floor and on the bathroom floor of their cramped apartment. They walked around partially naked in the small place. They ate while they were partially naked and they were happy and in "love" and nothing could go wrong.

A few weeks later after the move, Ruth began her "entry-level" accounting position, at Knopf & Global, in Beverly Hills. Within six months, the auditing firm promoted Ruth from a cubicle to an office, on the tenth floor, which overlooked Wilshire Blvd., and when she looked down at the cars and pedestrians below, she really wasn't excited about working, in an auditing firm, but she was "hungry" for power and success. And every morning that she entered the building, she wanted money and she could taste it. She would sit down at her office, on the tenth floor, and began to prepare for her morning meetings with senior-level mangers and created spreadsheets and "combed" over procedures so she knew what she was talking about; and when she wasn't in a meeting or auditing files at a client's business, she was with Francis or talking to him on the phone during a quick break.

Ruth was clearly in love and some of the older woman at Knopf & Global gossiped about her "look of love" and her "large" engagement ring. "She thinks she has it all, doesn't she?" One married woman said to another married woman in the lunch room. They wanted her happiness and her love and her slim figure. Ruth was now twenty-three years old and she could eat nachos, stay up late, get up early and have sex and do anything else and still look refreshed at work. Some of the bitter women in the firm didn't care what Ruth had or didn't have. They knew that one day she would become "old" and "wrinkled" and "broken hearted" and hoped they were around to witness it. Yet regardless of what other people thought about Ruth, she was on her way to earning "big bucks" and she wanted a large house and to live better than her parents. She was engaged to a handsome guy, with a thick mustache, who was in medical school and would eventually become a chest surgeon and she was proud of her life and she was ready for a family in a large white house; and she dreamed of picnics with her white family every Sunday after Church; and she envisioned the "white picket fence" in a conservative white neighborhood. She wanted it all; and Ruth was "inching" closer to her "white" dream.

And while Ruth was working her "way up" inside the auditing firm, Francis worked at a dumpy medical clinic, within the ethnic neighborhoods of Venice. And Francis was also like Ruth. He was eager for success. When Francis put on his lab coat, he felt strong and confident. He wanted to help his patients the best that he could and he knew one day that he was going to be a great chest surgeon. And he wanted the money and the great family which included two or three children. "It was going to be an awesome life," he thought. Francis imagined waking his children one at a time and he would play soccer with them and drive them to martial arts and take them horseback riding. He was going to "love" his children unlike his parents, who were distant and merely strangers in the shadows of a "medium-size" one story house, in Arcadia. Ironically his parents were both counselors for "troubled teens" and Francis knew "deep down" that he wanted to raise his family with love and patience unlike his parents who were constantly impatient.

A few months of working at the clinic, Francis became a popular doctor and his favorite" patient was Clara Turner, a black seventy-two year old woman, originally from Compton. She walked slowly and wore large framed glasses and always told the receptionist behind the front desk that Francis was a "great doctor." Clara looked forward to seeing Francis and always expressed her gratitude for Dr. Stevens' patience and she trusted his "diagnosis" and she considered him a "white" son that she never had.

"Are you married, Dr. Stevens?" Clara asked during a "routine" visit.

"Almost," Francis said, as he smiled and filled out paper work.

"I think every one should experience marriage at least once in their life. I've been married for over forty-five years and there are some bad times; and of course there are some very good times, and I wouldn't change a thing."

"That's great to know," Francis said. "I have a friend that needs to hear what you just said."

"Well he should follow in your footsteps," Clara said. "You know, I've been going to doctors for years and they're so cranky and so eager to get you out of their office before you could ask them another question. But you're different. You're going to do great things."

Francis smiled. It was the first time he heard a compliment from one of his patients who were mostly poor and expected "miracles" every time they entered the examining room. He rarely heard a "thank you" or "I appreciate your help." He heard the bitching and the complaining. Yet Clara's words encouraged him as he assisted her into the lobby, where her grandson, Jimmy, waited for her. Jimmy was a tall bulky construction worker who greeted Francis with a smile and a "bone-crushing" handshake. Clara and Jimmy invited him and his fiancée to dinner many times. Francis was appreciative of the numerous offers but he kept making excuses why he couldn't attend one of their dinners. And then Clara eventually moved to another part of the city.

And time "moved" forward and Francis and Ruth were about to get married. They hired a wedding planner and decided to marry in Santa Barbara, but they were unsure if their guests would be able to fly or drive two hours to attend their wedding, so they chose a small church, in Santa Monica. They wanted a small "inexpensive" ceremony, since they were saving money for a white house and a "large" white family.

The wedding finally arrived and so did the collection of gifts. After the dancing and celebrating in a hotel ballroom in Santa Monica, Francis and Ruth raced to their one bedroom apartment and put together the money they received as gifts and deposited it into their bank account. And then they drove to a cheap hotel, in Pismo Beach, that overlooked a dirty pool and a "barely" functional Jacuzzi, and they listened to the crashing waves in the ocean. For three days they "made love" and discussed their dream house and their "dream" family which would consist of two girls and one boy and maybe they would have a family dog that had a thick coat and nothing would change their dreams. And so they drove back home to Los Angeles after their three day trip, at Pismo Beach; and two months later they discovered their "dream home" with an actual white picket fence, on Fourth Street, in Santa Monica. The house was one and a half-million dollars. They entered the place and walked on the hardwood floors. "This had to be fate," Ruth thought. They ushered the real estate agent out of the house so they could view the three large bedrooms without being pestered. And now they stood in the empty living room and once Francis figured out what his monthly mortgage would be, he urged Ruth to find a house on the other side of the freeway, but Ruth refused. She had to have this house to raise their family and that is when she turned to her husband

and said "I'm pregnant."

On that afternoon, in 1994, in Santa Monica, on Fourth Street, Ruth and Francis were going to be parents. They hugged and kissed and they were the happiest couple on the planet and Ruth told her parents the "news" and her father was happy but Louise was apprehensive. She wanted Ruth to "wait" and get more established in her career before giving "birth" but Ruth ignored her mother's comments. Ruth was starting to live the life that she wanted; and once again, Knopf & Global promoted Ruth to a "lead" auditor and she befriended a supervisor at the auditing firm. Her name was Meredith and she was a tall stringy woman with brown frizzy hair who had already been married for over twenty years; and Ruth told her about her pregnancy and that is when Meredith warned Ruth about the emotional and physical changes that can occur in her body before and after pregnancy. But Ruth didn't care because she was prepared for anything at twenty-four years old.

Once Francis discovered that he was going to be a father, he had a drink at an Irish pub, in Santa Monica, and shared the "news" with his former roommate and former college classmate, Omar Morales. They sat at the bar and drank and Omar put his arm around Francis and said "You son of a bitch! How come you never told me about this?"

"Well, I'm telling you now," Francis said.

"When did you find out?"

"Are you referring to the house that I'm buying on Fourth Street?" Francis asked.

"Are you kidding! You're buying a house here, in Santa Monica?"

"Yeah. Why is that so hard to believe?" Francis asked, smiling.

"Because I want to buy a house on Fourth Street," Omar said.

"You'd rather blow your money on women you don't care

about."

"Yeah, so what's wrong with that?" Omar asked and smiled and they hugged and discussed Francis' new house and then a possible name for the child; and Omar paid the tab and patted Francis on the back. They were about to leave when Omar said "Oh, by the way, they're hiring at The Crenshaw District Hospital."

Francis stiffened when he heard the ominous name. "No, thanks," he said.

"I'm getting hired there," Omar said.

"Are you kidding? Don't you remember what happened there? That place is called 'House of Death' for a reason."

"That was ten years ago," Omar pleaded. "You have to get over that shit."

"Omar, a woman died on the lobby floor," Francis said. "She was spitting up blood and a janitor mopped up around her until she passed out and died. You don't just 'get over' that."

"What do you want me to say?" Omar asked. "This could be 'our' chance."

"Our chance for what?" Francis asked. "What are you talking about?"

"It's our fuckin' chance to do something great in that hospital," Omar said. He was becoming more impatient and excited. "You even said that you were getting stifled at the clinic, and how the hell are you going to pay the mortgage and raise a family working there?"

"I have money saved up and so does Ruth."

"And what if you can barely make the mortgage for a month or two, are you going to ask your parents or Ruth's parents for money?" Omar put his hand on Francis' shoulder. "Look, I can get you an interview. At least give it a chance."

Francis and Omar spoke a few more minutes about the hospital and then they left the Irish Pub and walked to their cars in back of the pub. The sun lowered and shadows evolved and they shook hands and Omar drove off in his Porsche as Francis sat in his pre-owned silver Mercedes and began to wonder how on Earth could he pay a monthly mortgage and raise two or three children and work at a clinic? Yes Francis and Ruth had saved enough money for the down payment for the house and a year of mortgage payments and bills; but that was it. He couldn't afford the "birth" of his child unless he worked at a large hospital and became the chest surgeon he always wanted to be. He knew if they encountered financial difficulties they could ask his parents for "cash" but he definitely didn't want to exercise that option. Francis had to make a quick decision. He would have to at least consider interviewing at "The House of Death" before the "birth" of his child.

CHAPTER 16

Francis endured the tedious interview process at The Crenshaw District Hospital, and on the fourth and final interview, Francis wore a charcoal gray suit and he looked "sharp" as he focused his attention on the medical director who sat behind a large tidy desk. His name was Jack Kennedy. He wore an Armani Suit and he was extremely intelligent and knew how to cleverly "bullshit" his way through any situation. He had a "smooth" persuasiveness and he wanted Francis on the hospital's staff. Jack definitely liked Francis' charisma and personality; and of course, Jack was highly impressed with his letters of recommendations.

By the final interview, the hospital decided to hire him; ironically Jack felt that he had to work "hard" to actually persuade Francis to work at the hospital.

"I hope I'm not being too bold" Jack asked politely. "But I clearly sense an apprehension."

Francis wanted to tell him that he was apprehensive because a black woman "bled to death" on the lobby floor; and ironically that person was Tamika Johnson. She was twenty-nine years old, and had three children who ranged from two years old to twelve years old; and Tamika was living on welfare and didn't have any medical insurance. And on an unfortunate night, in 1984, Tamika stumbled into the urgent care center, at The Crenshaw District Hospital, complaining about "extreme" stomach and chest pains. Once a black administrator discovered that Tamika didn't have medical insurance, she told Tamika to "have a seat" and Tamika told every medical staff member that strolled by that she needed medical attention "now" but she heard the standard response "Ma'am, someone will be right with you."

And finally Tamika went into convulsions on the heavily waxed floor and vomited blood, and the vomit and the blood began to smell so the janitor arrived and mopped it up, and the scene was videotaped from a surveillance camera in the corner of the lobby of the urgent care center, and the video was "leaked" to the media and The Crenshaw District Hospital endured several lawsuits by Tamika's family and they "settled" out of court, and the hospital suffered a horrible image; and so the hospital became known as "The House of Death" for several years. Ironically Tamika was Candy's aunt; and Candy would be one of Tyrone's victims years later, and so on and so on.

Now after a few moments of silence, Jack finally asked "Is it what happened here ten years ago?"

"That's correct," Francis said. He was slightly relieved that Jack knew why he was apprehensive without having to bring it up.

Jack leaned back into his chair and went into "bullshit mode" as if he had been preparing for this moment for several weeks. "That was all a hiring mistake," he said. "Nothing like that will ever happen again, at this hospital; and anyone involved with that situation, in urgent care, has since been removed including management." Jack leaned over his tidy desk to stress his message. "Nothing like that ever happened since then. I just want you to know this is still the largest HMO hospital in the city, and, unfortunate things do happen. I do understand what happened was a horrible incident but even if you decide for some reason that this place isn't for you, I want you to know this is a very safe hospital."

Francis knew Jack was a "smooth" talker and Francis liked Jack although he didn't completely trust him. Francis felt that Jack was the director of the hospital for a specific reason and that "reason" was in case another "horrible" incident occurred. The hospital needed a "smooth" talker to calmly explain the situation internally at the hospital. Although the hospital had a staff of publicists and general counsel to explain their "dirty laundry" to the media, the hospital needed Jack for "smoothing" out apprehensions to possible new staff members who worked at The Crenshaw District Hospital, or who were about to get hired.

"Let me discuss this with my wife and I'll get back to you." Francis said. They both stood and shook hands.

"I'm sure your wife is enjoying that beautiful house," Jack said, smiling.

"Excuse me," Francis responded.

"Omar told me that you bought a house four blocks from the beach, in Santa Monica. It's a very pricey area. I know, I used to live there myself. Well anyway, congratulations!"

Francis and Jack spoke for another moment and Francis said that he "would be in touch;" and Francis smiled as he left the office and rode the elevator to the lobby and thought "Man, is that guy smooth." And then as he passed by the Hispanics and blacks and "poor" whites that strolled through the government painted hallways, Francis' smile dissolved and he began to wonder where exactly Tamika "bled to death." But Francis had to "forget" about that incident. "He's probably right," Francis thought. "This is 'probably' a safe hospital."

And so Francis left the hospital and entered the parking structure; and as he approached his pre-owned silver Mercedes, he felt that he could accomplish "great" things in this hospital. He drove home and sunlight diminished and the sky darkened. His mind drifted and he wasn't really sure if he should accept the offer. He wanted to be the best chest surgeon in the city, but could he "really" become the best at an HMO hospital, where another person bled to death on the floor, in the urgent care center, because that person didn't have medical insurance? All Francis knew is that he had to pursue his dream, and he had to do that now.

The sky was nearly dark when Francis arrived home in the "white" pristine area. Ruth wasn't home yet, but he figured that she had another "last minute" meeting. He entered his partially empty one and half million dollar house. His footsteps echoed on the hardwood floor in the living room and the place seemed "too empty" for some reason. He turned on a ceiling light and walked in the bedroom. Boxes were still stacked in the corner since they moved in a few weeks ago. He turned on a lamp on Ruth's side of the bed and sat down and instantly felt a pain in his side; and then the phone rang and Francis quickly answered it and received "urgent" news from his Mother-in-law. He knew something was wrong.

Francis got into his pre-owned silver Mercedes and sped toward the Wilshire Medical Hospital, in Westwood, and into heavy traffic; and Louise's words echoed in his head. "It's Ruth. She's at the hospital. She had a miscarriage."

About twelve minutes later, Francis parked in a much cleaner parking structure than the parking structure at The Crenshaw District Hospital; and there wasn't any trash on the ground and the stairway didn't smell like piss. Francis moved by the various white families, in the pristine lobby; and the lobby was much quieter than the "other" hospital. Francis approached Louise and asked "Where is she? Is she okay?"

"She's okay. She'll be out soon. I tried to call you on your cell phone but you didn't pick up," Louise said.

Yet Francis wasn't listening anymore. He was pacing the clean waxed floor when a Filipino nurse appeared pushing Ruth in a wheel chair. Ruth appeared lost and disorientated for the moment. Francis hugged Ruth tightly and then he spoke to an

Indian doctor for a few minutes about Ruth's "condition" and a few minutes later, Francis received a prescription for Ruth; and a Chinese woman filled the prescription at the pharmacy before they closed.

Forty minutes later, Francis drove home as Ruth sat in the passenger seat and stared out of the window and the city lights slid off her face.

At home in his kitchen, Francis made tea and most of the items were still in boxes and he stood alone at the stove and the tea kettle began to whistle. He turned off the flame and poured hot water in a mug and dangled a tea bag inside of the mug for a moment, and he finally placed the tea bag on a paper towel, and that is when "horrible" thoughts began to fill his mind. "What happened to her body and the baby inside of her? Would she actually be able to have children? Would I have to adopt a child? How are we going to pay the mortgage if she is too weak to work?"

Francis tried to calm down. He reminded himself that miscarriages were sometimes a part of life as he carefully brought tea into the bedroom where Ruth was halfway under the covers, and her face was partially highlighted by a circle of yellow lamp light. The TV volume was on low and Francis carefully placed the hot tea on the night stand and sat down next to his wife and asked "How are you doing?"

"Better, I guess." Ruth tried to smile as she dabbed a tissue at her eyes. "Are you going to take the job?"

"Well, we do need the money."

"Do you want the job?" Ruth asked. She always asked the questions that made Francis feel important.

"I want the job," Francis said. He studied his wife's beauty for a moment within the circle of yellow lamp light. "I'm going to clean up the kitchen." He was about to stand when Ruth squeezed his hand.

"Why did this happen?" Ruth asked.

"I don't know," Francis said, softly. They both forced a smile. He kissed her on the forehead and left the bedroom and walked out of the house and moved the trash cans from the side of the house to the curb in front of his house. He stood and listened to the silence and peered at the various circles of yellow lights from the street lamps. And now Francis wasn't sure if the world around him was fake or real. He was almost twenty-eight years old and he was married and living in an expensive home in a "prominent" white neighborhood and he was about to accept a job at the largest HMO hospital, in Los Angeles. And although his wife "lost" their first child, he wondered what would happen to their next child if she got pregnant again?

Francis concentrated on the silence in the "white" neighborhood, and he finally turned and entered his house and got into his nighttime clothes and got into bed and Ruth turned off her lamp and they both laid together within moonlight and shadows.

"Francis?"

"Yeah?"

"Am I okay?"

"You're great," Francis said and turned toward her face and kissed her cheek. He wanted to make love to her. He slid his hand over her pajama bottom and felt the padding under her panties which was there to absorb the excess blood. He was going to love her forever which is a decision he made the moment that he saw her at the graduation party, two years ago, in 1992, when he was twenty-five years old.

"I want to try, again," she said. Her face was partially hidden by shadows.

"I do too," Francis said.

They began to kiss and he wanted her and she wanted him and nothing could split them apart and they were still in heaven, on Fourth Street, in Santa Monica.

A few days later, Ruth returned to work and nobody knew

what happened to her except her boss and her married co-worker, Meredith Walker, and Human Resources in which they had to be informed for "legal" purposes; and on the day of the unfortunate incident, Ruth was able to drive herself home and once she was home the pain became too "unbearable" and she called her mother, Louise, who drove her to the "clean" Wilshire Medical Hospital. And when anyone else at Knopf & Global asked about her sudden absence, she responded "It was probably the tuna sandwich in the café downstairs that made me sick."

A few weeks after the miscarriage, Ruth met her mother, Louise, for lunch at a cafe, in Brentwood, on Montana Avenue. They sat under a green patio umbrella outside and Ruth could tell that her mother was nervous about the prices on the menu, but Ruth reminded her mother that she was making "good" money and would "take care of the check." By the end of the meal, Ruth finally discussed the most important thing on her mind.

"Francis and I are going to try to have another child."

"What!"

"I said – "

"I heard what you said, but are you sure you want to do this now?"

"You know you always do this to me. You're always raining on my parade."

"Please calm down. I'm not going to tell you what to do. However I think you should wait."

"Wait for what?" Ruth asked. She was becoming irritated with her mother's bullshit once again.

"Bringing a child into this world isn't an easy task, nor will it ever be. This child doesn't go away at eighteen or at twenty-two or thirty-two. They're with you until the very end," Louise said. She was sincere and she loved Ruth dearly but she had "only" one child for a reason, and that was due to the fact that "raising" a child was difficult and expensive. And Louise wondered why on Earth would Ruth think about getting pregnant so soon after suffering a miscarriage, but Louise didn't bother to ask her daughter that question.

"Mom, Francis and I are going to have a child, probably a girl, and I'm going to love her to death."

"And what if you have a boy? You can't return him."

Ruth finally smiled within the shadow of the green patio umbrella.

And a few weeks later, Ruth was pregnant; and this time, Ruth made a mental decision that her body was only to accept a beautiful child; and the months moved forward, and Ruth was four months pregnant and employees, executives, and the managing partners, at Knopf & Global, pointed and smiled and waved at her protruding stomach; and then Ruth became six months pregnant and on a cold afternoon, she and Francis bought a crib and children's books; and at night, Francis read to the child inside of Ruth, as Ruth sat in a large chair in the child's room. Ruth smiled and felt the baby kick inside of her; and one night, when Ruth was nine months pregnant, she had a dream; and in this dream, Ruth was seventeen years old, and wearing a white dress. She was walking in the woods and discovered a beautiful eight year old girl with blue eyes and sandy blond hair.

The girl was crouched by a tree.

She finally stood and Ruth began to talk to the eight year old girl and they laughed and they finally approached a long road and Ruth said "It was nice talking to you."

"What's your name?" the eight year old girl asked.

"My name's Ruth. What's yours?"

"My name's Abigail."

They hugged and waved and Ruth watched the girl walk down the path, alone. And in that dream, Ruth felt like she actually knew that eight year old girl with blue eyes and sandy blond hair.

Ruth finally awoke from her dream and smiled.

CHAPTER 17

Ruth gave birth to Abigail Stevens, in 1995, at the Wilshire Medical Hospital and Ruth was twenty-five years old and Francis was twenty-eight years old, and they brought their daughter home a few days later and they took so many pictures of their daughter over the next few years that they instantly filled up numerous photo albums; and time moved quickly during the day and slowly at night. Francis and Ruth awoke for the crying that punctuated the late night silence. Yet the loss of sleep didn't "hinder" Ruth or Francis' careers.

Knopf & Global promoted Ruth from a "lead" auditor to a supervisor of one of the departments and she was glad that she didn't have to travel to the client's offices as much; and Francis began assisting on chest surgeries at The Crenshaw District Hospital, and he eventually became the chest surgeon that he always wanted to be. Francis was quick and firm with decisions, in the O.R., and he loved his job and his wife and his daughter.

Time moved forward and Abigail turned two years old and then three years old and then four years old; and finally at five years old, Ruth suddenly realized that Abigail was "gravitating" toward Francis.

Ruth would listen, in the hallway, as Francis read to Abigail, in her bedroom every night; and Ruth would watch

Francis and Abigail paint together, on the kitchen table, or she would watch them color in coloring books together, on the living room floor; or sometimes Ruth would once again stand in the hallway and listen as Abigail would talk to her father, in her bedroom, about her drawings or about her teacher, Ms. Robinson, or about her new friends; and as Ruth watched the bond strengthen between daughter and father, Ruth became jealous of being "left out." Yet Ruth tried to "befriend" and play with her five year old daughter, but she did not receive her daughter's warmth as Francis did; and then one day, Ruth was picking up her daughter's clothes from the floor, in Abigail's bedroom, when she heard laughter outside. Ruth peered through the bedroom window and noticed Francis playing with her five year old daughter in the backyard, where they were tossing gold colored leaves at each other; and Ruth placed Abigail's clothes to her face to stifle her tears but she cried for some strange reason; and Ruth was "officially" becoming jealous of Abigail's relationship with her father; and in effect, Ruth believed she was receiving less attention from her husband and she became tired of competing for her husband's attention with her daughter.

Francis relationship continued to grow with Abigail. He was constantly present in her life. He drove her to kindergarten and walked her to class almost every morning, except the mornings that he had to "prep" for surgery; and the mornings that he did drop off Abigail in kindergarten class, he would talk to Abigail's kindergarten teacher, Penny Robinson. She was thirty-five years old and just recently "broken-up" with her boyfriend. She was a wafer thin attractive blond haired woman with visible "dark roots" who lived alone with two cats, in a two bedroom townhouse, in Redondo Beach.

Penny knew Francis was married but she was attracted to him and she thought Abigail was intelligent and a great artist; and then Penny discovered Francis Stevens was a chest surgeon, and Penny would fantasize about Francis when she would lay in bed, at night, trying to forget about her ex-boyfriend; and she pleasured herself to the thoughts of making love to Francis, the chest surgeon. And in the morning, when she got dressed in her bathroom, she would spray an extra squirt of perfume above her medium-size breasts that were accentuated by a push up bra; and Francis noticed Penny's attraction toward him and he could smell her perfume scented breasts. Yet Francis knew that he would never be "completely" attracted to another woman, even during his "first" marital issue, which was just beginning. It started one night when Ruth decided not to have sex with Francis. She stated that she felt ugly; Ruth stood in her bra and panties, in front of the mirror, as if she was acting out a scene in a "shitty ass" movie. She would pull on her "love handles" and poke the fat on the back of her legs. She despised her body. "I will never give 'birth' again," Ruth thought, as she examined the stretch marks and sagging skin on the side of her stomach. She thought her body was "falling apart" at thirty years old. She even stopped pleasuring herself.

Now Ruth felt "dry" inside and out.

Yet Francis still "heavily" desired sex with Ruth and he would frequently think about when he would bend her over the bed "doggy style" and watch the flab jiggle in her butt. However those late nights of "doggy style" were momentarily over. And then on another night, Francis watched Ruth continue to poke and tug at her excess fat around her stomach while still wearing her bra and panties, and he finally asked "Could you please come to bed?"

"I feel gross," Ruth said, irritated.

"You look great."

"I look so fat," Ruth said. She secretly loved the attention that Francis would give her when she pouted; yet she didn't care that he was quickly losing his patience. Ruth removed her bra and put on a worn stained night gown and got into bed and was about to turn off the lamp.

"Ruth, where's the lingerie I bought you?" Francis asked.

"I don't feel like wearing it."

"If you don't like your body why don't you start working out?"

"Are you saying I'm fat?"

"I'm saying goodnight!" Francis said and grabbed a blue blanket from the closet.

"Why are you leaving?" Ruth asked. "Just because I don't want to have sex?"

"Think about it!" Francis said. He left the bedroom with the blue blanket while Ruth sat on the bed within a circle of yellow lamp light and folded her arms and pouted.

Francis tiptoed into Abigail's moonlit bedroom and closed the door and sat in the large chair where he watched his daughter sleep for a moment and then Francis eventually fell asleep; and over the next few weeks, Ruth's sexual frustration continued to grow. She still desired sex but not with her husband. She finally decided to confide in her co-worker, Meredith Walker, one afternoon, during their lunch hour, as they walked briskly, in their flat shoes, around the park, in Beverly Hills.

"What's the problem, Ruth?" Meredith asked.

"I just don't feel myself."

"Your body will bounce back from the 'birth,' but I warned you about the transition," Meredith said.

"Yeah, okay," Ruth said. "But it's been five years since I had Abigail."

Meredith slowed her pace and looked at Ruth and asked "What you are trying to do to your husband?"

"What do you mean?"

"You can't starve your husband from sex. Trust me."

"I'm not trying to do that," Ruth proclaimed.

"When was the last time you had sex with him?"

"I guess a month or so," Ruth said. Yet, she really couldn't remember.

"Jesus, Ruth. You have to start opening up and I mean that literally."

"I'm just not in the mood."

"Well, have you tried lingerie?" Meredith asked.

"Francis already bought me something."

"And?"

"And I didn't feel like putting it on."

"How about some toys?" Meredith asked. "Those always seemed to get me and John in the mood. You should have seen what I bought in Vegas. This thing had to be twelve inches."

"I tried it once and I felt liked I was being ripped apart."

"You didn't have to get twelve inches."

"It was smaller," Ruth said.

"You gotta do something, Ruth. I've been married long enough and when my husband wants sex, I'm on my knees in the bedroom, or the kitchen, or wherever; because if he's horny and he ain't getting it from me, well guess what? He's going to be thinking about getting it somewhere else, and you want to stop his urges while they're still in the thought process."

Ruth thought about Meredith's comments, as she drove from Beverly Hills to her house in Santa Monica after work. She knew that she was being selfish. She had to be more "giving" to Francis. However Ruth was no longer getting her husband's attention liked she used to before the "birth" of her daughter.

Now it was all about Abigail. So why on Earth did Ruth have to compete for her husband's attention? Yet Ruth loved Abigail, but her anger and frustration grew toward her five year old daughter. During one evening at the Stevens' dining table, Abigail began to eat without praying and Ruth snapped and said "Abby, how many times do I have to tell you to pray before you eat!"

"I'm sorry, mommy," Abigail said politely. She quickly prayed "Thank you, Lord, for my food, and for my mommy and daddy and for their food. Amen."

They began to eat and Ruth noticed her husband glaring at her and she instantly looked away and continued to eat without looking at her husband.

The tension was building.

It wasn't enough for Ruth that she required prayer before each meal, like her mother, now she brought tension to the table. Ruth realized Francis was angry, and she knew that she had "crossed the line." And after Francis put Abigail to bed, Ruth was picking out clothes for her meeting tomorrow, in her bedroom, when a discussion evolved into another argument with her husband.

"You know it wouldn't kill you to be a little nicer to Abigail. She's only five," Francis said angrily.

Ruth grimaced. She was tired of hearing about her daughter's fuckin' feelings and said "I have to start training her so she understands how to appreciate what she has."

"Jesus, Ruth. She's not a dog. She is our daughter."

"You're always protecting her!"

"Maybe I need to," Francis said. He needed to leave the bedroom again. It was something he was doing more often lately. "Sometimes, I don't know if I married you or your mother!"

"If you want to get laid, Francis, why don't you go fuck yourself!"

Francis finally grabbed the blue blanket from the closet and left the bedroom and tiptoed into his daughter's moonlit bedroom and softly closed the bedroom door behind him and sat in the large chair and watched Abigail sleep; and he eventually fell asleep; but before he did, he wondered if he was being "unfair" to his wife. He loved Ruth more than anything; and yes she could be a "moody pain in the ass," but he knew that he had his faults. Did he need to be rude and did he need to intervene with his wife's lessons for their daughter? Maybe it was important that Abigail prayed before every meal and before she goes to bed. Francis looked at his daughter sleeping, in the moonlit bed, and all he could "feel" was love for her, but he knew he had to "make nice" with his wife; and so the next morning, Ruth was in the bathroom at the sink, in her bra and panties, applying make-up when Francis snuck up behind her and kissed her shoulders and apologized and Ruth tried to forgive him and they hugged and kissed and tried to "make nice." Yet during the next few weeks, Ruth's jealousy and sexual frustrations only increased. She wanted to discuss her "issues" with Francis but she wondered what was she supposed to tell him? "I'm jealous of Abigail and the attention that you give her all the time and I 'need' the attention you gave me when we first met!" However instead of Ruth discussing her "issues" with her husband, she hid them and decided to continue to punish Francis by not having sex with him.

And of course, Ruth knew it was wrong.

Ruth just kept telling herself and her husband that she felt fat and that she wasn't "in the mood." She also decided to work until seven or eight p.m., almost every weeknight. She told Francis that it was tax season. "Things should die down in a few weeks." However the "few weeks" turned into a few months and then an unexpected event occurred. It happened in a Starbucks' parking lot, around six-thirty p.m. She decided to get out of the office one evening; and so she grabbed her laptop and drove to Starbucks and parked and walked across the parking lot where she met a very familiar looking male stranger.

Yet an hour before she met a very familiar looking male stranger, and before she decided to leave the office, she spoke to her mother on the phone who said "Ruth, I think you're jealous. That's that problem. You have to accept that Abigail is part of your life and your husband's life."

And of course Ruth denied the accusation and asked "Are you kidding me, mom? That's silly. I have to get out of here. I'll call you later."

Ruth hung up the phone and grabbed her laptop and drove to Starbucks and parked and grabbed her laptop and noticed the familiar looking male stranger in the parking lot.

"Ruth, Ruth Gordon?" the male stranger asked.

She instantly noticed this male stranger who was about thirty years old and well built; and yes that male stranger looked familiar but she couldn't place the face.

"You have no idea who I am. Do you?" he asked.

Ruth shook her head and said "Kind of, I guess."

"Let me save you some trouble. Phil Taylor, from UCLA. We had an accounting class with Professor Benedict, or some people would say Professor Dick?"

"Oh, yes, Phil! How are you? You look great. What happened?"

"I'll take that as a compliment," he said. They both smiled. "It's called joining a gym." He patted his stomach and said "I know you've been working out."

"I wish. The only working out I get is running from one meeting to another."

"Well, you look great!"

"Thank you," Ruth said.

Finally the moment arrived between the two familiar looking strangers when Phil asked "Are you going inside?"

"Oh, yeah, I just have to make a phone call really quick," Ruth said.

"Sure. Do you want me to save you a seat and a Frappuccino?"

Ruth hesitated for a moment. "Yeah, that would be great. But make it an Iced tea. I'm still watching my waist."

He smiled and she smiled and Phil turned and walked inside Starbucks and Ruth walked back to her car and took off her wedding ring and put it in her purse and thought about what she *should* do at this very moment; and she continued to think about what she should do as she walked across the Starbucks' parking lot.

Ruth and Phil sat down at a table and discussed life

during their college days and getting stoned together and discussing their former college friends, and during the near hour long conversation, Ruth never mentioned her marriage nor did she mention the "birth" of her daughter. At the moment, her family was nonexistent; and when Ruth finally left, she was "unusually" horny. She arrived home and dished out her casual kisses to her husband and her daughter as they played with toys on the living room floor. Ruth entered her bedroom and put her purse on the floor and went into the bathroom and locked the door and stripped off her clothes until she was in her bra and panties. She sat on the toilet lid and slid her hand under her damp panties and closed her eyes and she felt the wetness on her fingers tips. She came silently as her body shuddered. She cleaned herself in the shower and fell asleep after dinner. Francis laid awake next to her watching cable TV. He looked at her and thought "When the hell did she ever fall asleep that fast?"

As the following weeks passed, Ruth began to "hang out" with Phil Taylor. They "casually" met during their lunch hours at a park, in Beverly Hills, as Phil "conveniently" worked down the street, at another auditing firm, Manning & Finch. And as they met, they discussed life after college and their experiences of working at two of the largest auditing firms, in Beverly Hills. Yet during their numerous conversations in person and on their cell phones, Ruth "still" never mentioned her husband and her daughter; and on one afternoon when Phil asked Ruth at a sports bar if she was ever married, she stated "no" but she did mention that she had a miscarriage; and unfortunately that was the only indication that she attempted to give birth; and yes Ruth was nervous about lying but she told herself that she was "caught up" in the moment, and she was "caught up" in the moment as she decided to continue to take off her wedding ring and place it inside her desk drawer at work, or in the console of her newly purchased BMW. And Ruth was diligent of hiding her "true identity" as she continued to meet Phil in various sports bars or "cozy" dark lounges, in Beverly Hills. And when she was "done" meeting Phil for the evening, she would "diligently" put her wedding ring back on her finger before she entered her house, on Fourth Street, in Santa Monica, where she would kiss her husband and daughter on the cheek as they played with toys on the living room floor or colored in coloring books together.

And this scenario continued, until one afternoon when Francis received the cell phone bill and he decided to open it before Ruth came home from another "long" day at work; and when Francis opened the envelope of the cell phone bill and unfolded the monthly statement, he instantly noticed an unfamiliar phone number listed "numerous" times on the sheet. Francis walked into his bedroom and sat on the bed and "decided" to call the "mysterious" phone number since he had this strange feeling that his wife was doing something that she shouldn't be doing over the past few months; and Francis finally spoke to Phil on his cell phone for about three minutes and within that "brief" conversation, Francis told Phil that he would kill him if ever called his wife again; and ironically that was the same evening that Ruth "accidently" entered her house without her wedding ring.

CHAPTER 18

When Phil Taylor received the phone call from Ruth's husband who stated that he would kill him if he called his wife again, Phil instantly hung up. And at that moment, Phil could have told Ruth about Francis calling him, but instead Phil ignored her call since he was still in shock that Ruth never told him that she was married and that she had a five year old daughter; and the anger began to evolve in Phil's body as he recalled Francis screaming at him during the "brief" conversation, and then Phil thought "That cunt lied to me. She set me up." So Phil decided not to speak to Ruth about a "possible" trap that could be awaiting her at her house, on Fourth Street, in Santa Monica.

And when Ruth did come home that evening, she remembered seeing one suitcase by the dining room table. She instantly realized something was wrong; and as Francis entered the room with a few of his suits she immediately asked "What are you doing? Where are you going?"

"I would have never married you if I knew you were going to pull this shit on me!" Francis said. He was clearly disappointed. Ruth knew she fucked up and in the eight years that she had known Francis, he was never this angry.

She felt the shame and she finally pushed her husband

over an emotional cliff; and now she had to suffer her penitence. Ruth could only respond as any guilty person and asked "What are you talking about?"

"Where is your wedding ring, Ruth?"

It was at the very moment, during that evening, that Ruth Stevens was "busted." And where the fuck was her wedding ring? And then she remembered that she had left it in the middle console of her newly purchased BMW.

Shit! Shit!

Fuck! Fuck! Fuck!

She remembered the wedding ring too late and she heard him say "Tell Abigail I'll call her soon," and then he was gone.

And at the moment, after her husband left the house with his suitcase and a few of his suits, Ruth turned and noticed her daughter in the hallway who said "You made daddy mad."

Yet that moment was sort of a blur and Ruth didn't remember how she responded to her daughter. Ruth remembered walking into the dimly lit master bedroom and discovered the cell phone bill on the night stand within a circle of yellow lamp light, and Ruth sat down and grabbed the bill and read her husband's hand written words "Phil Taylor." And then she wondered what made her want to become "romantically involved" with another man? Wasn't she happy? She had a gorgeous five year old daughter and a handsome husband who was a chest surgeon who gave her respect, admiration, love and paid the majority of the monthly mortgage payments.

And now she was nearly destroying everything in her life, including her family solely because she wasn't getting her husband's attention like she "used to." So she had to punish her husband. And in this moment, near the circle of yellow lamp light, she felt nauseous. She knew in her heart that she had become a "selfish bitch" and this behavior originated because she wasn't getting attention "liked she used to." She had to "grow up." Ruth made nearly one hundred thousand dollars per year, at thirty years old, but there was more to life than making a large salary and living in a "nice" white house and the year was 2000, and Ruth had to change; and so a few days later, she decided to call Phil Taylor and he reluctantly "took" the call and they eventually met at the bar area of a seafood restaurant, in Beverly Hills, and the sky was gray and it was cold outside. They sat down at a table and Ruth told Phil the "truth." Phil sat calmly in his expensive suit drinking a glass of Bourbon. And she continued to tell him what she should have told him a few months earlier and Phil finally responded "You told me that you weren't married. You told me that you had a miscarriage!" He was trying not to cause a scene within the seafood restaurant. "You have a five year old daughter. How could you lie about that!'

"I did have a miscarriage," Ruth said. Her voice was barely above a whisper. She really didn't have to explain anything to Phil, but she "owed" it to him. Now she had to endure Phil's response. I'm sorry. I really am!"

"I'm sorry too, Ruth" Phil said. "You're a mess and you need a shrink!" Phil stood and up said "Please don't call me again" and before Ruth could respond, Phil left in his expensive suit; and at that very moment, Phil became another passing stranger who entered her life for a moment, and then he was gone; but this stranger left an emotional scar. Now Ruth sat alone in the bar area of the seafood restaurant, and she cried as customers gawked and some pointed but she didn't notice them. Ruth finally paid the bill and walked back to work and during the walk, she thought about the earlier days, the easier days, when she dated Francis and they talked for hours and there weren't any worries about mortgage payments and raising a child, but the "simple" days were in the past.

And time moved forward.

The next few weeks became exceedingly difficult for Ruth. During one morning, when Ruth walked Abigail into Ms. Robinson's kindergarten class, Ruth kissed her daughter and watched her play with other kids and that is when Penny Robinson approached Ruth and said "Mrs. Stevens, I'm sorry for asking, but I haven't seen your husband in a few weeks. Is he okay?

"He's fine. He's just, um, out of town for business."

"Oh, I told your husband a few months ago that Abigail is a wonderful student. She's going to be something great one day," Penny said. She inhaled deeply as she had something on her mind. "I actually tried to have children but the doctor told me that I couldn't, and my boyfriend suddenly changed his mind about marrying me, so I broke up with him." Penny stopped for a moment, paused, and finally said "You're a lucky woman."

Ruth hated this sudden guilt trip and quickly excused herself and Ruth couldn't remember what she had told Penny but she had to leave and she drove to work and it started to rain and the words "You're a lucky woman" repeated in Ruth's mind. "Was it true?" Ruth asked herself. "Am I lucky?"

Yes Ruth was "still" a lucky woman.

And when Ruth arrived home that evening, her mother, Louise, was at the stove cooking meat. Ruth changed from her work clothes in her bedroom and put on some loose fitting clothing and entered the kitchen and began cutting vegetables; and during that moment, Ruth thought about when she was seventeen years old and helped her mother cook and prepare food, in the house, on Del Rey Avenue, in Sherman Oaks, and how the aroma made the dusty curtains smell like garlic.

"Have you heard from Francis?" Louise asked.

"Mom, am I a bad person?"

Louise lowered the flame on the stove and approached her daughter. Louise knew she had to be sensitive and she couldn't tell her daughter that she wasn't "mature" enough to raise a child or a family. Instead Louise grabbed her daughter's shoulders and said "Listen, Ruth you're a great person."

"I lied to this guy, this stranger, for no reason. I didn't tell him the complete truth. All I told him about my life was that I had a miscarriage."

"What is the truth?" Louise asked her daughter.

"I don't know anymore," Ruth said, defeated.

"The truth is that you gave 'birth' to a beautiful daughter and you have a great husband."

And at that very moment, they both smiled and Ruth was surprised that her mother had come to her aid when life kicked her in the ass; and now a new light "burned" inside of Ruth Stevens. She had to get her husband back and show him that she really truly loved him. She instantly remembered what her father told her during that warm August afternoon, in 1992. "You have to be tough like I always taught you. It's hard to tell what's around each corner."

After dinner Ruth drove to Omar's townhouse, in Westwood. Francis was sitting on a red couch. He appeared depressed and his stubble was thick and his mustache appeared unkempt. Ruth asked if he wanted to take a walk and he said "sure" and they walked together on the lit residential streets of Westwood and passed students who played touch football in the street under various circles of yellow street lights.

"Abigail keeps asking about you," Ruth said.

"Tell her I'll call her soon," Francis said.

"She's not your patient."

"I need more time."

"More time for what?" Ruth asked. "It's been nearly three weeks and you called twice. She needs you and I need you."

Francis stopped in front of Omar's townhouse and he faced his wife. "Ruth, you have no idea what you have done to me. How am I ever going to trust you?"

"I didn't do anything, I swear!"

"How come we never had more children, like we planned? Remember those days, when we discussed having a large family?" Francis asked. He was emotionally hurt and distraught. "It was because you're so worried about your damn figure!"

"Is this what you really want to talk about now?"

"You're selfish, Ruth," Francis said. He was burning with anger.

"I'm sorry. I mean it. I really am."

"You made your choice and now I have to make mine," Francis said. He walked up the stairs of the townhouse and unlocked the glass door and entered; and Ruth stood on the sidewalk and cried.

A few minutes later, in Omar's townhouse, Francis laid on the red couch. Omar approached and said "You can't stay here, buddy."

"Fine, then I'll get a hotel," Francis said. He stood and was about to leave.

"That's not what I'm saying."

"Then what are you saying?" Francis asked. He was losing his patience once again.

"I'm saying you have a family to go back to."

"What do you know about a family, Omar? What is the longest relationship you ever had? Six months? Eight months?"

"This isn't about me," Omar pleaded. "This is about you. It's all about you!"

"I can't go back," Francis said. He sounded desperate, it was a feeling he never quite experienced before.

"She knows she fucked up," Omar said.

"Oh, yeah! Does she really know that?"

"She isn't going to pull this shit, again. I promise."

"Yeah, how do you know?" Francis asked.

"What about forgiveness? Isn't that what they teach you in Church every Sunday?" Omar asked. "Listen, you can do what you want, but I've known Ruth as long as you have, and I've never seen that look in her eyes like she had tonight. She is lost without you and you're 'really' lost without her."

Francis was mentally drained. He drove to a café and

sat alone in a booth under a glow of white ceiling light and he drank coffee and ate a slice of cherry pie. Francis hated that Ruth "might" have fooled around with another man; but Francis was mostly disgusted that Ruth would pull off her fuckin' wedding ring, as if the symbol of their marriage could be discarded into a drawer for the sole purpose of cheating. The anger grew inside of Francis but he had to "forgive." Maybe Omar was correct. Didn't he learn about "forgiveness" in Church?

It was past midnight when Francis arrived at Omar's townhouse. He entered the bathroom and turned on the faucet and splashed water on his face and applied shaving cream on his stubble and mustache and picked up a clean razor and began shaving.

The days moved forward and Ruth did her best as a single parent to care for her daughter. She poured cereal and milk for Abigail each and every morning and that is usually when Ruth heard the routine questions "When is daddy coming back?" and "Why did daddy leave?" and "Did you make daddy leave?"

And it was the last question "Did you make daddy leave?" that echoed in her mind. Ruth wanted to say "One day you'll understand, you little brat." But Ruth usually remained quiet or quickly responded "He'll be back shortly." Yet Ruth started to believe that her marriage was definitely over. She was only thirty years old and was mentally preparing herself to tell her five year old daughter that "daddy is not going to live with us anymore." And then she would have to explain the living situation to her parents and tell her co-workers about the separation and the looming divorce when Francis didn't show up at the Christmas party. The embarrassment and guilt choked her. She realized all these problems were her fault for getting involved with another man. She told Francis that she didn't do "anything" with Phil, but that was another lie. No she didn't have sex with Phil, but even holding hands and the "light" kissing and caressing was considered cheating. Or was it?

Now Ruth stood at the bathroom sink, in her work attire, and cried. She still had to make dinner for Abigail and get her ready for bed and read to her. Ruth felt sick to her stomach. She couldn't contain her emotions and she began to cry when she heard her daughter's soft voice "Mommy, where's dinner? I'm hungry."

Ruth turned to Abigail in the doorway and wiped her eyes. She looked at her daughter and thought she was so adorable in her short dress and a white T-shirt that had short puffy sleeves. "Dinner will be ready soon. Go color in your book," Ruth said.

"Okay," Abigail said and left the bathroom.

Ruth sat down on the toilet lid and resumed crying and that is when she realized that her daughter didn't ask her what was wrong like she had always asked her father when he wasn't smiling or appeared unhappy. Yet Ruth didn't have time to ponder about the past. Ruth knew she had to be strong. She changed into her sweats and a long T-shirt and began preparing ravioli dinner at the stove, in the kitchen. Her mind wandered and then she heard footsteps from the foyer.

"Abby, dinner isn't ready," Ruth said. She was becoming irritated until Francis appeared in the kitchen. His face was clean shaven. He looked much younger and more handsome without the mustache. They hugged tightly and Ruth said "I'm sorry."

"Me too," Francis said.

They kissed passionately in the kitchen and Ruth said "You finally shaved your mustache."

"Yeah, it's for good luck."

"It looks great," Ruth said.

They continued to kiss and once again Francis, Ruth, and Abigail were a complete family; and after dinner, Francis sat on Abigail's bed, near a circle of yellow lamp light, reading a story to her. He finally finished it and put the book down and Abigail asked "Daddy, why did you leave?"

"It's something we do as adults, sometimes," Francis said.

"Are you going to leave again, daddy?"

"No. I'll never leave you or mommy again."

"Promise, daddy?"

"I promise," Francis said. He leaned over and kissed his five year old daughter on her forehead and they both said "goodnight" and he turned off the lamp and he left her dark bedroom, as she quietly prayed to herself.

CHAPTER 19

On Abigail's eighth birthday, Ruth took pictures of Abigail as she made a wish in front of her birthday cake and was about to blow out the candles in the living room. Her teeth were starting to "grow" in and her hair was in a ponytail. Francis sat next to her and they both smiled at the camera and they were both very happy, father and daughter; and this was the picture that was eventually framed and hung on Abigail's bedroom wall; and as more birthdays followed, one after the other, Abigail made the same wish year after year, before blowing out her candles; and she wanted to tell someone about her wish; and one day at the park, when Abigail was about to turn thirteen years old, she decided to tell her father about her "birthday wish" that she made every year before blowing out the candles on the cake; and at the moment, the sun lowered and the shadows extended over the dried dead grass and the leaves drifted across their feet and Abigail asked her father "Do you know what I wish for every year before I blow out the candles on my birthday cake?"

"Abby, your wishes are a secret. If you tell someone they may not come true."

"Don't say that! I need this wish to come true."

"You're not 'really' supposed to tell anyone. You know that, right?" Francis asked and he smiled and loved the innocent conversations that he had with his daughter.

"Just let me tell you this one time, please?" Abigail begged. "It's important."

"Okay, this one time," Francis said and smiled again.

"Every year before I blow out the candles, I wish that you'll never leave again and that you'll always be around.

Francis stopped walking and faced his daughter and said "Listen, Abby, I'm not going anywhere."

"I know, but you left before. Was it because what mom did?"

"What are you referring to?" Francis asked. He wondered how on Earth did she remember what happened over seven years ago.

"I heard you and mom talking about it one day with the bedroom door open and I still remember that night you left with your suitcase."

"Listen, Abby, that was in the past," Francis said. He realized at that moment that his daughter was growing up and becoming more perceptive and she was starting to ask a "shit load" of questions.

"So you'll always be around?"

"I promise, just like I promised you years ago," Francis said.

They resumed walking together as the sun lowered and time continued to move forward.

Abigail entered St. Susan Catholic High School, in Brentwood, when she was in ninth grade. Ruth had to decide if she wanted to enroll Abigail in a "pricey" all girls private Catholic high school. Yet Ruth secretly wanted to keep Abigail away from boys and have her in a religious "setting."

"I think this is important," Ruth said one night to her husband, in the bedroom, while she ironed her clothes and Francis laid on the bed in his shorts trying to focus on the TV, but he wasn't able to do so at this moment.

"She's not going to be around any boys. Is that what you really want? How is she going to learn about love and relationships?" Francis asked. "All she will know are those 'catty' girls."

"Our daughter is fourteen not twenty," Ruth said, angrily. The frustration consumed her once again when she thought she wasn't getting her way. So she "bitched" and "moaned" until she got her way.

Abigail started attending St. Susan in Brentwood, in 2009; and it seemed like a "good idea" to Ruth. Her daughter wore the conservative school uniform and learned philosophy; and she eventually learned to speak and write in Spanish and French; and she learned complex mathematical equations and read and deconstructed literature. She memorized passages from the Bible; and Ruth became excited when Abigail's prayers became lengthy at breakfast and dinner. And what made Ruth the happiest is that she was getting her way once again.

However in her sophomore year, at St. Susan, Abigail met Barbara and Janey and she eventually became one of the "gossip girls" by her junior year. Almost every night, the Stevens' phone rang, and numerous girls called to trade school "gossip" with Abigail. Francis bought her a cell phone against his wife's wishes, but hoped that the cell phone would eliminate the numerous phone calls to the house. However Barbara and Janey began coming over to "study" with Abigail, in her bedroom. Ruth would stand behind the closed bedroom door listening to the girls giggle while discussing about "weird professors" and "kissing boys."

Ruth cringed in the hallway as she sporadically listened to the "school gossip" and heard laughter and she began to despise it, and she couldn't allow Abigail to be "happy." Ruth was becoming "jealous" of Abigail again. Yet at forty-two years old, Ruth was becoming angrier and more annoyed and irritated around her family. She would "snap" at Abigail for leaving clothes on her bedroom floor, and then Ruth would direct her frustration toward her husband for "sticking up" for Abigail. And then the "bottom" fell out for Ruth Stevens.

On a warm afternoon, in January, and after twenty years of working at Knopf & Global, Ruth was "laid off" and by the time she was "laid off" she was a senior manager and was responsible for a team of six auditors while earning nearly two hundred thousand dollars per year, which did not include bonuses. Ruth would speak to the clients and budget the project and "handpick" her auditors which usually consisted of fresh and hungry "twenty something" accountants. Within that search, Ruth picked an accountant named, Kenny LaGrange, to work on her team. Yet Kenny worked "too slow" auditing the client's records which caused the auditing job to go over Ruth's quote; and the client refused to pay the "extra" amount, so Knopf & Global lost over fifty thousand dollars and Ruth's "ass" was put on the corporate butcher's block. Ruth spoke to Kenny about his "slowness" and she should have demoted Kenny after the first "fuck-up" on the auditing team, but good ol' Ruth kept Kenny on her auditing team because she believed that Kenny was a smart and hard working auditor who had a "bad break" in life. Both of his parents were dying from cancer and he had to assist with their medical bills and purchase their medicine; and it was always medication that his dying parents needed. Yet none of this "personal business" mattered to the partners, at Knopf & Global. It was only about pure "white" competition within the corporate glass walls.

The five partners of the Beverly Hills firm were known as the "white wrecking crew" which consisted of white Republicans and they met every Tuesday to have their "cut-throat" business meetings. The ages of the partners ranged from forty to sixty-five years old and they mostly drove Mercedes, BMWs, Teslas, Ferraris and Corvettes; and the "white wrecking crew" lived in Palisades, Malibu, Brentwood, Santa Monica, and Bel Air; and the "white wrecking crew" never called in sick. Most importantly the partners at Knopf & Global liked Ruth and "considered" making her a partner "one day." They always thought she displayed a "solid" work ethic and dedication to the firm. She was quick with decisions and she treated everyone in the firm with respect. So the issues of causing the firm to lose over fifty thousand dollars and keeping a "slow auditor" on her team began to "blow over" until the firm decided to hire a new partner who became a part of the "white wrecking crew." His name was Brad Davis. He was in his mid-forties and wore tailored suits and drove a Ferrari to work. He graduated with "honors" from an Ivy League school and he never got married. Single women loved him and so did married women. Within weeks of being hired, Brad was considered a "prick" and wanted everything his way. He was a perfect addition to the "white wrecking crew."

Brad believed he was "fitting in" at the firm until he discovered Ruth was a senior manager. Although Brad earned significantly more than Ruth and he was a partner and she was not, Brad secretly disliked her. There were only a few things that made Brad Davis nervous in this world, and that was a smart and attractive woman; and he "secretly" believed that she would eventually "outsmart" him in the firm. It was his "little secret" of insecurity under his expensive suit. So once Brad discovered that Ruth was the source of causing the firm to lose a "significant" sum of money, he spoke to the other partners and he showed them the "financial loss" on graphs and how much more money Ruth could "lose" for the firm for keeping a "dipshit" on her auditing team. And when the partners were still "unsure" that they should "cut her," Brad Davis pulled out his "secret weapon" and told the rest of the "white wrecking crew" how many more clients he would bring to the firm if they just do what he wants.

And so on that warm afternoon, in January, Brad and the rest of the "white wrecking crew" decided to "layoff" Ruth Stevens. Brad gladly initiated the task and poked his head in Ruth's office on that warm afternoon, in January, and invited her into his glass office with John Fleming who was another partner of the firm. Ruth knew something was wrong once she entered Brad's office and noticed Brad's "plastic smile" and John Fleming who sat nervously in a large chair. Ruth didn't bother to sit down. She knew the end was coming and she knew Brad was looking forward to this moment, and he wanted to make Ruth "squirm" before swinging down the "corporate" axe down on her "skinny white ass." He wanted to make this a difficult process for her.

"Ruth, there's things that we have to do in this company," Brad said, tugging on his newly purchased tie. Ruth was not new to office politics and she knew she was facing the inevitable.

"Are you laying me off or firing me?" Ruth asked. She knew Knopf & Global would never fire a high-level female manager unless they either murdered someone or embezzled money from the firm; so she knew an unlawful firing would equal a law suit and "bad press" in the media, and firing a high-level female executive would not "look good" among the "white" auditing firms, on Wilshire Blvd., in Beverly Hills.

"We're doing some shifting around," Brad said. He was actually expecting Ruth to "lose it" but the opposite occurred. Brad continued to say "We have to make some cutbacks."

"If you have to make cutbacks, why did you hire another secretary?"

"Well, there's some organizing we have to do in the firm," Brad said. He tugged at his newly purchased tie, again. He was becoming nervous but he still loved this moment, although he hated confrontation, especially with a "high-level" female employee.

Ruth was tired of the "corporate bullshit" and said "If you're going to get rid of me then just do it, but you owe me!"

Brad and John were unprepared for the mild confrontation and they both looked at each other for a moment, slightly confused. "What? What do we you? Please, Ruth, this is already difficult," Brad said.

"Three years of severance pay."

"Are you kidding me? You know how much you've lost for the company?"

"And do you know how much I have made for this company. I've been here for over twenty years. Who were you brown-nosing twenty years ago?"

John Fleming adjusted himself in the large chair but he remained quiet as he feared confrontation more than Brad; and so twenty minutes later, after Ruth politely threatened to seek an attorney, Brad "choked" and offered her a two year severance package, and he did so without seeking advice from general counsel and from the "white wrecking crew" and from Human Resources.

Ruth left the glass office with a "little" dignity. Yet as she carried her boxes of "shit" from her office, Ruth was relieved that she was "finished" at the large corporate auditing firm, but she did enjoy earning "lots of money" which helped her purchase an expensive house, in Santa Monica, and put a teenage daughter in an all girls private Catholic high school, in Brentwood. And Ruth drove home in her Lexus SUV, filled with over twenty years of crap.

Ruth was quiet during dinner and she finally told Francis what had occurred at work, as she washed dishes. She expected Francis to be angry, but he wasn't. And why should he be? He was earning "plenty of money" as a chest surgeon, in the largest HMO hospital, in Los Angeles; and after learning about her two year severance package, Francis told her to finish the novel that she had started over twenty years ago.

"That was so long ago," Ruth said.

"It's never too late to start over," Francis said.

He knew his wife wanted to make excuses as to why she shouldn't make a change in her life, but now Ruth was pissed off and wanted revenge. However Ruth didn't want revenge against Brad or the "white wrecking crew" at Knopf & Global. Ironically

Ruth wanted revenge against her daughter and said "I think Abigail should get a job!"

"Oh, please, Ruth. Not this shit, again."

"Yeah it's always shit when I want Abigail to do something," Ruth said.

"Jesus, Ruth. We agreed that Abigail is not going to work after school."

"No, you decided. Remember?"

Francis tossed the blue sponge on the counter and left the kitchen. Ruth sat in a chair and folded her arms for a moment. She wanted everything her way once again.

Ruth finally left the kitchen and time moved forward.

At The Crenshaw District Hospital, Francis discovered that his patient, Sal Williams, had lung cancer, which was possibly due to smoking for over thirty years. Francis needed to operate and he told Sal about his cancer and Sal asked "Can you talk to my brother?" And so Francis spoke to Tyrone in the hallway and Tyrone was very angry and difficult and believed that "another" white man was taking advantage of the black man.

And time moved forward and Sal agreed to have the tumor removed from his chest; and as he placed the clothes into his suitcase, inside of his bedroom, in his Inglewood apartment before his surgery, he "secretly" knew that he would never return to his place. And then Sal died less than twenty-eight hours after the surgery.

And time continued to move forward; and Tyrone discovered that his brother died when someone from the hospital contacted him at work. So Tyrone was angry and pissed off again as he drove his sister, Wanda, to the Crenshaw District Hospital and he saw his older brother, laying motionless on a gurney, in the ICU. And Tyrone noticed a long scar on Sal's chest. His body was cold and then Tyrone wanted "black" justice, and before he "snapped" he told his boss, Don Blue, at Eric's Auto Garage, that he needed a few days off because of his brother's death.

And as Tyrone sat in his Buick Regal, in front of a church, he held a knife with a six inch blade and realized that he "needed" to create a funeral for the "white ass surgeon." He was ready to murder and he was hoping the Lord would stop him, but he realized that the Lord never stopped him before when he murdered one, two, three, four, five, six, seven, eight, nine, and ten black prostitutes. So Tyrone drove a few blocks away from the parking structure, at The Crenshaw District Hospital, to seek revenge on that "white ass motherfucker." And it was in the employee section of the parking structure where he waited for his "white" prey.

And it was during this "time" that Carmen Espinoza was thinking about what she would eat for dinner and then she thought about sitting in her bathtub and soaking her feet and "possibly" pleasuring herself in the warm water, and then her twelve hour shift ended, at the hospital. She was exhausted and it was after six p.m. and sunlight was almost "gone" for the day and heavy thick shadows grew over the gum marked pavement, as she headed toward the crowd that waited outside of the elevator and she didn't feel like being "stuffed" in the elevator with a dozen "smelly ass" strangers.

And this is when she entered the stairway of the parking structure and ascended the first floor and the second floor and the third floor. She finally ascended the stairs of the fourth floor and stood on the landing when the door smashed open and she saw the angry eyes and large nostrils of the black man, in a green hoodie. And he bumped into Carmen.

Yes for a moment, she looked at the black man, in the green hoodie.

And then he was gone.

Carmen yelled "HEY!" but it didn't matter at that moment and she was slightly dazed when she entered the fourth floor of the parking structure, in the employee area. And when she walked across long shadows, Carmen discovered blood on the ground, near a white Mercedes. She slowed her pace around the white Mercedes, but the moment happened way too fast. Francis lay bleeding to death. Blood soaked through his clothes. His hands and neck and face were cut and bleeding. And there was so much blood. Carmen screamed and she dropped her purse and ran toward the stairway and away from Francis who lay in his own blood. His eyes were closed and his breath stopped. He was gone. He was dead. No heart beat. And a shadow emerged over the lifeless body of Francis Sevens.

The shadow moved slowly at first.

AFTER LIFE

CHAPTER 20

Once Francis Stevens died, his spirit stood over his bloody and lifeless body in the parking structure, of The Crenshaw District Hospital, and his spirit looked identical to his dead body. Yes Francis wore the same clothes that he bled in and died in, but these clothes were clean; after Francis' spirit entered the after life, everything was bright and blurry with white and yellow circles of light. He was a new soul in this world; and initially in this world, Francis could not remain still in the after life. He was now listening to Carmen speak to Detectives Preston and Johnson in the interrogation room.

And everything happened so fast.

And that's because a few minutes ago, Francis was walking to his white BMW to drive home and to eat dinner with his wife, Ruth, and his seventeen year old daughter, Abigail.

And now he was dead.

And his spirit was watching the living but everything was bright with white and yellow circles of light that filled his vision in the after life.

And once Francis arrived in the interrogation room, he was unsure how he got there and he could only discern words and shapes of the detectives in the interrogation room and he saw a large blob of brown flesh that was Carmen; and what Francis heard was disjointed and muffled. "How tall was he?" and "What did he look like, specifically?" and "How black was he?" and "Would you recognize him if you saw him again?"

And then Francis was gone.

He couldn't stay.

He was new in the after life and he had difficulties controlling his ability to move from one place to another, and everything was bright with white and yellow and circles of light; and a few weeks later after his murder, Francis was in the motel room, in South L.A., and his vision had "cleared up" by this time; and now he was standing near a bright yellow lamp light and he watched Tyrone straddle Candy, the black prostitute, on the bed; and Francis watched in "disbelief" as Tyrone attempted to suffocate Candy by placing his hand over her mouth and that is when Candy bit into Tyrone's hand and he looked at his hand and saw the blood oozing from the cut on his palm and he grabbed Candy's head and "snapped" her neck.

Her body instantly went limp and Candy died with her eyes open and Francis watched Tyrone grab a washcloth and wipe fingerprints from the bathroom door knob and he wiped every place he could think of including the front door knob.

Tyrone was about to leave and he turned and "glanced" at Candy's lifeless body on the bed within a circle of yellow lamp light for a moment and calmly closed the door with the washcloth and pocketed it. Francis then walked through the door and followed Tyrone down the hallway until Tyrone sensed someone or something. He turned and noticed a moving shadow on the yellow painted wall. Tyrone didn't see Francis' spirit but he felt a presence; and it was the same presence that he felt in his bedroom two weeks earlier, the night of Francis murder. Now Tyrone turned and hurried down the narrow stairway and left the fuckin' motel from the rear door; and he walked around the motel and dropped the washcloth in the gutter and got into his Buick Regal and he fumbled with his car keys for a moment and drove away from the motel and down Crenshaw Blvd and toward his house.

And as Tyrone drove, he felt that same fuckin' presence that he had felt in the motel hallway. Tyrone adjusted the rear view mirror and peered into the backseat where Francis was sitting but Tyrone couldn't see anyone.

Francis wanted to continue and sit and terrorize Tyrone but his spirit left the car and he hovered above the Buick Regal, on Crenshaw Blvd. for a moment; and it was during that moment that he remembered his promise to Abigail since she was five years old. And it was the same promise that he had made when she was almost thirteen years old when they walked together in the park, on an afternoon, and the leaves blew across their feet and it was that same promise that he made to Abigail when she was seventeen when they were both sitting on the brown leather couch, in the living room, at night, and the TV was on; and during those moments, those lost moments in his life, he promised that he would always be around for her and Ruth.

Three days after his murder, Francis attended his own funeral. He stood in the back, behind the last aisle under the canopy tent. His vision was still blurry and filled with white and yellow circles of light as he listened to his daughter thank everyone for coming and he heard her mention how great he was and how loving he was and then he finally heard Abigail read the short handwritten eulogy.

> "*Birth and death are like a puzzle. What actually comes first? Who really knows? Every moment, every part of life feels out of order; but, in the end, life and death come together, within the after life.*"

Francis felt her emotion and he noticed family members that he hadn't seen in years, even though everything was still bright with circles of white and yellow light, but he thought he did see his parents, and he thought he saw his aunts, and uncles, and cousins; and people were crying and they finally stood and gathered around the coffin and Francis finally noticed Ruth again. She was now standing next to her daughter and they watched the coffin lower into the ground; and that is when Francis believed that he could get his wife's attention from the after life. He softly placed his hand on Ruth's shoulder. She turned and Francis smiled at her but his wife peered through her dead husband.

"It's me, Ruth," Francis said.

There was no response from Ruth and the same thing happened a few hours later, when Francis watched Louise and Ruth argue after the service, in Ruth's bedroom.

"I'm not the enemy, Ruth," Louise said.

"My fuckin' husband was just murdered! Excuse me if I'm a little impatient here!"

Their attention was quickly diverted to Abigail who stood in the doorway and said "Uncle Albert wants to know where his decaffeinated coffee is that he asked for nearly a half hour ago."

"Don't you know how to knock?" Ruth snapped.

"I'll be right there, honey," Louise intervened. "Just give us a second." Abigail closed the bedroom door and Louise focused on her daughter. "Jesus, Ruth, you have to get a hold of yourself. You're going to scare Abigail right out of this house."

"Is that a threat?"

"I'll be in the kitchen making decaffeinated coffee," Louise said, calmly. She left the room and closed the door, and Ruth resumed playing with her wedding ring. Francis stood in the corner of the room and he had to make his presence known and an instant chill filled the room. She rubbed her arms.

The hardwood floor creaked in the corner of the room as Francis approached Ruth. She instantly felt a presence and turned and looked in his direction; yet she didn't see her husband nor did she hear Francis say "Ruth, you have to listen to your mother. You're going to scare Abigail away from you."

Ruth knew someone was definitely in this room. Ruth quickly left and Francis stood still as he realized that once again he failed to communicate with his wife, at this moment; but he would "not" stop trying."

As Francis continued to watch Ruth and Abigail weeks after his death, he wondered what he would say to them. Didn't he say everything that he needed to when he was alive?

And after a few weeks in the after life, Francis began to see images clearly and the white and yellow circles of light slowly dissipated, but Francis began to feel a withdrawal from watching the living. He felt the loneliness of just being an "observer" in the after life. He had no impact on the situation when Ruth forced Abigail into a public high school; nor could he try to stop Ruth when she forced Abigail to find a "shitty ass" job after school. And Francis stood and watched when Abigail met Danny, at Rite-Aide, and he stood and watched when Abigail began to snort cocaine and had unprotected sex with her boyfriend; and Francis stood and watched as Danny and Abigail devised a "botched" plan to rob Lester Jackson, the night manager, of Rite-Aide. And Francis watched Ruth drink Scotch while she wrote her novel during the day. He would momentarily "grab" her attention by making the floorboards creak and making it much "cooler" in the room and rattling the door knobs or opening the bathroom door when she was applying make-up or showering, or crying or vomiting; and he watched Ruth date Norm Jacobs, the high school counselor. And he watched Ruth and Norm in a cheap diner, in Santa Monica, when she admitted that she had an affair when she was married.

Over the few months after his death, Francis began to focus on his wife every day and he continued to believe that he could communicate with Ruth, somehow, someway; and one day, Francis encountered a "breakthrough" and this breakthrough occurred during Ruth and Norm's visit to the mall. Ruth was trying on the most "beautiful" brown suede jacket, in an "upscale" clothing store; and she tried on the brown suede jacket and loved the feeling of it, and she walked to a mirror and posed in the brown suede jacket; and that's when she saw her dead husband in the mirror.

Francis was "excited" that Ruth noticed him, but Ruth was horrified and then she said to Norm "I can't do this anymore." She "peeled" off the brown suede jacket and threw it at him and left the store.

"Wait, Ruth!" Norm yelled and hung up the jacket and followed Ruth into the mall and Francis watched Norm catch up with Ruth; and Norm was partially out of breath when he said "Talk to me, Ruth. Is it Abigail?"

And Francis listened to Ruth explain that it was her husband and that he was following her "everywhere" and Norm responded "Maybe he is trying to tell you something and that everything will be okay" and that is when Francis pleaded to Ruth and said "I'm here, Ruth. I know you can see me" but Ruth and Norm couldn't hear Francis; and Ruth and Norm hugged within the thick crowd of strangers and some of them stopped and stared; and Ruth and Norm walked out of the mall; and Francis was angry for a moment, because he couldn't change the "living" but he now knew that his wife "had" seen him. Yet all Francis could do was watch his family live without him and he now watched Ruth and Norm hold hands as they walked among the living, in the mall; and that is when Francis finally realized that he "lost" the love of his life.

During his life, Francis prayed, attended church and never "touched" his wife and daughter inappropriately and he saved people's lives for a living; and in return someone took his life and he died a terrible and violent death. His throat was cut and the pathologist stated in his report that Dr. Stevens died from choking on his own blood.

One day in the after life, Francis wondered that if he never operated on Sal, would he still be living and avoid the painful death that Tyrone inflicted upon him.

From the after life, Francis periodically watched Tyrone after he murdered Candy in the motel room, in South L.A. He watched when the judge denied Tyrone's bail and Francis was in the courtroom when Tyrone was found guilty in the first degree for murdering Francis. And Francis was in the court room years later when Tyrone was found guilty for murdering the ten black prostitutes, in South L.A. and he was sentenced to "death." And Francis was in Tyrone's cell when Tyrone read a letter from his daughter, Keisha, who denounced him as a "piece of shit" and hoped that he would "die in hell." And Francis watched Tyrone throughout the years as every family member stopped visiting him in prison, and Francis watched as "the city" tore down Tyrone's house, and Francis heard the death threats from various inmates in prison who wanted to kill Tyrone for murdering the prostitutes, because someone knew someone who was related to one of the prostitutes.

However in the after life, Francis talked to some of the black prostitutes that Tyrone had murdered, in South L.A. Candy was the first victim he met in the after life. Her real name was Candice Thompson. At one time, Candice was considered a "gifted" student in middle school, until her brother, Dwayne, forced her to smoke marijuana, at twelve years old; and a year later, she "tried" cocaine and then she "tried" crack; and she couldn't stop smoking crack and she needed money to buy more crack, so she began to "sell" her body on the streets year after year until she met Tyrone on Crenshaw Blvd.

Now in the afterlife, Candice was an angry spirit. She wanted revenge on that "black piece of shit;" and so she roamed the halls of the motel where she was murdered hoping to find his "dumb black ass" so she could try to stop him from murdering someone else in the motel.

And then Francis finally met the other black prostitutes that Tyrone murdered. Most of them were angry spirits as their lives ended in various tragedies. Tyrone murdered Monique Carter by blowing a hole in her stomach with a .22 shot gun, at "point blank range." Another woman named LaSandra Simmons was suffocated to death as Tyrone put a plastic shopping bag around her head until she lost unconsciousness and he raped her and then disposed of her body in an alleyway in South L.A., and Rashida Johnson was shot in the back of the head with a .38 handgun and then there was Shante, Taniqua, Monet, Bridget, Porsche and Rhonda who had succumbed to Tyrone's wrath with his infamous six inch blade.

The black angry spirits now wanted revenge from the after life. They were hoping to find him somewhere among the living and try to murder him from the after life. Yet during their plan of revenge, Francis spoke to Tyrone's victims and discovered that they were "good people" who became a "product" of poverty, abuse and neglect. Most of the victim's fathers had left them when they were young and some of the women were sexually abused by their fathers or their uncles or their brothers or their brother's friends; and most of the victims lived in "roach infested" apartment buildings with their siblings as their mother worked two jobs, or some of the mothers were smoking crack and selling their own bodies for a "hit" instead of taking care of them "dumb ass kids."

After hearing the discouraging stories from Tyrone's victims, Francis "firmly" believed that they were possibly "better off" in the after life. They were no longer subjected to prostitution and drugs and violence, and some of the women had their own kids to raise; but now they were alone and angry in the after life; but Francis realized that he didn't want to be angry in the after life, and after speaking to the dead black prostitutes, Francis realized he was "fortunate" to spend his brief time on Earth with a loving family.

Most of the prostitutes never really knew what love was and what it meant to be "in love;" and now Francis knew that he could not be distracted from watching his family; and so he resumed watching Ruth and Abigail, but Francis was unprepared for what he was about to witness in the living world after his death.

Francis sat in the backseat of Danny's green 1973 Pontiac Trans Am, as Danny drove "high" on cocaine and Abigail sat "high as shit" in the passenger seat staring out of the window, as the Motorhead song, Fast and Loose cranked from the "shitty ass" speakers; and then Francis watched as Ruth became a drunk and "kicked" her daughter out of the house. And Francis watched when Abigail pointed a gun at her black night manager, Lester Jackson, at the community park, in Mar Vista.

"No, Abigail! He didn't do it. Please don't shoot him!" Francis said as he pleaded a few feet away from her and Abigail lowered the gun for some reason.

Maybe she heard her father but then Danny emerged from the shadows of darkness. He grabbed the 9mm Smith & Wesson from Abigail and shot Lester Jackson four times in the chest.

BLAM! BLAM! BLAM! BLAM!

Lester died instantly as Francis watched the incident. And Francis was there when Danny and Abigail drove to a motel, in Palm Springs. He watched as Danny stood by the dusty drapes in the motel room that overlooked the "shitty ass" parking lot and Francis entered the motel bathroom as Abigail urinated and washed her hands and peered at her image in the mirror. She was about to leave when she stopped and felt a chill and rubbed her hands. She was completely unaware that her father was watching her. And Francis was there when a sheriff shot and killed Danny, on the side of the highway, near the Arizona border. And Francis watched as police officers arrested his daughter on a street in Palm Springs, while people "stared" and "pointed." Francis watched investigators "dust" for prints in Lester's blue Prius, in the parking lot, of the community park, in Mar Vista, and they discovered a few strands of Abigail's blond hair in the backseat.

Francis witnessed Abigail tell Ruth in the visiting room of the juvenile detention center that she was pregnant. And of course Francis was in court when Abigail was sentenced as an "adult" for being an accomplice for murder and robbery. And Francis was there when Ruth placed flowers, at the cemetery, of the first anniversary of his death; and on the drive home, from the cemetery, Francis watched Ruth from the passenger seat, as Ruth took off her seat belt and thought of veering into oncoming traffic, at seventy miles per hour. However she realized that she may not die in the auto accident; and she may actually kill someone else, which would result in a pricey law suit; or she may suffer severe head trauma and possibly bleed to death on the way to the hospital while choking on glass and her own blood. So Ruth decided to possibly save her plan of suicide for another day. Ruth buckled her seat belt and she drove to church and prayed on her knees; and she finally arrived home and it was dark and most of the media had left for the night and she decided to skip dinner since she was much too "distraught" to eat. She poured herself a glass of Scotch from her "emergency supply" that she kept under the sink; and then she stood at the doorway of her daughter's dark bedroom and she "immediately" felt the cold still air and then she eventually entered her bedroom and turned on the lamp and placed her glass of Scotch on the night stand and sat on the edge of her bed away from the circle of yellow lamp light. She looked at her wedding ring for a moment and realized that she needed to make a "change" in her life. She finally removed her wedding ring; and on the first anniversary of her husband's death, Ruth said "I love you, Francis Stevens."

Ruth stood up and kissed her wedding ring and walked to the dresser and placed her ring inside the drawer.

"I love you too, Ruth," Francis said.

Ruth heard the floorboards creak behind her and she felt the sudden chill in the room. Francis stood behind her and she felt the touch of her husband and she closed her eyes and smiled.

CHAPTER 21

A few years after Francis' murder, Ruth's depression began to slowly dissipate. She finished her manuscript, *The After Life*. She submitted it to over fifty agents. She read some of the rejections and the comments ranged from "the plot is way too slow" and "an amateur effort" to "The story is completely unbelievable and the characters seem more stagnant than the plot." Yet on the fifty-first submission, Ruth found an interest from a mid-level agency, in Orange County, and received a "small advance" from a publishing company a few months later, and her novel became a "massive" hit after it was featured as the "Book of the Month" by a popular talk show host; and then numerous bookstores were constantly "out of stock" for weeks.

Readers across the country were engaged by the story's plot which revolved around the heroine, Corinne Dolan, a housewife, in a small Midwestern town, who has an affair with Dale Hartmen, the "local" sheriff who is eventually "gunned down" by a "cokehead" while on duty. The sheriff watches over Corinne as she attempts to have a "normal" relationship with her husband and children after the murder.

The novel became a "best seller" and literary agencies were desperate to represent Ruth; and journalists interviewed her about the process of writing a "best seller" and they inquired about her own husband's murder; and ironically as Ruth discussed her husband's murder, her books sales increased; and in between the money and the fame for writing a "best seller," Ruth met Stan Wisenberg, at a book convention. Stan was a Jewish accountant, from New York, who became a literary agent, in New York, over twenty years ago; and now he had an impressive roster of best selling writers. And so Stan flew to L.A. ever other week to visit Ruth. She admired his work ethic, his charm, and of course, his success. The "long distance fling" lasted a few years.

Ruth was in her mid-fifties and Stan was nearing his mid-sixties. She was "free" to love anyone without guilt. Yet in between the sex with Stan and her success as a best selling author, Ruth had a new responsibility. She was a grandmother to Marcus Stevens. He was born in 2013. Ruth raised him while her daughter served a ten year sentence in prison. Ruth became a grandmother at forty-three years old; and over the years, Marcus became a "shy boy" as he entered the public school system. And when Marcus entered second grade, his teacher, Mrs. Hinderheart, a frumpy woman who smelled like fabric softener and pickle juice described Marcus as a "slow student" who could not compute "simple" addition and write "simple" sentences. "It's beyond me why he can't figure this stuff out," Mrs. Hinderheart said one morning to Ruth, in a private conference.

Yet Ruth learned to ignore the "bullshit;" and on a rainy morning, when Ruth walked Marcus to class, she kneeled in front of him under a green awning and said "I want you to listen to me, Marcus. You're not slow. You're a nice person." She was serious about what she had told him and when she walked back to her car, she remembered walking Abigail to kindergarten when she was five years old, and then she remembered her mother, Louise, walking her to kindergarten class.

And the cycle of life moved round and round.

Throughout grade school and middle school, Marcus sat in the back of the classroom unable to make eye contact with anyone and he was scared to raise his hand when he knew the answer to the teacher's questions. And during recess, Marcus sat alone on a bench outside with his head down. And then the bullies came after him. He was unable to defend himself. He was small and had very "little" confidence. So he got used to the "pushing" and the "punching." He hid the bruises from his grandmother the best that he could and never told the teachers or anyone else about the bullying.

Marcus was an easy target as he was shy and emotionally scarred and teachers and students were completely unaware that his mother was serving a ten year prison sentence and that his father was shot and killed by a sheriff; and nobody knew that his grandfather was murdered, in a hospital parking structure, at a HMO hospital, years ago. "Maybe my family is cursed," Marcus thought to himself years later.

However at seven years old, when other children spoke to their mother before they went to bed, Marcus was unable to do so since his mother was in prison. So who could he speak to about his problems? He felt shy around his grandmother and year after year, he was considered the "oddball" with a mental handicap by teachers and the school administration. He had very little motivation to complete his homework. He had a "D" average and Ruth listened to the so-called expert teachers who said "I think your grandson needs help" or "I know a great school for him that would assist him with his 'problems.'" And on a certain afternoon, Ruth heard "I'm sorry, but I think your grandson has a learning disability." Over the years, Ruth listened to the excuses from teachers, counselors, and therapists as to why Marcus was a "D" student. Ruth didn't believe the comments. She thought that all the comments were bullshit and she knew that she would never place Marcus into a "special needs" class or school. She knew her grandson just needed confidence. So at night in her bedroom, near a circle of yellow lamp light, Ruth prayed for Marcus to obtain confidence and then she decided to introduce Marcus to prayer. Before every meal, Marcus prayed for his family, his own life, and the food that he was about eat; and as Ruth watched him across the table, Ruth believed that Marcus needed more than prayer to fix his "social" issues. So she took him to the mall to buy new clothes. "Dressing well would definitely improve his confidence," she thought; and during an excursion to the mall, when Marcus was almost nine years old, he asked his grandmother if something was wrong with him.

"There is absolutely nothing wrong with you, Marcus. Like my father used to tell me, 'you have to be tough. It's hard to tell what's around each corner," Ruth said.

"What happened to my dad?"

Ruth finally parked her car and turned off the engine and faced her grandson. She knew that she would have to answer that question one day, so she told him the first thing she could think of at that moment. "He was killed in a car accident."

"Did a sheriff kill my dad?"

"Who told you this?"

"I looked it up on the Internet," Marcus said. "Is it true?"

Ruth realized that she couldn't lie to Marcus and she said "Your father did something very bad. He pointed a gun at a sheriff and that's why your father isn't here anymore."

A long silence ensued between them and Marcus finally asked "Why would he do that?"

"I don't know, Marcus."

They were silent for a moment. They both wanted to know the answer to that question. Yet nobody really knew that Danny was desperate when he pointed a 9mm at a sheriff, on the side of a highway, near the Arizona border.

Marcus thought about his mother being sentenced as an accessory to murder, and then he thought about his father being a possible murderer and it was difficult for a nine year old to comprehend. However Marcus appeared to have only one way to go in life and that was down; but Ruth was determined to make sure that Marcus' life was not going to spiral out of control like her daughter's life; and Ruth never wanted to explain the "truth" to Marcus about his father, his mother, and his grandfather; but as he turned ten years old, the "truth" was scarring him socially; and as Marcus began to grow taller than the other kids, he walked clumsily down the school hallway with his large shoes and avoided eye contact with everyone, although he was becoming a very handsome boy and he had blue eyes like his mother and he had mulatto skin like his father. However Marcus was "lost" among his classmates. He was still very shy and was considered "slow" by various teachers and the administration. And then the "secret" about his mother was eventually coerced from Marcus after showing up year after year to "open house" with his grandmother; so one day afterschool, when Marcus was ten years old, three of the biggest fifth graders cornered Marcus in the courtyard, next to a bungalow. "Where's your mom, asshole?" Marcus remembered hearing "Don't lie to us or we'll beat the shit out of you." So after threats of physical violence, Marcus told them that his mother was in prison and then one of the three kids asked if she was a "hooker" but Marcus didn't know what a hooker was so he shrugged his shoulders; and within a few days, most of the students in the fifth grade knew that Marcus' mother was in prison and Marcus was constantly teased and Marcus got into a "pushing match" with another student and Ruth came to school and heard "more bullshit" from teachers and the administration like "Your son seems very angry" followed by "Have you considered a special school for your grandson where he would be around other kids 'like' himself?" Ruth felt the sting and the harshness of the public school system and realized why Abigail hated the public high school that she had attended. Yet Ruth didn't remember public schools being so "screwed up" when she attended them in the early 1980s.

After Marcus' "pushing match" with another student, Ruth believed that something had to change within her family but she didn't know what needed change at the moment; and then Ruth was still occupied with the phenomenal success of *The After Life*. Ruth received a five million dollar advance payment for her next two books. And her agent Stan was negotiating with attorneys and producers for a movie adaption of her novel.

Ruth quickly became the wealthiest person in the entire Gordon and Stevens' family, but she couldn't hide from the "truth" about her family; and she wished that the worst thing that Abigail could have done was break a vase or a curfew. However Ruth's past resembled a nightmare. And with all of her wealth, she still had to raise her grandson because her daughter was in prison.

The year was 2023 and Ruth was emotionally drained from raising her grandson and now she was preparing for another anniversary of Francis' death; and on that dreadful day, Ruth drove Marcus to the cemetery and they placed flowers near Francis headstone that read "Beloved Husband and Father 1965 – 2012," which was further proof that Francis had left the Earth much too soon. And Francis stood a few feet away from Ruth and Marcus; and Francis noticed the "other spirits" that lingered near their own headstones wishing they could come back to the living. But Francis no longer wanted to stay in the after life filled with regret like other spirits. After the fifth year or so in the after life, Francis finally "accepted" this place after a spirit named Joseph told him to enjoy where he is because he will never leave; and so Francis thought about what Joseph had told him so he decided to enjoy the after life without any "regrets."

After the visit to the cemetery, Ruth drove home with Marcus. They had dinner and Marcus fell asleep a few hours later. Ruth finally fell asleep and dreamed of Francis. He was underwater and he was trying to tell her something as she watched him through a small window in a room, but she was unable to decipher what he was saying. And then Ruth was lost in the woods, and she noticed Francis in dry clothes. He told her that someone was coming to stay with her for a while.

Ruth woke up from the dream and the morning light glowed within the curtains above the bed, and Ruth put on her robe and entered her home office and turned on her laptop and typed the words, *The After Life Part II.*

The story burned inside of her and she could not stop writing the new story as she felt a new twist was about to happen in this new book.

Yet Ruth didn't know what that twist would be.

But it was coming.

CHAPTER 22

Ruth and Marcus stood in the driveway of her house and they were both nervous about something and the sun was bright in the sky and it was a hot morning. They were both dressed for a certain occasion. Marcus had combed his hair back and it was still wet from the shower. He wore khaki pants and a white collar shirt. Ruth wore black pants and a "nice" sweater. She faced her grandson and asked "How do I look?"

"Fine, Grandma. Why are you asking?"

"Maybe I should change," Ruth said. She felt like a teenager again, even though she was nearly fifty-four years old.

They entered her BMW and Marcus sat in the passenger seat. Ruth drove out of the city and toward Bakersfield and the air became warmer and she turned on the air conditioner; and outside the terrain was brown and dry and various large boulders dotted the bleak landscape.

"Do you remember what we spoke about, Marcus?" Ruth asked interrupting the low sounds of the music that droned endlessly for an hour.

"Yeah, I know," he said softly.

"Remember she's going to be in shock, so don't ask her too many questions."

"I know, Grandma."

"She knows that she made a mistake, but she's going to be very glad to see you, so let's leave it at that for now, okay?"

"Okay," Marcus said and continued to focus on the bare desolate area.

Ruth continued to drive. She was silent for the remainder of the trip. Her heart pounded as she neared the prison. She was slightly relieved that she would no longer be solely responsible for Marcus. Yes Ruth was going to miss taking him shopping for clothes, talking to him at night, before bedtime, and watching TV with him, but she needed her "old" life back.

An hour later, Ruth and Marcus arrived at the prison. Numerous female inmates were meeting their family members, and husbands, and boyfriends and friends; and in the distance, Ruth noticed Abigail who now had short hair. She was wearing tattered clothes and was twenty pounds heavier than when she first entered prison ten years ago. Abigail approached and hugged her mother and her son, and Ruth instantly discovered the innocent teenager within the eyes of her twenty-eight year old daughter. She was still attractive but she had a penetrative glare in her eyes and she walked stiffly, which were things she didn't have before she entered prison; and although Abigail had spent ten years in prison, she "narrowly" missed a twenty-five year prison sentence for being an accomplice to first degree murder, aggravated assault, and robbery and other charges. During her trial, the prosecution desperately tried to prove that this "clean white adolescent" murdered Lester Jackson out of "rage" but they were unable to prove to the jury that Abigail fired the gun since Danny's and Abigail's finger prints were both found on the weapon. Throughout the three week trial, the jury remembered hearing the testimony from the crying eighteen year old woman who had suffered a "great" traumatic loss after her father was murdered. Abigail's attorney realized that her "crying" made her "appear" sympathetic in the eyes of the jury. So when it was her time for her to take the stand after lunch one day, her attorney told her to keep crying. And Abigail got on the stand and cried so much that most of her statements were unclear, and she had to repeat most of it. However Abigail was not acting. She was nearly delirious and the jury had to decide if Abigail was the "actual" shooter or an accomplice to murdering and robbing a black man. And now at twenty-eight years old, she stood outside of the prison after serving a ten year sentence instead of a twenty-five year sentence.

Ruth drove her grandson and her daughter back to the city and nobody said anything. The silence was deafening. Although nobody really knew what to say and Marcus was clearly afraid to speak to his mom. Abigail just stared out of the window, in the backseat, of the BMW. She wanted to adjust to the changing world in silence.

And the year was 2023.

Before she actually knew it, Abigail was in the house she grew up in, on Fourth Street, in Santa Monica. Everything was the same inside, but the home felt different for some strange reason.

A few hours later, Abigail and Ruth sat at the dining room table eating a "late" dinner. And under the bright yellow light in the dining room, Ruth carefully studied her daughter's face and she still saw the defiant teenager who snorted cocaine and wanted to do things "her own way." Yes Ruth wanted to say "see what happens when you don't listen to your mother." Ruth stopped the spiteful thoughts since she knew that she had to be "easy" on her daughter, but she couldn't pretend as if nothing ever happened.

"I read your book. It's really good," Abigail said.

"I'm glad you're back," Ruth said. She chewed a piece of tough steak for a moment. She was suddenly nervous about something and said "I was speaking to a friend and she knows somebody at a warehouse. They need people in the back." Ruth shifted in her seat. "It's a simple job, but they'll hire you." She was clearly uncomfortable with the subject of her daughter working so soon, but she felt like she "needed" to mention the opportunity.

"Mom, can I at least finish dinner?" Abigail asked. She was clearly exasperated.

"I know, Abby. I was just trying to help."

"Oh, is that what you were doing? Are we done talking about work?"

Ruth said forcefully "You have to work. Don't you think?"

"Just like I did when I was seventeen? You can't even wait twenty-four hours before you make me get another shitty job!"

Their voices were raised and Ruth and Abigail were already in their first argument as Ruth said "We have to start growing up."

"Are you including yourself? Last time I checked, you kicked me out of the house!" Abigail was already unable to endure her mother's bullshit.

Ruth reached across the table and grabbed her daughter's hand and said "Listen, Abby, I'm glad you're back and I would do everything in this world for you and Marcus; but life has changed, and that's something you 'must' realize."

They stared at each other for a long moment and Ruth finally grabbed the empty dinner plates and brought them into the kitchen as Abigail sat alone at the table and listened to her mother washing dishes just like the night that her father was murdered. Abigail hadn't been in this house in over ten years; and now it was 2023. Abigail wondered what life would be like in ten more years. And then she wondered what could she actually do with her life? She had spent most of her twenties in prison. She was now a mother of a ten year old boy.

Abigail entered her "old" bedroom and closed the door and sat on the edge of the bed and looked at her son, Marcus, who was watching TV. His face was bathed in a circle of yellow lamp light.

"Mom, is Grandma mad at us because we're here?"

"No, not at all, sweetheart. We're just discussing living

arrangements, that's all," Abigail explained.

"Are we going to leave here one day?"

"You bet," Abigail said. She kissed his forehead. When she leaned back from the circle of yellow lamp light, she noticed how her son was beginning to resemble his father, Danny, the "out of control" cokehead who shot and killed an innocent black man, in a community park, in Mar Vista, and then he committed suicide by pointing a gun at a sheriff, on the side of a desert highway, near the Arizona border. Abigail had to forget the past and put it behind her, but it was only a "matter of time" that Marcus would turn into his father, or that's what Abigail feared.

Now Abigail brushed her teeth in the guest bathroom and while she brushed her teeth, she wished that she could close her eyes and forget about her past mistakes, but her son and her mother were a constant reminder of them.

Abigail returned to the kitchen and spoke with her mother. She didn't want to end the first night back in the house on a "sour note." Ruth began to pour a glass of Scotch when Abigail entered and she was quickly reminded of the past once again. She finally said "I heard the prisoners talking about your book one day in the yard."

Ruth turned and looked at her daughter as if Abigail hadn't said anything. She kissed her on the forehead and said "goodnight" and was about to leave.

"Why did you take me out of private school? Was it because you hated that I was young and happy and I had friends?"

Ruth thought she could hide her "secret" feelings about her daughter, but she was wrong. Yes Ruth was definitely jealous of her daughter just like Louise was jealous of Ruth over thirty years ago, and the vicious cycle continued. Ruth left the kitchen with her glass of Scotch unwilling to continue to trade "verbal blows" with her daughter. Ruth entered her bedroom and sat on the edge of her bed and held her glass of Scotch, with a shaking hand, within a circle of yellow lamp light; and she remembered the night that Abigail came into her room hours after her husband was murdered wanting to see his body at the morgue; and then Ruth realized that nothing has changed between her and Abigail, in over ten years.

What Ruth hated the most, at this very moment, is that Abigail was correct. Yes Ruth disliked when Abigail was a teenager and happy and had friends; and of course, she hated that she was beautiful. Yet for some strange reason, Ruth didn't have any animosity toward her grandson; however when Abigail entered Ruth's house after ten years of being in prison, the "old" jealous feelings surged inside of Ruth. It was true that Abigail was an ex-con without any job skills. She was broke and almost twenty-nine years old. Oddly enough Ruth was unable to forget that Abigail stole Francis' attention away from her over two decades ago. Ruth was also jealous of Abigail's current age. Ruth disliked getting older even though she was still considered "attractive" among the elderly neighbors. Yet Ruth still desired a youthful appearance with perky breasts and a flat stomach. She wanted a face without wrinkles and stress lines. Most of all she wanted Francis back and she wanted everything her way. And there was a selfishness that she still couldn't get rid of even though she was fifty-three years old.

Ruth peered in the mirror above her dresser, across the foot of the bed, as she continued to hold her glass of Scotch in her shaking hand. She knew that she had to control her emotions. Her grandson slept in one bedroom and her daughter slept on the couch, in the living room. Ruth encountered a new chapter in her life and had to embrace it and try to be understanding.

And on the moonlit couch, in the living room, Abigail laid awake and wondered if she might be "better off" in prison, which may be easier than facing reality. She knew "deep down" that she still despised her mother for what she had done to her when she was a teenager. However Abigail loved her son, yet when she looked at Marcus she was instantly reminded of Danny, the Mexican-American who was her first and only love. The Mexican-American "took" her virginity and made her bleed in her private area. She started to relive the moments when Danny introduced her to cocaine and how Danny left her alone, at the Desert Lodge Motel, and how she ended up pregnant and in prison. Abigail had spent more than ten horrible and lonely years in prison; it was a place of shattered dreams; it was a place where only nightmares lived, and these nightmares consisted of rapes and fights with weapons. And during the living nightmares, there were visiting hours where family members cried and blamed each other for a life that went inexplicably wrong. Abigail snapped from her horrible claustrophobic thoughts. She realized now that partying with Danny and snorting cocaine and ditching high school classes were no longer part of her world. She had to be a responsible parent. She could never touch drugs again. She was also on probation for five years which consisted of "random drug tests" and discussing her progress with her parole officer. And she needed to do something productive in her life, so a few weeks later she applied for a warehouse position, at Supreme Industries, in Van Nuys, located on Sherman Way and Van Owen. And this was the company where Ruth knew someone that knew someone, and Abigail would eventually work in the warehouse area, which was a rat and roach infested "shit hole" but it was still a job with medical benefits for her and Marcus; and before Abigail started her job at Supreme Industries, in Van Nuys, she received her driver's license. Ruth bought her daughter a new car. And before Ruth purchased the vehicle for her daughter, Abigail studied for the written driving exam and once she passed the test, she began practicing how to drive, in Ruth's BMW, in an empty parking lot and then on the busy streets of L.A. and then she drove on traffic-jammed freeways during rush hour.

And two weeks before the interview, at Supreme Industries, Abigail practiced interviewing with her mother, who coached her carefully. Ruth instructed her to sit up straight and make great eye contact "and never look like you're timid or shy. Sometimes supervisors and managers intimidate employees if they can," Ruth said. Abigail remembered the corporate "words of wisdom" from her mother. Abigail also realized that she needed to "improve" her appearance. She no longer wanted to look like a "poor ex-con." She lost extra weight around her stomach and hips. Abigail grew her hair longer; and then one morning after stepping from the shower, she wiped away the mist on the mirror, and realized that she was still attractive and she had to leave the memories of incarceration behind her. She now needed a purpose in life; and that purpose was to "stay clean" and to raise her son the best that she could.

The first interview finally arrived and she interviewed with her direct boss, the warehouse manager, and then she was invited back for another interview with the Director of Operations, Jess Parker. On the day of her second and last interview, Abigail arrived early and wore slacks and a blue and white striped blouse. She entered Jess' office and realized that this was the interview that could "make" or "break" her in trying to get hired in this rat and roach infested "shit hole." Jess was a white handsome well-built guy about forty-five years old with light stubble on his face. His hair was closely cropped; and at first, Jess didn't bother to glance at Abigail. Jess knew Abigail was an ex-con and he was doing a "favor" for someone who knew someone; and Jess could have chosen any other candidate from a "stack" of resumes on his desk for the "shitty ass" position, but he didn't; and Abigail stood in the doorway of his office, Jess continued to work and said "Have a seat." Abigail entered and sat down across him and she had a fast heartbeat. She was clearly nervous and she expected the worst, and to be treated like an "abused" child. Ten years of her life was spent taking orders from angry prison guards and she was always on alert for some "bitch" to rape or stab her. That was then and now she peered at the dusty cheap art work on the blue painted walls, as she waited for Jess to look at her. All he said was "Have a seat" while pretending to read her application, but when Jess looked up at Abigail, he instantly discovered the prettiest woman who ever sat in his office. He was momentarily speechless. Jess Parker had spent nearly fifteen years in the military and fought in two wars and breathed blood. He smelled death from rotting corpses that littered the barren landscape of the Middle East. At this moment, it was a woman who had made him nervous. He glanced at her application that laid next to his "other" work.

"Is there something wrong?" Abigail asked. She remembered to make eye contact and never look "timid or shy" like her mother had instructed her weeks ago.

"Well," Jess said. He cleared his throat and said "I didn't expect to see you here." He was loss for words for a moment.

"You mean someone like me sitting here?"

They both smiled nervously. "It's just, well, you have a criminal record. Is that a mistake?"

Abigail's smile dissolved. It was the two words that haunted her, "criminal record." How should she respond? What could she say? "Oh, I also watched my ex-boyfriend kill someone in front of me and I still have nightmares about it, and no pills in the world can help me deal with it." Instead she remained silent.

Jess realized that her application was correct as Abigail sat silently. "How come someone this pretty could spend time in prison?" He thought to himself. He wanted to ask her a million questions. He knew people "screwed up" in life, as he did when he was younger. So why should this woman with blue eyes and sandy blond hair be any different?

"Okay," Jess said clearing his throat and trying to concentrate on the situation. "The job pays twelve dollars per hour. You'll be responsible for packing boxes, loading and unloading trailers on eighteen wheeler trucks. Oh, have you ever driven a forklift before?"

She shook her head and said "No."

They both smiled as they were both trying to "fight" an attraction.

"Well you'll learn quickly," Jess said. He leaned back in his chair. "After a year of working in the back, I might be able to get you up here, in the office area. I'll see what I can do."

"That sounds fine," Abigail said. She thought that the interview was over and she was about to stand.

"Listen," Jess said and at that very moment. Abigail feared that she was going to have to explain exactly how she "ended up" in prison, or if she ever killed someone. The thought filled her mind until Jess cleared his throat and said "I know this isn't the most prestigious job, but just hang tough."

"I will," she said, softly. For some reason, she actually started to believe that this guy in the large leather chair was a "nice" person. Maybe her mother was incorrect to believe that most supervisors and managers try to intimidate employees if they can.

"Oh, by the way, I noticed you went to St. Susan in Brentwood."

"Yes, yes I did," Abigail said. She smiled proudly.

"My niece goes there," Jess said. "She loves it. Can you picture a teenager loving high school?"

Yet Abigail was one of those teenagers that did love high school until her "cunt of a mother" pulled her out of school.

Jess and Abigail shook hands and she was officially hired the next day. Her days were long in the warehouse. For eight hours in the stifling heat in the warehouse, Abigail unloaded freight from semi-trailer trucks with a forklift, she separated the freight on the dock after the trailer was entirely unloaded, and then she had to label the freight, and move it once again with the forklift; and then she would have to fill out the "proper" paperwork and when the company mail arrived, Abigail would have to distribute mail throughout the large company and on and on; and by nighttime, she was exhausted but she still had to help her ten year old son with his homework. One night while Abigail sat with Marcus at the dining room table, she reviewed a barely comprehensible composition that Marcus wrote. She had a strange feeling about something and she instructed Marcus to read a paragraph in a textbook and he struggled to pronounce simple words. "What a fuckin' mess," Abigail thought. "He's about to enter sixth grade and he could barely read!" Abigail panicked. Her son definitely had some sort of problem. She was unsure what was wrong with him. "Maybe it's his brain," she thought. "Maybe it was all the coke I used to snort." Abigail knew her son was quiet, even when he visited her in prison; and she knew that Marcus never had any "real" friends.

"Marcus, are you concentrating?" Abigail asked her son almost every night.

And his response was always the same "Yes I am."

Abigail leaned back in her chair one night after helping Marcus with his homework and wondered why her mother never mentioned that Marcus had a "possible" learning problem. One morning Ruth and Abigail went grocery shopping and Abigail asked the inevitable question "Mom, does Marcus have some sort of learning disability? And please don't bullshit me! I've been trying to get him to concentrate on his homework for weeks. His homework is a mess. It's been so difficult, and he could barely read."

"The teachers said a few things, but what do they know?"

"What do you mean they said a few things? What things? And thanks for letting me know!"

"You have enough problems, Abby," Ruth said. "This is the last thing you needed to hear in prison."

"Jesus, mom. I've been home for over two months! Marcus is nothing more than a "D" student. His teacher wants to hold him back next year."

"Oh, they're not going to do that," Ruth said.

"Bullshit! How could you be so calm?"

"His grades were actually improving until – "

"Until what?" Abigail snapped.

"Well until you got home," Ruth said.

"So now this is my fault!"

"Look Abby, the school is going to pass him like any other student. This is public school, not private school," Ruth said. "I've spent enough time with Marcus. His problem is that he lacks confidence, pure and simple. He's troubled about his father and not having his mother around."

"Well, is there anything else you need to tell me?" Abigail asked.

"If you really want to know, students have been teasing him about you and Danny."

"Wait, how does anyone know about us?" Abigail asked. And then she thought about Danny and his olive skin and his shoulder-length hair and the "I don't give a fuck" attitude. She had to fight the memories and move forward.

"These are ten and eleven year kids, Abby. You could find everything on the Internet. You have to start understanding that the older Marcus becomes, the more he's going to have to live with what happened to you and his father."

"And I need you reminding me of this?" Abigail asked. She wanted to cry at this moment. "So what do you want me to do?" She was officially lost. She naively believed that her difficulties were behind her, but now the "old mistakes" terrorized her and Abigail wiped her eyes and left the supermarket.

Ruth watched her daughter leave and she felt bad for her, but there was nothing that she could do to "fix" the past. They drove home in silence. Abigail stared outside and she realized that she could not "sit back" and feel sorry for herself and her son. She had to "start over" and she had to improve her son's life. She was not going to allow anyone to fuck around with Marcus' education.

A few weeks later, Abigail met with Marcus' fifth grade

teacher who stated that Marcus needed "professional help" since he was continuously "falling" behind. Abigail was dissatisfied with the conversation and met with the assistant vice principal and the principal in the school. Abigail didn't know much about teaching, but she realized after previous conversations with the staff that public education was all about pushing responsibility onto another school, or it was the parent's responsibility to help the child, and if a child "fell behind" it was always the parent's fault; and then Abigail remembered her professors at St. Susan. They were all graduates from Ivy League schools and actually "cared" about a student's progress. They tried to motivate students.
It was all about motivation in the private Catholic School, in Brentwood. Abigail quickly began to believe that in the world of public education, nobody "really" cared about Marcus. It was all about the paycheck; and Abigail refused to listen to the mediocre teachers and school officials. Instead she finally listened to her mother and started to believe that Marcus just lacked confidence; and so every night, when Abigail tucked her son into bed, she told him how smart he was and how he was going to make her proud one day.

At first Marcus didn't believe his mother and he certainly didn't believe that he was smart. Yet over time, Marcus grades slowly improved and near the end of the semester, Marcus became a "C" student. And when he finished sixth grade, Marcus finally became a "B" student, and Abigail finally realized that her mother was finally correct about something. Marcus' confidence slowly improved and Abigail started to believe that anything is possible with faith. Although Abigail had spent over ten years in prison, she believed that she could still improve her life and Marcus' life; and every weekday, Abigail worked diligently in the stifling warehouse, packing boxes, sweeping floors, and driving a forklift loading and unloading containers on eighteen wheeler trucks and sometimes her boss would send her to the pallet yard to sort the bad pallets from the good ones. The sweat burned her eyes and she was always thirsty in the heat; and within the dismal world of working in a warehouse, the Hispanic employees never spoke to her since she was the only "white bitch" who worked in the warehouse and in the pallet yard. Abigail listened to their conversations in Spanish, and she understood most of it, since she studied Spanish, at St. Susan. She heard them say that white people don't drive forklifts and unload trucks and work in the pallet yard. The "gringos" worked in the air-conditioned offices up front, earning "fat" paychecks and the "gringos" didn't have criminal records, but they knew Abigail did. Yet Abigail wasn't discouraged by the hatred. She still believed that she could improve her life and her son's life; and although Marcus wasn't a "planned" pregnancy, Abigail loved him unconditionally; and with her faith, Abigail worked month after month saving her money, and finally one day, Abigail located a two bedroom apartment, in West L.A., a few miles from where Danny used to live. She was hesitant to live so close to her former boyfriend and the horrible memories, but it was her first step toward a successful life with her son. Abigail believed that happiness was unfolding in front of her.

CHAPTER 23

After five years of unloading containers on eighteen-wheeler trucks and sorting pallets and counting steering wheel covers and distributing the company mail and on and on, Abigail finally received a promotion, at Supreme Industries. She was almost thirty-three years old, and during a stifling hot afternoon, in the warehouse, Abigail wiped the sweat from her forehead while sifting through a recently delivered box of office supplies and she discovered Jess approaching her. He smiled and was wearing a blue collar shirt and said "If you're interested there is a position up front, in accounting."

Abigail was slightly hesitant as she expected the promotion a year after she started the company, but it had been five "solid" years of exhausting work and inquiring from Human Resources about an "opening up front" but there was nothing for her; and when she felt "disgusted" about "moving up" at Supreme Industries, Abigail had sent her resume to other companies. She had a few interviews, but she had "no luck" in receiving a new job with a larger salary, so she stayed working in the warehouse, at Supreme Industries; and now she finally received the chance to move forward and to escape the grueling work in the heat and the mistreatment by the Hispanic employees who hated her for being a "gringo" and Abigail now faced Jess and asked "What will I be doing up front?"

"It's an entry-level position. It's mostly data entry for now, and after a few months, they'll give you more responsibility. I'll make sure of it," Jess said, smiling.

"Okay, let me discuss it with my mom."

"All right, but I need to tell you something," Jess said. "You know you don't belong back here."

They both agreed and Abigail interviewed with the accounting manager, Patrick Owens and two weeks later, Abigail had her own desk and cubicle in the air conditioned office area. She sat in front of a computer for nearly eight hours entering product codes of steering wheel covers and aftermarket rims into Excel spreadsheets. She was excited for the change and she no longer had to wear a dirty blue warehouse uniform which made her feel like an inmate. However in the accounting department, Abigail encountered "new" problems. Co-workers gawked and commented in hushed tones about her, whether it was about her skirt or the way she wore her hair or spoke or coughed or breathed. She attempted to ignore the "cattiness" which continued week after week, until Jess appeared at her cubicle one day to see how she was "handling" the new position.

Abigail smiled as she quickly realized that after Jess left that she was no longer "prey" to the vicious heavyset women in the department for the moment; and coincidentally Jess made his presence known weekly and he made sure that Abigail received the most money that the company would allow for that position. The other women finally stopped gawking and "talkin' shit" about her for now. Abigail knew that Jess Parker was her only friend in the company. She smiled as she thought of him while typing product codes into Excel spreadsheets. Abigail learned that the corporate world, like prison, was shark infested with older women who despised her because she was "young" and "attractive" and "smart." Now in the accounting department, she was surrounded by mostly venomous heavyset middle age women who resumed tormenting her when Jess would not come by for a few weeks; and then they eventually discovered that Abigail was a single mother so they privately criticized her for being thirty-three years old and having a fifteen year old son; but after six months in the department, the venomous middle age women discovered that she was an ex-con and wanted to know why on Earth she was working in the accounting department.

Most of the women and a few of the men wondered if they were safe with an ex-con in their department. "What if this crazy bitch started to shoot up the place?" A hefty Hispanic woman asked a thin pale Cuban woman who had a mole above her right nostril and on the left side of her forehead, during a morning break. The fear became rampant in the accounting department, as Abigail quietly worked in her cubicle entering product codes month after month into Excel spreadsheets and distributed them to various executives throughout the company. Yes Abigail heard the complaints as she walked through the maze of cubicles every morning once they discovered her "true" identity. The paranoia increased and the manager, Patrick, had to do something about the situation since productivity was decreasing. So one day, when Abigail was on her morning break, he gathered the employees into his glass office and listened to the numerous complaints. He heard concerns about their safety and "voiced" their concerns that she "might" steal items out of their purse or drawers and so on and so on. Patrick felt "overpowered" by his staff. He eventually gained the courage to confront his boss, Jess. So when Patrick walked to Jess' office, he imagined that Jess would instantly comply with his concerns and have Abigail instantly moved back to the warehouse with the other "derelicts." However Patrick was shocked when Jess said "She deserves a chance like everyone else in this place. And if there's a problem we can go upstairs and talk to my boss." Patrick instantly "backed off" since Jess' boss was Ray Tucker, a large muscle-bound former wrestler who spoke in a thick Texas accent and who pulled at his beefy mustache when he was angry. And Jess knew everyone in the company feared Ray except for the President, Wes Jackhorn. Now Patrick realized that his subordinates were "stuck" with an ex-con and he told his staff that Abigail was "here to stay."

Employees grumbled in their cubicles after they heard the news. They knew that Abigail was intelligent and followed orders quickly. However they didn't care how helpful this new "ex-con bitch" was in the department. They considered her an "outcast." However the employees were secretly displeased and jealous that Jess protected Abigail. "Yeah, she's cute and smart but what is so great about her?" said a hefty accounts payable clerk to a balding middle age male staff accountant, during their lunch break. Yet Abigail ignored the "cattiness" and the negative comments since she had to focus on raising Marcus who was now a teenager.

At fifteen years old, Marcus was nearly six feet tall and he was taller and stronger than most of the other students in public high school and the anger began to "emerge" inside of him and he quickly attracted the wrong crowd and one day when Marcus walked across the court yard, in high school, he met three teenage thugs who were the most feared students on campus.

"Hey, homie," Franklin De La Rosa said. Marcus stopped and faced the leader of the clique. Franklin was a short Mexican-Italian "scrapper." He was sixteen in the tenth grade and already had a full grown goatee. He had the most fights after school than any other student and he was "motherfuckin' proud of it." He picked on smaller kids and taller kids and bigger kids and they were all too afraid to tell school officials that they were on his "shit list" so they endured their beating with displeasure after school. Yet the few students who stood up to Franklin were usually flattened with a quick uppercut.

And now Marcus focused his attention on Franklin and asked "What's up?"

"You in my first period math class, right?" Franklin asked. His chin was raised up from years of being a total bad ass.

"Yeah, that's me," Marcus said.

"You wanna smoke, homie?" Franklin asked and pulled out a pack of cigarettes.

Marcus instantly looked at them and then peered at Franklin. He should have said "Fuck, no! I'm not into that shit" and walked away or he should have said "No, I'm cool homie." Yet Marcus was like any other teenager and he wanted "real" friends and responded "Yeah, sure."

Franklin gave Marcus a cigarette and lit it for him and said "I'm Franklin. These are my homies, Rock and Skinny." Marcus "bumped" knuckles with two thin Mexican-American teenagers with shaved heads and Franklin said "If you ever need anything or if someone's giving you shit just let us know and we'll take care of it." Marcus nodded his head and they walked behind an empty tennis court with their lit cigarettes and smoked. And before he knew it, Marcus was in "Franklin's clique."

Marcus continued to smoke cigarettes over the following weeks with his "homies" and then one warm afternoon Franklin brought out some "red hair" marijuana, at his aunt's shitty apartment, in West L.A., where he slept on the couch; and now he smoked the "red hair" with Marcus and Rock and Skinny and they began drinking beers and they listened to a rap song by a rapper named Biggie; and Franklin asked Marcus if he thought his father, Danny, was shot and killed because he was Mexican, and Marcus thought about the situation and he started to believe that his father was murdered because he had brown skin. Although Marcus didn't mention to his stoned and drunk "homies" that his father was probably "high" on something and that he was speeding in his car and then pointed a 9mm at a sheriff, on the side of a dusty road in the desert; but none of that "shit" mattered to young Marcus, and so he believed that his father was shot and killed because he was Mexican. "Shit, his gun didn't even have any bullets," Marcus said to his homies. "They were on the motherfuckin' car seat." Marcus found out about the bullets on the passenger seat from Abigail who found out from Ruth who found out from the police report in which the attorney obtained back in "motherfuckin'" 2013; and now the anger grew inside of Marcus Stevens and he was pissed off that he never got to see his father. He began to ditch school and listen to gangsta' rap and he listened to songs that included the lyrics "smokin' niggas" and "fuckin' bitches." He loved the music and he heard the words "nigga', nigga', nigga', nigga', nigga'," in his head everyday and his grades "lowered" and Abigail pleaded with Marcus to start studying, again. She reminded him that he was something "special" but he didn't care anymore.

Marcus was no longer shy and innocent. He was angry and pissed off and he continued to hang out with Franklin, Rock and Skinny; but Abigail didn't give up on her son. She repeatedly pleaded with him to study and so Marcus decided to "appease" his mother and he finally went into the school library one day during lunch time and his hair was now in braids and his life was all about smoking marijuana and drinking alcohol and listening to gangsta' rap and he continued to hear the words "nigga', nigga', nigga', nigga', nigga'" in his head over and over. And now in the school library, he was reading a book by an author whose last name was Salinger and Marcus tried to understand what he read so far and he looked up from this book and discovered the most "sought" after girl in high school. Her name was Blue Sky Garcia and she was Mexican-American. She was nearly five feet eight inches tall and she wore tight jeans and had a "large chest" which proportionally filled any small or large shirt. She was in tenth grade and every boy in school loved her and fantasized about her and every girl admired her "well-built" frame. Yet Blue Sky wasn't a typical fifteen year old teenager. She could have hung around the cheerleaders and the "loose" bitches on a Friday night and dated jocks and drank and smoked "red hair" and lost her virginity to "some" guy on the football or baseball team.

Blue Sky was different. She never missed a school day

and she attended church "almost" every Sunday and she wrote poetry and read many poems by Dickinson and Whitman and Frost. And Blue Sky lived with her parents and her younger sister, Lolita, in a two bedroom apartment. She wasn't bitter or angry about the living situation. She loved life and she was very confident; and now she noticed Marcus in the library reading a book by an author whose last name was Salinger; and her and Marcus made eye contact and she smiled and approached one of the most feared students in high school. They introduced themselves and began talking and Marcus finally asked "What do you do for fun?"

"I write poetry."

"Poetry? Isn't that for sissys?"

"Do you know what poetry is?" Blue Sky asked and Marcus was silent. "Let me guess, you're just another cute guy who sags his pants and doesn't have a brain."

"Shit, I've gotta brain," Marcus sat up in his chair. He had to show that he was tough.

"Well then tell me something," Blue Sky said.

"Tell you what?" Marcus asked, slightly irritated.

"Tell me what poetry is?" Blue Sky asked.

Marcus thought about that question and tried to remember what he learned from poems that he had to read for a few "shity ass" English classes and he finally said "Okay, poetry is about sunsets, it's about life. It's about beauty and romance."

"Great, that's a start," she said.

"Now can I show you what I'm all about?" Marcus asked.

"I'm not into drinking and I don't watch porn. So you better think of something else to show me."

Marcus smiled. He liked her personality. "Nah, that's not what I'm talking about."

And a few hours later, after school, Blue Sky walked with Marcus to his mom's apartment and she didn't expect a challenging intellectual conversation with Marcus, but she was attracted to him and maybe because he was one of the most feared guys in high school and he hung around with other feared guys in high school; and then Marcus and Blue Sky entered his mother's apartment and she stopped in front of his bedroom door and said "If you try anything I'll kick you in the nuts and call the police."

Marcus smiled and he liked that he couldn't fuck with this "bitch." Blue Sky was not intimidated or weak but neither was Marcus. They entered his bedroom and he put on a CD and listened to a rapper named Dre; and Marcus brought out his glass bong and "packed" the bowl with "red hair" and instructed her how to smoke from the glass bong and to put her finger on the carb hole and that she needed to "suck in" the smoke into her lungs; and he lit the bowl for her and she put her finger on the carb hole and sucked in the "red hair" and she instantly coughed out the smoke; and Marcus watched the "hottest chick" in high school, in his bedroom, getting stoned. And the rumors spread throughout the crowded hallways in high school that Marcus and Blue Sky were "fooling around," but Blue Sky didn't care about rumors since she secretly loved the attention.

And over time Blue Sky became more attracted to Marcus and she discovered that Marcus was intelligent and that he could name most of the American Presidents and list which ones were shot and which ones served in wars and which ones served two terms in office and so on and so on. Blue Sky and Marcus hung around together at lunch and they spoke at night on the phone and sometimes during the phone conversations, Blue Sky painted her toenails and Marcus would lay on his bed, in his boxers, and look at the cracked ceiling. She realized that under his angry persona, Marcus was a "nice guy." Ironically his anger intrigued her as she didn't "really" want someone too nice. On a few occasions, her parents introduced her to "nice" Latin guys who wore collar shirts and were in math clubs and brought her flowers. She was nearly sixteen years old and she wanted a "challenge" and someone that she didn't always understand and she became "smitten" over her new boyfriend and she began to include Marcus in her poetry.

> *"Have I found the love of my night?*
> *Does he therefore trick me for his sheepish grin?"*
> *And would he therefore steal my world without me knowing it?*
> *I will only know in the light of the world.*
> *And within this circle of light, does he really want me?"*

As time moved forward, Blue Sky wondered if she would ever marry Marcus one day. She imagined herself, at eighteen, walking down the aisle, in her wedding gown, about to marry Marcus who would still have his hair in braids and he would be wearing a three piece wool suit that he bought from Sears; and she would fantasize about a "great life" with Marcus; and then she remembered that her parents used to tell her that "dreaming was a bad thing since dreams don't 'normally' come true" but she continued to "day dream" about her boyfriend.

Yet as Blue Sky was in love with Marcus, Abigail was becoming troubled by Marcus, as he was now sixteen years old and continued to "hang out" with the wrong crowd. Abigail felt the stress of trying to keep Marcus focused on his homework while trying to pay her bills and she even needed financial assistance from her mother every month, but Abigail also needed a "break" from being a single mother and working with co-workers who despised her for being an ex-con. She knew she was a cog in a wheel of a "shitty ass" company that manufactured rims for various automotive companies while she was trying to keep her life together. However Marcus continued to defy his mother and he became more rebellious and continued to "ditch" school and he would come into his mother's apartment smelling like cigarettes and alcohol and marijuana. Abigail constantly pleaded with Marcus to improve his grades and her dream of Marcus becoming a "honors" student began to slowly dissipate and Marcus didn't care about how smart he was "'cause that shit was in the past" and the year was 2029.

Abigail also had to try to forget about Marcus' bullshit. It was her last day on probation. She stayed "clean and sober" for five years and she was able to "keep" her job. She avoided breaking the law and now she was eager to love someone. She secretly wished that Danny was still around and she would love him like she did when she was seventeen; and now Abigail rode the elevator to see her parole officer and Abigail thought about how Danny was a troubled piece of shit and that is why she was in the situation that she is in now and because of him she snorted coke and drank beer and listened to Motorhead's 1980 album, Ace of Spades, over and over; and then she remembered Danny "taking" her virginity and exposing her to robbery and murder and she instantly became sickened by the past, as the elevator doors opened and she momentarily forced herself to "forget" about the past when she met her parole officer one last time. And for some strange reason, she couldn't remember if her parole officer's name was Steve or John; and for what seemed like a long time, Steve or John warned her about continuing to stay "clean and sober." And she finally shook Steve or John's hand and he congratulated her and she was "officially" off parole and she left the red brick building and then she resumed thinking of the past again and then she blamed herself for staying with Danny and she had the chance to leave his apartment, in 2012, when her mother arrived at his door, frantic and pale. She pleaded with Abigail to come back home.

But she didn't.

She stayed.

And time moved forward and Abigail stood at the

vending machine one afternoon, at Supreme Industries, in the break room, when she noticed Jess Parker who asked "How are you doing today?"

"Fine, I guess," Abigail said.

Jess felt something wasn't right with her and asked her something that she thought would excite her. "I was wondering if you were interested in another promotion within the department? Well, it's kind of a promotion."

"Really? What is it?" Abigail asked. She smiled and instantly felt better.

"It's a temporary supervisor position. Patrick is leaving and we need someone to be an assistant while a new manager comes in and gets up to speed."

Abigail was baffled and said "I, I didn't know he was even leaving." She was surprised but excited, since she didn't like Patrick because she believed that he was a wimp and couldn't "control" his staff and she finally asked "Are you sure about this?"

"I wouldn't have asked if I didn't think you could do it," Jess said, smiling.

"What about my background?"

"What about it?" Jess asked. "Look, don't worry. I can make most anything work in this place?" He was cocky and Abigail was attracted to that; but she also felt there was something else on his mind.

"Okay, well let me think about it," Abigail said. She was a nervous teenager again, but life was so different since she was seventeen. She was an ex-con but she had to be strong. Her mind drifted into the distance for a moment.

"Oh, I was also wondering if you were interested in going out for a drink," Jess said.

Abigail was momentarily stunned that the Manager of Operations asked her out for a "drink." She believed for some strange reason that she had "lost her looks" at thirty-four years old since nobody "formally" asked her out. She only dated one person in her life, which led to a murder, an unplanned pregnancy and a ten year prison sentence; but that was in the past and she said "Sure, if it's legal."

They both laughed and then she wondered if this so-called date had something to do with the "temporary" supervisor position in accounting.

Abigail left work an hour later and drove home to get ready for her date; and when she arrived to her two bedroom apartment, in West L.A., she instantly smelled marijuana as she entered the apartment and the smell came from her son's bedroom and she heard the "thump" of the base pounding against the closed bedroom door. Abigail stammered across thick shadows and yanked opened the bedroom door and discovered Marcus on the bed packing "red hair" into a glass bong while Franklin, Rock and Skinny were on the floor playing video games and gangsta' rap music blasted from the stereo and they instantly turned and glared at Abigail as if she was disturbing them. She kicked his friends out of the apartment and turned off the music and yelled at Marcus, but he didn't care because he was "tough" and "high" and he was nearly seventeen years old and a "bully" at high school. He intimidated students and took their money and other "shit" that he wanted and his anger never frightened Abigail, but she realized one morning that Marcus was becoming more like her than his father; and now as she stood over Marcus who sat on the bed, he finally put the glass bong gown and she said "I told you a million times Marcus, that I don't want anyone over here on a weekday. You hear me? And why are you smoking pot in here!"

Marcus shrugged off her yelling and bitching since he shrugged everything else off. He was tough and part Mexican-American like his father and he said "I thought you said it was 'okay' to smoke in here."

"Are you kidding me, Marcus! I thought you told me that you were smart," Abigail said.

"Yeah, I'm smart. Of course I'm smart."

"Then why are you hanging around those clowns? They're just going to get you in trouble. Is that what you want?"

"They're my homies. What's wrong with that?"

"Yeah, and what are your homies names?"

"Franklin, Rock, and Skinny," Marcus said proudly. He raised his chin feeling tough in front of his mother.

"What kind of names are Rock and Skinny?"

"It's their nicknames," Marcus said.

"Fine, Rock and Skinny. What are their God-given names?"

"Seth and Efron."

"Listen," Abigail said, "I care about you, Marcus. Their parents may not care about them, but I care about you."

"They don't have parents," Marcus said, as he continued to keep his chin raised up; and in that moment, Abigail realized that the sweet ten year old boy she once saw when she got out of prison was gone; and now her son was filled with anger.

"Stand up, Marcus," Abigail said.

Her son stood up and towered over his mother and she grabbed his chin and said "Please don't let me down, Marcus. You're all I have. And get a belt for your pants."
And in that very moment, she felt his anger when she stared in his eyes but she wasn't afraid of her son and she said "Grandma will be over in a few minutes." She turned to leave his messy room that smelled like marijuana smoke. "And please open a window."

"I don't want her here," Marcus said.

"Then please let her know that," Abigail said and she left the bedroom and closed the door behind her; and then she heard the rap music again along with the bass that pounded against the bedroom door. She couldn't handle his "bullshit" right now. She had to prepare for her first post-prison date and she picked out clothes and showered and dried her body with a dirty blue towel and she put on tight jeans, a clean "tight" shirt and she added a bit of "makeup" on her face in the bathroom and she now heard Marcus slamming things in his room. She blocked the "shit out" and focused on her image and believed that she was still attractive and believed that her life would improve. Yeah she was an ex-con with a "rotten son," but her life had to have some meaning somewhere and in someway.

Sometimes Abigail believed that the bullshit she endured "day in" and "day out" was all part of a dream and she would eventually wake up in her "old" bed and join her father at the breakfast table and she would be wearing her school uniform and her father would lower his newspaper to reveal his smile that she greatly missed and she would smell the scent of his cologne, and she absolutely missed every fuckin' thing about him; and now in her bedroom of her apartment, Abigail finished preparing for her date and she felt a chill, and then she felt her father's presence in the room; and in the corner of the bedroom, Francis stood within heavy shadows and watched his daughter for a moment and he smiled and he said "I'm proud of you, Abby, just hang in there" but of course Abigail didn't hear him but she rubbed her hands together and Francis finally said "I'm here, Abby. Don't ever forget it" and then he disappeared from the corner of the bedroom and the chill dissipated. Abigail smiled for a moment and then the rap music from her son's bedroom began to piss her off again, and she thought that Marcus was a great looking kid but was becoming increasingly difficult. She would receive weekly calls from his high school that he missed "fifth" and "sixth" periods. She talked to Marcus numerous times about leaving school early but he didn't care what his mother had to say.

Marcus despised his mother along with his teachers and everything else just like Abigail did when she was seventeen years old. Now she was thirty-four years old, and she was amazed how life repeated itself in various ways. Abigail snapped from her trance in her sunlit bedroom as she stared at her image in the mirror and heard the front door open and slam shut which was followed by her mother complaining about something. Abigail entered the living room.

"My God, Abby, you're looking thinner. What have you been doing? And why don't you open some windows in here. It's stifling. Are you smoking cigarettes? You know how bad those are for you?"

Abigail inhaled deeply as exhaustion momentarily took over and she said "No, mom, I'm not smoking and I'm not losing any weight."

"Well, it sure looks like it," Ruth said as she put her purse down. She followed her daughter into the bedroom. Abigail tried to calm down since she would be meeting Jess in less than two hours. Ruth and Abigail spoke for a few minutes and then Ruth fixed her hair in the mirror and then looked at her daughter and then she looked at the clothes that she was wearing and asked "Are you sure you want to do this, Abby?"

"Mom, please don't start. It's a date, not a marriage."

"Well, God, I hope not. And if you decide to fool around please make sure he wears a condom this time."

"You didn't just say that, did you?"

"Are you sure you didn't lose weight. I swear you look thinner. Are you on this new diet? All the women seem to be going on this. I forgot the name of it."

"I'm fine," Abigail said.

"Fine," Ruth said as she started playing with her hair in the mirror again.

"And if you want to really know how I'm doing, why don't you look around," Abigail said.

"You know, your father used to say that things get worse before they get better," Ruth said. She adjusted her daughter's shirt. "Are you sure you don't have anything nicer than this?" Ruth leaned back and examined her daughter's attire. She thought Abigail looked a little "cheap" with the thick black eyeliner and "heavy" mascara. Ruth knew she couldn't tell Abigail what she really thought so she said "I'm sorry, you look great."

Abigail peered suspiciously at her mother and asked "Okay, what's wrong? You're looking at me funny."

"Nothing," Ruth said.

Abigail grabbed her purse and told her mother that Marcus wasn't allowed to watch TV or play video games, and he wasn't allowed to use his cell phone until he finished his homework. Yet Ruth and Abigail both knew that Marcus rarely paid attention in school and rarely finished his homework.

A few minutes later, Ruth kissed Abigail on the cheek and said "good luck" and Abigail drove to Reseda and sat in a "shit hole" bar and waited for Jess. The place was tiny and there was a juke box against the back wall that played classic rock songs. The music was muffled and the speakers rattled during a "heavy" guitar riff. Abigail looked around the place and she wished that Jess had picked a nicer establishment with clean tables and candle light, but Jess wanted to meet here. Abigail could have chosen a place on the west side, but she wanted to get far away from her apartment; and now she waited and he finally arrived wearing a white collar shirt and dark colored jeans that covered a portion of his cowboy boots. She smelled his cologne as they hugged. They ordered beers as this would be her "first" drink in over fifteen years. They said "cheers" and drank their beers and the conversation was awkward as they asked the standard bullshit questions. "Where did you grow up?" followed by "Do you have any brothers or sisters?" and so on and so on.

Abigail thought this so-called date was a mistake until Jess asked "Are you still on probation?"

"Why?" Abigail said. She was surprised by the question. She wondered what was going on at this moment.

"Can you keep a secret?" Jess asked.

She instantly recognized his concerned tone. She wondered if this "meeting" was a trap. "Maybe he's a cop," she thought and then she remembered what her mother had told her about some supervisors and managers "who want to intimidate employees if they can." Abigail finally responded cautiously and said "Depends what you're talking about."

"Is that a 'yes,' that I can trust you?" Jess asked.

"It's a maybe," Abigail said firmly.

"Okay, fine," Jess said. "Do you party?"

Abigail remembered hearing the words "Do you party?" as she got in her car in front of the bar a few minutes later and followed Jess in his Ford truck. Her heart raced within her thin chest. Why was she following the Manager of Operations to his one-story house, in Reseda? There were only a few more miles before she arrived to his place and she should have called him on his cell phone and said "I don't think this is a good idea."

But she didn't.

She should have called him and said "This doesn't feel comfortable, buddy."

But she didn't.

Or she should have told him in the bar that she was "too tired" after he invited her over to his house to "party."

Yet she didn't.

Abigail now sat on Jess' red couch, in his living room, listening to a Rolling Stones' song while snorting cocaine on a glass table. She leaned back on the red couch. She couldn't believe that she was "high" again and she forgot how great it was to be "high." "Nothing feels better in this shitty ass world than to snort some 'good shit'," she thought after she snorted her second line.

Abigail remembered drinking beer on the red couch with Jess and she remembered seeing Jess snorting lines of coke on the glass table. He joked. She laughed. And they began kissing and then they had sex on the red couch near the red brick fire place. He wore a condom and she was in heaven for now and they were both "coked up" and drunk and she loved this moment with the Manager of Operations; and she came and she wanted him to come inside of her, in the condom; and where were the condoms when she had sex with Danny?

She couldn't think of the past now, could she?

Jess finally came inside of her and he laid his sweaty body on her within the dim circle of yellow lamp light. The night was over; and Abigail awoke half-naked on the white shaggy carpet. She looked at her large breasts and noticed her bra was shoved halfway underneath the red couch and she noticed Jess sleeping on the red couch. His snoring punctuated the calm morning silence; and then her cell phone rang. She gathered her bra and her shirt as she answered her cell phone. Her mother's raging voice blared from the cell phone and Abigail was trying to understand what her mother was saying as Abigail was "coming out" of a hazy night of drug use and drinking and sex.

Now she was once again, a mother, a daughter, and an employee, in the accounting department, at Supreme Industries, in the valley; and yes she was enduring a quick conversation with her mother on the cell phone and she finally said to her mom "I was going to call you. We were catching up on things. I'm, I'm fine. I'm sorry I didn't call. Stop screaming at me, mom. I hear you! Okay, fine, I told you that I was going to call. I'm fine. I'll be home shortly. Can you bring Marcus to school?" and the call was over before she knew it, and she put on her clothes and grabbed her purse and stumbled to her car that was parked on the street and the air was already hot and she got into her car and strapped on the seat belt; and the bright valley sunlight glowed on the dirty windshield which made her feel dizzier. She was in no "legal" condition to drive since she snorted coke and drank part of a six pack last night, but she had to get home to West L.A. She started the car and was instantly startled by Jess banging on the driver's side window. He was shirtless and smiling and he was still drunk and high and the smile exemplified his happiness that he got laid, and she rolled down her window and she smelled the alcohol on his breath and he said "Don't forget you have work in a few hours, little lady."

"Can I get a doctor's note?" Abigail smiled.

"How was last night?"

"How about you get a shirt on?" Abigail said. "And I don't kiss and tell."

They kissed and she drove away and drove south on the 405 Freeway to West L.A., and her hangover slowly dissipated as she drove into the cool air that blew into her car as she moved further toward the beach, but now she had to deal with her mother's wrath. Abigail finally parked her car in the back of the apartment complex; and when Abigail entered her shitty two bedroom apartment, Ruth appeared from the small kitchen. A new anger evolved in Ruth. She raised her grandson for ten years while her daughter was in prison; and now she had to take care of two irresponsible children. "That is not going to happen," Ruth thought as Abigail stumbled through the front door.

"This is how you start you life over, by leaving your son with me all night while you do God knows what!"

"Are you kidding me, mom?" Abigail said angrily. "And you're telling me how to run my life! Let's start with your mistakes."

"When you start paying for a babysitter and no longer have to rely on me for financial assistance then we can talk about my past mistakes."

"So it's all about the money? Is that it?" Abigail screamed.

"Lower your voice, Abby. You have no right to talk to me like that! Do you hear me? You need to clean up your life!"

"I told you I was out with a friend," Abigail said. She was exhausted and now she was lying to her mother.

"I know you were getting high, again. I see it in your eyes!"

"You know everything, don't you? You're such a great mother. I still smell the whisky on your breath sometimes. Or is it Scotch?" Abigail asked. "That's what you call being a good parent? Kicking me out of the house at seventeen?"

Ruth tried to calm down. She realized "years ago" that she was not the "perfect" parent. She was a "functional" alcoholic who still dealt with the memories of her husband's murder and she had a daughter who spent over a decade in prison for being an accomplice to murder and robbery. Ruth achieved accomplishments in the literary world and she managed to earn over three million dollars in book sales and a large advance for her next book and a "nice" payday from a production company, which "officially" purchased *The After Life*. Yet her success didn't matter at this moment since her daughter and grandson's life was currently derailing. Ruth inhaled deeply and said "You need help, Abby, or you're going to end up in prison again!"

"You know everything, don't you? You know when to take me out of private school and force me into a public school and when to tell me to get a shitty night job."

"I did what I thought was right, dammit! Now you can really see how easy it is to raise a child."

"You know dad didn't want me to work. I heard the arguments, but you had to always get your way. And look what happened. You're a great example of what I should become!"

"Fine, fuck it! Blame me for everything, Abby!" Ruth snapped. She realized that Abigail was still a "lost" seventeen year old girl. Yes Abigail had gained wisdom but that didn't "really" change her life at all. And not only was Abigail "lost" but so was her son. Ruth finally grabbed her purse and left the apartment and entered her 2028 Mercedes that was parked at the far end of the driveway. She cried as she sat in the plush leather seat. Ruth knew her daughter was "possibly" headed back to prison. She felt it. And Ruth didn't know if she could "handle" visiting Abigail in prison for another five to ten years with her grandson, while she had to raise his "crazy ass."

Ruth started the car and drove to her house; and during the drive is when she thought about how selfish she was when Abigail was young and how she "always" needed everything her way; and then she remembered what her mother, Louise, had told her outside under a green patio umbrella, at a café, in Brentwood, in 1994. "Bringing a child into this world isn't an easy task, nor will it ever be. This child doesn't go away at eighteen or at twenty-two or thirty-two. They're with you until the very end." But Ruth didn't care what her mother had to say because Ruth knew everything back then. Now over thirty years later, Ruth still felt clueless about life.

Meanwhile in her apartment, Abigail prepared for work and she stripped off her "dirty" clothes in her bedroom and she should have felt like a "slut" for having sex with the Manager of Operations and she should have felt disgraced and angry for snorting cocaine and getting drunk and she should have felt guilty for being a terrible "role model" to her son, but she didn't care. She peered at her naked body in the mirror, above the dresser and realized that she really didn't care about much anymore. Abigail was mentally exhausted from constantly judging herself and she was almost thirty-five years old and had been out of prison for over six years.

She wanted a career.

Maybe, just maybe, she might still become a "temporary" supervisor as Jess initially offered her and then the company would see her as a competent team leader and promote her as a "permanent" supervisor. Or did Jess "bait" Abigail with a new opportunity just to get her in the sack? Could she "really" trust him? One guy had ruined a part of her life. She had to move forward. She could still obtain her GED. And then she can enroll into a community college and study business management at night. She suddenly felt peace in the bedroom. She didn't know that her father stood in the corner and it was only when she rubbed her arms that she finally realized that he was there; and then after a few moments in the room, Abigail entered the bathroom and showered. The warm water brought her temporary relief from the drug induced night and she grabbed the soap and washed the memories of last night away and she imagined washing away her years of drug use and the murder and robbery of Lester Jackson and the unplanned pregnancy.

And she imagined her past sins were momentarily gone.

She was clean of dirt and filth in her mind and she quickly imagined what it would feel like if her father wasn't murdered and her mother didn't pull her from Catholic School and didn't kick her out of the house and if she never met Danny Ruiz. She imagined herself graduating from St. Susan with "honors" and wearing a blue gown; and in the fall she would begin classes at UCLA and she would become a pre-med student and she would meet a wealthy stockbroker named Dean Willis, at a party; and she would become a surgeon like her father; and Dean and her would eventually purchase a five million dollar bedroom house, in the Palisades; and Abigail would give "birth" to two sandy blond hair boys named Blake and Sean; and during the summer, the family would travel to Europe and sail off the coast of Spain, in a private yacht. Everything would be great and she would love Dean, Blake and Sean and they would love her.

Abigail snapped from the dream and she realized that she was still in the moldy shower that had cracked tile and she still lived in a shitty two bedroom apartment. Abigail was still an ex-con living with her "rotten son" and the anger grew and life was the same as it was last week and last year and so on and so on. And as Abigail continued to wash her body, she discovered a "lump" in her right breast. She gently poked at it and turned off the water and dried herself in front of the large bathroom mirror that was covered with mist and she continued to push at the lump again, as she raised her arm; but the lump didn't disappear since she discovered it in the shower, a few moments ago.

She was late for work but she didn't care. She should have called and told her boss, but she didn't. Nothing mattered to Abigail anymore. She felt like her spirit began to die inside of her.

Slowly.

Abigail felt the chill in the bathroom as she finished dressing for work and she had sensed her father was in the small hot bathroom. And he was just a few inches from her and she smiled and she remembered when she was seventeen, on the brown leather couch, at night, in the living room of the "old" house and she asked her father within the glow of the TV "Are you always going to be around?" and then she mentioned that she was "reading about all this life and death stuff and nothing seems to make sense," and Francis said "Unfortunately, life doesn't always make sense, but like I told you before, I'm always going to be around for you and mom." And the chill dissipated in the hot bathroom and she finished getting dressed and she finally opened the bathroom door and she was suddenly ready for work, or so she thought.

CHAPTER 24

After a night of sex and snorting cocaine and drinking beer, Abigail waited for Jess to "stroll" by her cubicle, in the accounting department, at Supreme Industries; and as she waited, Abigail thought of his smile and his messy hair in the morning when he banged on her driver's side window. She expected him to kiss her on the cheek, in the hallway, when nobody was looking. And why would she expect that? She fucked Jess Parker, the Manager of Operations. She enjoyed being desired by a successful handsome man. Yet the morning evolved into the afternoon. She left the department wondering if she would see his Ford flatbed truck, in the parking lot, but she didn't see him or his truck and for the next few days she waited patiently for Jess with a smile on her face, but he never came around nor did he call; and during the "waiting period" she believed Jess would say "Hello, my love" and bring her roses or a card, which would make the "heavyset" women jealous in the department and Abigail thought that she would have sex with Jess in her car or in the cab of his Ford flatbed truck; but none of this happened.

A few days after the sex and the drugs, Abigail began to wonder why Jess never came by her desk and why he never called. They "made" love and she "wanted" to be loved by Jess. After a painstaking week, she decided to speak to Jess' assistant,

Sarah, but her "usual" response was "he's out" as she read her Cosmopolitan magazine. Yet when Sarah left her desk to go to the bathroom, Abigail peeked inside Jess' office and Jess was not in there and she thought of calling him but she couldn't leave a "trail" that would lead back to her. And nobody in the company could know what happened between her and Jess that night, in his house, on his red couch.

A few weeks later, Abigail finally noticed Jess in the hallway. It was on a Thursday morning and he was walking and talking to an executive who was wearing a suit. Jess looked at her and quickly looked away and continued to walk with the executive; and that is when Abigail realized she was literally "fucked." She let this piece of shit have sex with her. In her mind, she was a corporate slut and the anger surged inside of her and she didn't give up. The next week she tried again to talk to Jess but he was on the phone in his office and "good ol'" Sarah told her that he was "super" busy. Yeah Sarah was probably getting suspicious of Abigail's persistence to speak to Jess. Ironically Abigail didn't realize that Sarah was used to women "strolling" by and "inquiring" about Jess' whereabouts; and Abigail walked back to her cubicle and she felt like trash on the bathroom floor. Yet while she was working in her cubicle, she knew that she was "not" going to give up that easy. No. She had survived the harshest nights in prison for over ten years without her family. "Fuck him," she thought. She would contact him somehow, someway; so one night when Abigail was in bed and a circle of yellow lamp light highlighted a portion of her face, she finally picked up her cell phone and dialed his cell phone number. "Fuck him," she thought again while his cell phone rang and a woman suddenly answered and said "Hello" and Abigail said "Um, I was looking for Jess Parker." She didn't expect a woman to answer his cell phone; and there was momentary silence and then the woman asked "Who is this?' and the woman's voice was cold and harsh and Abigail responded harshly and said "Who the hell is this?"

and Abigail heard "This is his wife! Who the hell is this? How did you get this number?" Abigail snapped at her and said "How the fuck do you think I got it!"

And the conversation was over.

The crazy ass bitch on the other line hung up and Abigail hung up her cell phone and she sat motionless within the threshold of yellow lamp light.

It was true that another guy had taken advantage of her, but she was not going to allow this "mistake" to fuck up the second part of her life.

She had to be smart this time.

The next day, Abigail could barely concentrate on her "shitty ass" paperwork, in her cubicle; nor could she concentrate when vendors told her over the phone why they were delinquent with their payments and so on and so on.

She didn't care what they had to say nor did she care about anything. She wanted blood. She cautiously stood up in her cubicle around eleven a.m. and slowly walked by Sarah, the petite "white bitch" and she knocked hard on Jess' office door and she expected Jess to swing open the door and scream "What the fuck do you want?" She expected intimidation. And why not? She had been "used" and "discarded" and so what did anything else matter now? She opened the door and she noticed Jess sitting calmly behind his desk. He was leaning back in his chair possibly hoping that the person on the other side of the door would disappear. But it didn't happen and Abigail instantly noticed Jess appeared thinner and "stressed" out and Jess finally said "We need to talk," and that is when Sarah, the petite "white bitch" stood behind Abigail in the doorway. Jess assured his assistant that everything was "okay."

Ten minutes later, Abigail and Jess walked across the company parking lot filled with weeds and cheap vehicles. They entered her car and Jess sat in the passenger seat. She noticed a "weakness" in his eyes, as if he was "pussy-whipped." He could barely look at Abigail. The cockiness was gone and he was nearly a living corpse. Yet a month ago, Jess Parker could "eat nails" for breakfast, lunch and dinner.

"I'm married," Jess softly said.

She wondered at that moment if she should be more sensitive toward his situation. "Fuck him," she thought. "This guy doesn't care about anyone but himself, so fuck him again." She was pissed and tired of life "pissing" on her; and so her anger instantly emerged and she said "How the fuck could you pull this shit on me!"

"I really like you, Abigail. I wanted to speak to you when I saw you in the hallway a few weeks ago, but I couldn't. I am separated and was planning on getting a divorce, but – "

"Planning? You were planning to get a divorce?" Abigail said. The "old" fire of hatred burned inside of her.

"Will you please listen?" Jess asked.

"Why? It's probably bullshit anyway!" Abigail snapped.

"I have children and my wife wanted full custody if I wasn't going to 'work' things out."

"So that's it. You wanted to work things out? What about us? Did you have this brilliant idea of working things out before or after you fucked me!" Abigail waited for a response but she knew his words were all the same to her. It was all the same "bullshit" she had heard in her life since her father was murdered. She heard numerous lies from her mother, from Danny and from her teenage son; and now she heard the "lies" from this spineless corporate "piece of shit."

The lies continued and so did the endless trail of crap that was flung over her eyes day after day; and she kept wiping the crap away but one day she would see the truth. And then one day the sun would eventually shine on her life again; but now her life was a constant battle of struggle and rage in a two bedroom apartment while living with her "rotten" teenage son.

Now she took her anger and "flung" it back on Jess Parker

and said "If you grew a pair of balls you would be dangerous. How could you fuck me over like this? You didn't think I had any feelings because I was an ex-con? You get me high and have sex with me. What would your boss say? What would Human Resources think of what you did? What would your wife and kids think of this crap, if they even fuckin' exist?"

Yes Jess knew Abigail had justification to be angry. He "fucked" her and he "fucked her over." And it was true. Jess didn't care about her. What the fuck for? He had his own problems. He was quiet for a moment and he listened to Abigail "rant" and "rave," which sounded as if she read dialogue from an award winning screenplay.

Jess inhaled deeply and put his hand on the passenger door. He looked at her and said "You could tell anyone you want, Abigail. But how would it sound to the court that you were using drugs again? Would you get another job? Would you lose custody of your son?"

Abigail was trapped. Her anger dissipated. Jess had indeed pulled his "last escape" from his corporate parachute and left the car. She could barely breathe as she watched him walk across the parking lot that was filled with weeds and cheap vehicles. She was literally "fucked" and she knew it. What if a judge or anyone aside from her mother knew that she was "using" again?" Yes she was no longer on parole, so she didn't have to "piss" in a cup, but what if she went back to prison? She would probably lose custody of her "rotten" teenage son and she may never get a job, again.

She lost this battle. She had to be smarter next time. She wanted to cry but she was tired of crying and she felt hollow inside. She had to be tough. The struggle wasn't over for Abigail Stevens, the ex-con. Abigail stepped from her car and went back to her cubicle, in the accounting department, and then she realized that she was never "considered" for the "temporary supervisor position" since they had already "selected" a temp while the new supervisor was "getting up to speed" and Abigail realized "too late" that Jess' bullshit was all a ploy for getting her in the sack. "How could I not see that?" she thought as she sat at her desk and stared at the computer screen. How would she endure this difficult time?

Luckily nobody knew about this incident and then a few months later, Abigail learned that Jess had miraculously resigned from the company. Abigail's immediate reaction was to be excited but she thought it was "odd" that a "high-level" executive departed the company inconspicuously. Usually the standard procedure was for employees to circulate a "good luck" card throughout the company and write something positive and the "soon-to-be" former employee would be the first to receive his or her piece of the corporate cake, as numerous employees awaited their slab of cake.

However there had to be something that Abigail didn't know about Jess' situation. There had to be something that Jess never mentioned to her before. Yet she needed proof that Jess actually resigned and not just relocated to another part of the building or to another "plant" in another state. She walked to his office and noticed it was empty and even the cheap dusty furniture was gone.

The surprise wasn't over.

She discovered that Jess' secretary, Sarah, was also gone.

Everyone in the company was "tight-lipped" about the situation.

Yet a few months later after Jess and Sarah "disappeared" from the company, employees began to discuss Jess' situation and on a cool morning, in the break room, Abigail overhead from a "bitter" employee that Jess was actually dating Sarah and she became pregnant. They decided to both quit and move to another state and Abigail finally realized the night she called Jess' cell phone that it was not his wife that answered, it was Sarah.

Abigail never knew if Jess was ever married, since she never saw pictures of his kids or wife or noticed a wedding band on his finger. His life appeared to be a big "fat" lie, but Abigail had to put Jess behind her.

However a month before Abigail discovered that Jess resigned from the company, she became severely depressed and hit a "low" in her life. She didn't know what to do. She didn't speak to her mother about the situation.

Abigail believed that she would have to see Jess for the rest of her life, walking down the hall, having to be subjected to the "smug" look on his fuckin' face.

And during one of her "depressed" days, Abigail drove to her apartment after work. She should have cleaned the mess in the sink, or vacuumed, or she should have prepared dinner. However she noticed that Marcus was not home, yet; and his bedroom door was open and Abigail peered inside and noticed clothes strewn on the carpet and his bed was unmade. The wastebasket over flowed with wrappers and trash. She wanted him to clean this "shit hole" but she was on a secret mission after she discovered his desk drawer partially open. She opened the drawer further and discovered a "white powdery substance" inside a small zip-lock bag.

She held the bag in her hand and noticed it appeared like some "good shit" and she left his son's bedroom and entered her bedroom and locked the door and carefully emptied some of the cocaine from the zip-lock bag onto the dresser. She grabbed her credit card from her purse and "cut" a few lines of coke and she snorted the first line with a rolled up twenty dollar bill and she closed her eyes and "loved" the moment; and she should have known that only the devil "himself" could make something so destructive and she snorted another line and then another. She couldn't believe how strong this "shit" was as it stung inside her nostril. She was really "high" and feeling good. But she couldn't stop herself and she snorted the entire supply. She needed more. She officially snorted all her son's cocaine. "This fucker must have more," she thought, as she sat on the edge of the bed and peered into the mirror; and in that moment of looking at herself in the mirror, she realized that she had "officially" fucked up her life.

She knew it.

Abigail Stevens was an ex-con and a "cokehead" while trying to raise her "rotten" seventeen year old son.

And yes it was at that very moment that Abigail realized how far she had "fallen" after snorting all of her son's supply of cocaine. She should have done like any other caring mother and called the police after discovering her son's supply of cocaine or show it to her son and "threaten" to call the police and flush the "white powdery substance" down the toilet and urge him to get counseling.

Instead she was a "junkie" who didn't care if Marcus had a drug problem or if he was selling it.

She snorted her son's cocaine. She needed help. She could barely recognize herself in the mirror. And in that very moment, she decided that she would never "touch" another drug.

She tossed the empty zip-lock bag in the dumpster outside and time moved forward and Marcus was seventeen and he became much like his mother when she was seventeen years old and Marcus Stevens was now "God awful trouble." He was now six feet two inches tall and full of muscle from lifting weights in the high school gym and he glared at every stranger on the street or in the high school hallway.

Nobody fucked with Marcus Stevens as he would walk down the crowded high school hallway with Blue Sky; and the students created a path for them as if they were "royalty."

Girls respected Blue Sky and were eager to associate with her; and Blue Sky loved the "attention" but aside from the "perks" of being Marcus' girlfriend, it was becoming a "struggle" to be around Marcus. She never "touched" drugs nor did she "abuse" alcohol and her mother told her to "dump" Marcus, but Blue Sky didn't listen.

She was seventeen and she knew everything there was to

know about life.

"He's a good guy," Blue Sky said to her mother one day in the kitchen.

"You're crazy," her mother said in English. "You have no idea what you're talking about. Marcus is the devil," her mother finally said in Spanish.

Blue Sky didn't care what her parents or her sister, Lola, said to her about Marcus. She tried to see the "best" in Marcus and she continued to include him in her poetry.

"To the error in my way, I see blindly.
For why don't I see the danger in the road ahead?
But my heart bleeds for this stranger.
For this stranger in my dreams is the same stranger in my heart.
So how do I ever continue my life without him,
Since he is my armor and my knight?"

Yet one night, Blue Sky invited Marcus into the apartment when her parents were visiting relatives in Mexico and before they left they had forbidden her to bring that "devil" into the apartment. Blue Sky knew everything there was to know about life and so Marcus came in and he was "high" and he spoke incoherently. "I can't believe this shit is happenin, you know what I'm sayin'? And if you think I'm gonna take that shit you're wrong. I know what's up in this place? Ya' know what I'm saying'?" And so Blue Sky became angry and looked at the guy who she included in her poetry. Now this "stranger in my heart" stumbled around in her parent's apartment. She thought it all had to be a dream. Marcus was nothing but a "clone" of the thugs that he hung around with and Blue Sky was like any teenage girl in love. She was "clearly" naïve. She loved the guy that her parents hated; and she realized that she wasn't dreaming at this moment when she noticed a gun tucked into his waistband when he leaned over and she realized that her parents were "right" that Marcus was the "devil" and he was nothing but trouble.

She screamed at Marcus to leave and he hesitated for a moment, but she screamed louder and he left the cramped two bedroom apartment and she locked the door, and she walked into her bedroom and started to write in her notebook on the bottom bunk, but the paper became too wet from her tears and her sister asked her why she was screaming at Marcus; but Blue Sky didn't answer her. Yes her life was a mess, even though she led a "clean life" and she was still a virgin. She was about to attend community college, in the fall of 2030, and she was going to transfer to a university and study journalism.

Yet her "clean life" and her goals didn't stop her from doing "stupid shit" like dating a thug and inviting him over to her parent's place when they told her not to.

She was seventeen and had "horrible" judgment and sometimes life became about working around mistakes rather than trying to "fix" them.

However she needed to "fix" her life and a few weeks later after kicking Marcus out of her parent's apartment, she used her allowance money to pay the submission fees to enter her poems into numerous poetry contests; and Blue Sky believed that one day she would be recognized for her talent: yet the more she tried to obtain the recognition that she wanted, she received more rejections. Sometimes she believed that she was "doomed" to poverty like her parents. Although after months of rejections, she believed that if she never "gave up" on writing poetry, or loving Marcus, she would get the life she desired, and all her "dreams" would come true.

Yet the more she dreamed the worst things became in her life. Marcus' drug use got worse and he "officially" dropped out of high school and he started selling drugs with Franklin, Rock, and Skinny and he began to carry his 9mm every where; and then one day, he realized it was the same "type" of weapon that his father used to murder Lester Jackson many years ago; and it was only a matter of time that Marcus became involved with the police.

And it finally happened.

One night he was partying with Franklin who was driving his Uncle's Monte Carlo and Marcus was in the passenger seat and a few "hot bitches" were smoking a joint in the backseat and they were "stoned" and giggling and luckily Franklin and Marcus forgot their weapons at a "party house" in Venice; and Franklin noticed the siren lights in the rear view mirror and he carefully parked the Monte Carlo at the curb and everyone in the car was seventeen, except for one of the Mexican girls in the backseat, who may have been fourteen but nobody could remember. And the car wasn't "reported" stolen and they were all cited for illegal use of marijuana and the car was impounded and they were all brought to a "holding cell" and so on and so on.

Abigail received a call from the police around five a.m. and she picked Marcus up over an hour later from the police station and she walked with Marcus across the parking lot in the early sunlight and she said "I can't believe you, Marcus. How could you be so stupid?"

"Like you any better?"

Abigail stopped and faced her son for a moment and she wanted to slap the shit out of him and instead she said "I want to show you something."

"What?"

"Marcus, get your ass in the car and please don't let me tell you again," Abigail said. She glared at her son and she hated his braided hair and his "saggin'" pants and the tattoos on his hands and arms. She started to hate everything about him. Marcus felt his mother's anger and he got in the car and she drove him to the community park, in Mar Vista, and Marcus looked around in the parking lot.

He was puzzled and asked "What are we doin' here?"

Abigail remained silent and she got out of the car and Marcus followed her across the wet grass and across a shaft of early sunlight, but it was still cold outside and Abigail continued to walk into an unknown direction. She hadn't been at this park in more than eighteen years and she felt strange and horrible since this place was the source of her nightmares. She stopped and said "This is it."

"So what are we doin' here!" Marcus asked, demanding to know.

"This is where it happened," Abigail said and focused her attention on her son.

"What are you talkin' bout'?"

"You know what I'm talking about, Marcus. Don't play fuckin' stupid with me. This is where your father killed Lester Jackson."

"So what!"

"You know everything don't you, Marcus?" Abigail asked. "Just take a good look at this very spot!"

"It was an accident!" Marcus said.

"Is that what you think?" Abigail asked. "Is that what your friends are telling you? Can't you think for yourself?" Abigail asked. She was beyond angry. "I was there, Marcus. Danny murdered an innocent black man before he pulled a gun on a sheriff a few hours later. Do you really know who you are idolizing?"

"I don't care!"

"He wasn't a hero, Marcus. I wish he was. He couldn't deal with what he did and he couldn't deal with being a father," Abigail said and she realized what she was saying was harsh but she had to say it. "I know this all sucks but he was a bad person."

"I don't give a shit!" Marcus said. His so-called "toughness" was wearing off and he wasn't the strong intimidating person that other students saw in the high school hallway, nor was it the "side" that Franklin, Rock, and Skinny had ever seen. Abigail was exposing the truth about his father. Marcus knew that his father murdered a black man, but Marcus wanted to believe that his father was a "hero" who was murdered by a "trigger-happy" sheriff, on a highway, in the desert, because of the color of his skin.

But Marcus couldn't endure the truth.

"I could have gotten over twenty-five years in prison for something that I didn't do," Abigail said.

"Then why are you here?"

"Because the prosecution couldn't prove to the jury that I fired the gun, so I served ten years in prison. And that is where you're headed if you don't change. Do you understand what I'm saying?"

Marcus understood what she was saying, but he didn't care.

And why should he?

Marcus the "bad ass" was almost eighteen years old and he was about to be a man and he knew everything about life and he continued to hear the words "nigga', nigga', nigga', nigga', nigga'" in his head and he said to his mother "I'm not like you. I'm nothing like you! Don't you understand that!"

"That's the same thing I said to my mom before I held a gun to someone's head in this very spot. Think about what I'm saying, Marcus. Please. We only get one chance at life." Abigail realized that she was "finally" getting his attention, but Marcus was trying his best to stifle his tears but he couldn't stifle them any longer, and so he started to cry and he wiped his eyes.

Abigail turned and walked to her car and sat inside and waited for Marcus and she was exhausted and she didn't know what time of day it was now; and then a few moments later, Marcus entered the car and he sat in the passenger seat. He was unable to look at his mother.

She saw the sweet ten year old son for a moment; but that

moment quickly dissipated as she glanced at his son's braids and the small numerous tattoos on his arms and hands and she said "Marcus, I love you. I just don't want to see anything happen to you. Do you hear me?"

"Take me home. I'm tired," Marcus said coldly.

Abigail knew now that she was wasting her time. She had to be at work in an hour, or maybe it was a half hour. She wasn't sure. She drove back to her apartment and she started to feel nauseous. Abigail called her boss, at Supreme Industries, and her name was Susan or Debbie or Vicky but she wasn't really sure. She just remembered telling Susan or Debbie or Vicky that she wasn't feeling well and Abigail fell asleep in her bed a few minutes later. She woke up an hour later and vomited in the toilet. She thought she was getting the flu even though she didn't have a fever.

A few days later, Abigail met Ruth for lunch, in Brentwood. It was probably on a Saturday. Ruth instantly noticed that her daughter "looked" thinner and pale and asked "Are you okay?"

"Mom, please don't start with me. I can't deal with this right now."

"I'm serious, Abby," Ruth said. "Did you ever consider seeing a doctor? It's probably your diet. I swear, the women today think they're always fat and they'll do anything to stay thin."

"No, I didn't change my diet," Abigail said. She finally smiled and knew her mother was a "royal" pain in the ass but Ruth could still make her daughter smile.

"You have to get more rest," Ruth said. She started to eat her fifteen dollar salad when she reminded herself that she would not be a selfish person anymore. She was now sixty-one years old and she wanted to change and she said "Listen, Abby, I want you and Marcus to move in with me."

"I thought you weren't interested in raising another grandson."

"I'm sorry," Ruth said.

"So that makes it okay?

"Stop it, Abby." Ruth said. She was losing her patience once again. "You know my mother once told me that bringing a child into this world isn't an easy task. I thought I knew everything when I was twenty-four years old."

Abigail looked at her food and didn't feel like eating and she looked at her mother and said "I think Marcus is lost, mom."

"He's just going through a difficult time," Ruth said. "That's all."

"No, that's not all," Abigail said. "He was hauled into jail. Look at him. He could barely wear his pants."

"It's not going on his permanent record," Ruth said. "He'll be fine." She sipped her lemon water. She didn't really want to tell Abigail that she believed that Marcus was probably "destined" for prison if he didn't change; and Ruth remained silent as she didn't want to say what she really felt. Ruth Stevens was trying to finally change from being a vindictive angry person toward her daughter and she was trying to be caring and loving all the time; and it was an exhausting process for her.

CHAPTER 25

After years of delay and numerous drafts and changes by her editor, Ruth's second novel, *The After Life Part Two*, was finally released; and it was critically acclaimed and she gained a larger audience who were "thrilled" about the plot which continued to center around the main character, Corinne Dolan. In this book, Corinne began to communicate with Dale Hartmen's spirit who was the "local" sheriff who was shot and killed in the line of duty by a "cokehead" in Part One. Now in this book, Corinne finally admitted to her husband, Steven Dolans, about the affair with the police man. And then Corinne decided to leave him and her two kids and drive from the Midwest to California, in a purple Prius, in hopes of a "new" life, while interacting with Dale's sprit.

Audiences were intrigued and women wrote thousands of letters to Ruth stating they wanted to leave their spouse and have an affair and some admitted they already had an affair and wanted another one.

Ruth admired her devoted fans and she finally admitted on a morning talk show that she had an "affair" during her marriage when she was thirty years old and her book sales "rocketed" through the roof and Ruth became the literary hero, in 2031.

And her first book, *The After Life,* was "finally" going to be produced into a film which earned Ruth another "seven-figure paycheck" and Ruth was now "truly" wealthy; and at sixty-one years old, Ruth became a "middle age" sex symbol. She was on the cover of various glamour magazines and she appeared twenty years younger and a "bit" thinner in the glossy photos.

Now Ruth began her book tour which started in L.A. and she drove to various book stores to promote and sign her new novel and she signed numerous copies and it became so tedious that she stopped looking at the faces of her readers, as she scribbled her name on the inside of her book. It became routine like brushing her teeth or cleaning her bathroom. "Maybe being a celebrity writer isn't for me," Ruth thought as she prepared for another book signing which was a few miles from her house; and on this certain afternoon, she was signing her book and gave it back to the person when she heard a very familiar sounding "Thank you."

Ruth knew that voice and looked up from the table to discover the gaunt face of her daughter framed by tangled sandy blond hair. It had been nearly three weeks since she had lunch with her daughter, in Brentwood, and she appeared sicker and Ruth was instantly concerned.

"You have a moment for a fan?" Abigail asked.

"Give me a moment," Ruth said and nodded her head. "I'll meet you outside." Ruth signed a few more copies of her book and she told her publicist that she had to "step outside" for a moment and the publicist made an announcement that Ruth Stevens will be back shortly after a "brief break" and the fans were slightly pissed off that they had to wait longer to get their book signed but Ruth didn't care; and she went outside to the patio area and she noticed that her daughter's face appeared even thinner in the afternoon sunlight. Ruth was worried about Abigail's health but she was also worried that her daughter would never adapt to "real" life after prison. She heard that some ex-cons come out of prison eager to improve their life. Some of them returned to prison while others just meandered through the sea of life unsure what to do with themselves, and Ruth believed that was Abigail's problem. She was meandering through life, being bumped around in any direction.

"Thanks for coming out here," Abigail said.

"You are my daughter," Ruth said.

"Is that the only reason you came out?"

"Abby, please. Don't start," Ruth said. "Tell me what's on your mind."

Her daughter inhaled deeply. She stared into the parking lot and finally said "I don't know what to do." She finally looked at her mother. "Since dad was killed, I lost a sense of who I really am, like I lost my balance and I can't regain my footing for some reason." She shook her head and said "I just don't know what to do with myself. I don't want to work anymore."

"Abby, I think you should see a doctor."

"Jesus, mom."

"I'm serious, Abigail. You don't look good. I'm not going to lie to you, you know that."

"I'm stressed that's all. Is that a crime?"

Ruth was about to respond to her daughter when her publicist appeared and told her that she needed to come back inside to her "awaiting" fans. Ruth nodded and the publicist went back inside and Ruth said to Abigail "Go get checked out."

Abigail watched her mother enter the bookstore and then Abigail turned and wiped her eyes as she walked back to her car and wondered what she really had to be proud of in life. She had an eighteen year old son who constantly disobeyed her. She had overdue bills; and as she drove home, her mother's words "Go get checked out" echoed in her mind; and later that night, Abigail dreamed that Jess was at her front door and she drove him to his house, in Reseda, and they snorted lines of coke from a glass table while listening to The Rolling Stones, but she couldn't tell what song it was and then she was in Danny's apartment, again; she was still thirty-six years old and she was snorting cocaine while a Motorhead song played and it was a song she remembered hearing many times before, but she couldn't remember the name of the song; and then she was standing on the wet grass at the community park, at night, with Danny; and she was still thirty-six years old as she watched Danny shoot Lester Jackson repeatedly. The gun shots were deafening. The Mexican-American shot the African-American in slow motion as he slowly collapsed; and Abigail stared at the whites of the African-American's eyes until they slowly disappeared behind his closing eye lids and Abigail woke up from her dream and she was sweaty and she rushed to the bathroom and vomited in the toilet.

She was sick and she knew it.

Something in her mind and in her body wasn't right.

The next day Abigail saw a doctor named Dr. Westcott. He was a short man with a bald spot and he put on latex gloves and examined Abigail under her medical gown. She told him about the "lump" in her right breast, which she had for nearly six months or maybe it was a year, but she wasn't sure; and she said that it felt like it got bigger but she wasn't sure and she mentioned her nausea and her vomiting and the weight loss and the nightmares.

"Why did you wait so long to come see me?" Dr. Westcott asked as he examined the lump in her right breast with his latex hands.

"I thought it was a sweat gland or something."

"Well you're definitely too young for cancer," the doctor said confidently and took off the latex gloves and typed Abigail's health issues into a computer and finally said to Abigail "I want you to go downstairs and get a X-ray and a blood test, and we'll move from there." Dr. Westcott noticed Abigail's apprehension. "Don't worry, you'll be fine. This is all routine."

Abigail changed out of the medical gown and into her clothes and rode the elevator to the lab on the first floor and the words "Don't worry, you'll be fine" echoed in her mind.

She finally had the blood test and got a X-ray and drove back to work. She was thirty-six years old and Marcus was eighteen years old; and on a Thursday night, Marcus was partying at a house, in Venice, or, maybe it was a Tuesday. Marcus was a proud high school dropout who graduated to selling coke full time with Franklin, Rock and Skinny.

And the year was still 2031.

At this party, in Venice, on a Tuesday or Thursday night, Marcus noticed Blue Sky who sat on a brown couch with a few of her friends and he was surprised to see her because he thought the relationship was over and so did Blue Sky, but she wanted to give Marcus one "more" chance, so she waited on the brown couch with a few of her friends.

Marcus approached Blue Sky and grabbed her hand and led her into a tiny bathroom of the party house and locked the door behind him and he tried to "make out" with her but she was finally disgusted with Marcus.

And that was it.

Blue Sky realized that Marcus wasn't the guy that she would stay with forever. Yeah he was still in her dreams and in her poetry. But now Marcus was indeed disgusting and Blue Sky was disgusted. He wasn't a "real" person anymore. He was a thug who intimidated other people. Blue Sky wanted more from Marcus but she was not going to get what she wanted from him and she pushed Marcus away in the tiny bathroom and Marcus said "What the hell is a matter with you, girl!"

"I'm not your girl," Blue Sky said. "Do you do everything that your friends tell you to do?" She was "pissed off" and she wasn't afraid to tell him how she felt.

"What, you think you're better than me 'cause you write poetry?"

"I'm going to college soon and what are you gonna do? Hang out with those losers and sell drugs?"

"It don't matter, 'cause I don't need college, when I got this," Marcus said as he pulled out a wad of cash.

"We're done, Marcus!" She screamed and unlocked the bathroom door and left and the music from the living room was much louder inside the tiny bathroom; and Franklin, Rock and Skinny advised him to "forget that bitch" and he tried to do so and Marcus drank a lot that night and he snorted cocaine in a bedroom and remembered seeing girls on the bed and he thought somebody said that "bitch over there, she's fourteen and she likes it up the ass," but he wasn't sure what he "actually" heard.

A few hours later, he stumbled into his mom's dark apartment and he fell over something and a light turned on in the hallway and Abigail appeared in a night gown and then she turned on a lamp in the living room and saw Marcus on the floor and he muttered something incoherently. He suddenly held his stomach and got up from the floor and placed his 9mm on the table and rushed into the bathroom and vomited in the toilet.

Abigail cried and wanted to kick him out of the apartment but she was "too weak" to argue with her six feet two inch son who now weighed over two hundred and fifteen pounds. And she didn't want to make the same mistake as her mother did nearly twenty years ago by kicking her child out into the world. So she went back to her bedroom.

Around eight a.m., Abigail approached her son who was eating cereal at the small card table and he had a "massive" hangover. Abigail was wearing a robe and she was pissed off at her son and she said "How dare you come into my house drunk and bring a gun in here. Where's your head?"

"You call this place a house? This ain't no house. It's a shithole! I have friends that have nicer places than this."

"Who? Drug dealers? You call them friends?" Abigail asked. "What are you going to do with your life?"

"Maybe I'll become just like you," Marcus said. He glared at his mother and she felt the "full-blown" anger.

"Don't worry, Marcus," Abigail said. "I'm not going to kick you out of here. I'm just going to wait until the police knock on my door and tell me you're in jail or dead."

Marcus stopped eating.

He was hurt and Abigail saw it in his eyes.

But she knew his toughness was derived from fear and that's why he carried a loaded gun and sold drugs and hung out with thugs.

He was scared and stubborn like his father and his mother; and now the vicious cycle continued.

Abigail turned and entered the bathroom and slammed the door.

Marcus was lost as he continued to sit at the kitchen table for a moment.

But he wasn't going to "take shit" from nobody so he grabbed his weapon from the drawer in his bedroom and left as his mother cried in the bathroom; and an hour later, Abigail sat in Dr. Westcott's office and it was on a Wednesday but Abigail wasn't sure.

And the year was still 2031.

She felt weak and exhausted and her beauty had begun to fade and she stared into a stream of morning light. She listened to the update on the blood test and she learned that she had breast cancer and the cancer had already spread through a portion of her body and she found out one week after her doctor told her that she was "too young for cancer" and the words "It had spread" echoed within her mind and those were the words she remembered throughout the following nights and weeks. However the next few minutes, Abigail pondered the doctor's conversation which included the words "mastectomy" and "surgery" and "radiation" and "chemotherapy" and "in order to save the other breast."

Yes Abigail was devastated as she walked across the lobby, in the medical building, and noticed her mother reading a magazine; and Ruth put the magazine down when she noticed her daughter's pale face and she recognized the scared and "dazed" looked in Abigail's eyes; and Ruth was alarmed and Abigail walked like a zombie; and during the drive home from the medical clinic, Abigail wondered if she had went to see the doctor after she first felt the lump in her right breast, would the cancer have "actually" spread?

Maybe Abigail was secretly hoping that she had cancer and that it would spread so it would end her "crappy ass" life and she could avoid all responsibility. But Abigail had to "fight" the discouraging thoughts about her illness and about her "shitty ass" day job and about her "rotten son" who bitched at her all the fuckin' time.

And maybe, just maybe, this cancer actually was her secret suicide like Danny's secret suicide was pointing a 9mm at a sheriff on the side of a highway in the desert and Abigail snapped from her trance.

She wanted to live.

She *had* to live.

She was determined to survive her treatment; and yes it was possible, at the end of the treatment, she would only have one breast but she was going to win against this life-threatening problem and that's all she was going to do.

She calmed herself down as she sat in the passenger seat of her mother's BMW and stared outside not realizing that she was already in her mother's driveway; and a few minutes later, Abigail sliced vegetables at the counter in her mother's kitchen, as Ruth turned the flame down on the stove to allow the rice to simmer and she approached her daughter and said "I want you to stay here, Abby, and I don't want an argument."

"I can't," Abigail said.

"Listen, Abby," Ruth said as she parted her daughter's bangs. Ruth wanted to say more but she couldn't since she was also an emotional "wreck." She thought on the way home from the hospital that she could "lose" her daughter. Before Ruth could finish her sentence, in the kitchen, Ruth tightly hugged her daughter and they both started to cry and they now had to work together as a team.

Francis had been dead for almost twenty years and Ruth realized that she had another challenge in her life. She had been prepared for this moment. Her years of selfishness and jealousy were gone and Abigail's anger and resentment toward her mother had instantly dissolved, and within the tears and the uncontrollable emotions, Abigail broke from her mother's grasp and wiped her eyes and said "There's something that I have to do."

"What is it?"

"It's something I should have done a long time ago," Abigail said as she continued to wipe her eyes.

CHAPTER 26

A year had nearly passed since Abigail had been diagnosed with breast cancer and she was almost thirty-eight years old and she weighed less than one hundred pounds. Her hair had fallen out from treatment but she was still on a mission, as she walked slowly down the corridor of a maximum security prison, on death row, with two large guards. She felt strange being back in a prison, but it was something that she had to do. She had to finish this mission so she could "finally" live in peace.

Abigail reached the visiting room and sat down slowly, partially out of breath, in front of a bullet proof glass and picked up the receiver and on the other side of the bullet proof glass was Tyrone Williams. He was nearly seventy years old and he wore thick glasses and he was thinner and he was completely bald. His shoulders were permanently slouched and he finally looked directly at Abigail as he picked up the receiver. He remembered her from court nearly twenty years ago. In Tyrone's mind, she was still the seventeen year old daughter of the "white surgeon" who was murdered in the parking structure of The Crenshaw District Hospital.

It was his infamous murder and it was his morbid masterpiece that made him a "household" name for several years.

"Thanks for seeing me," Abigail said.

"What could I do for you?" Tyrone asked. He still had the cold angry tone in his voice and the cold glare in his eyes.

"There's something I wanted to tell you," Abigail said. She practiced her speech with her mother and in the shower and in her bedroom within the past few weeks. However at this moment, she was nearly "loss" for words.

"I'm not sure what you wanna hear? You wanna here me say I'm sorry, is that it?"

Abigail felt his anger but she still had a mission which her father gave her years ago. She heard her father's soft voice as she slept. He patiently instructed her to forgive the man that murdered him; and here she was in prison visiting a convicted killer; and so she finally said to Tyrone "I'm not going to argue with you. I just want to tell you that that I forgive you before I run out of time."

"What do you mean?" Tyrone asked.

"I've got cancer."

Tyrone finally averted eye contact from Abigail. "My wife had cancer. The doctors told her that she was fine and then she died. I knew they were taking advantage of her. I just knew it."

"Is that what you thought my father was doing to your brother? You thought he was taking advantage of him?" Abigail asked. She was momentarily regaining her strength as the anger began to evolve inside of her.

"What does it matter?" Tyrone asked.

"I guess it doesn't matter," Abigail said. "But I just want to let you know that my father also forgives you. He told me every night for years while I was sleeping and he told me that he forgave you, in my dreams; but I didn't listen because I hated you, I hated everyone; but then I realized that I wasn't going to be around forever; and I didn't want to die with hatred inside of me. I lived with it for so long, I couldn't do it anymore, so I forgive you now."

Tyrone had never heard the words "I forgive you." They

were the most powerful words that he had ever heard and then he thought for a quick second that maybe life was all about forgiveness and then he remembered the families of the black prostitutes inside of the court room who hoped that he would endure a quick death, but it didn't happen. His life would most likely continue for years until he died of sickness or until his appeals "ran out" and he would die quietly from a lethal injection.

"Why did you 'really' come here?" Tyrone asked.

"Because I wanted to let you know that I was just like you after you murdered my father. I hated everything just like you did, but I guess I learned too late that hatred is evil; and I wanted to tell you that I forgive you."

"I'm sixty-nine years old. I haven't seen my daughter and my son in maybe ten, fifteen years. I can't even remember. I heard I had grandchildren but I've never seen them. I'm just another black man in this place and you think I care about you or your father," Tyrone said. "You don't know nothin' I've been through. You don't know what it's like to raise kids on your own. We just come from two different worlds."

"I had things, Tyrone. I had a family. I had a father before you lost your temper. I have a son that hates me, and I don't know how much longer I'll be around, and you tell me I don't understand heartbreak, I don't understand pain," Abigail said. "I watched a black man die hoping that it was the same person that murdered my father; and that's what anger is all about, right? It makes you do fucked up things. It makes you do things that are evil, right?"

Maybe for a moment, Tyrone wanted to apologize to her and maybe he wanted to apologize to the numerous families that he destroyed by murdering their daughters; and maybe he wanted to apologize for being a horrible father to his son and daughter, but none of that mattered now.

Abigail calmly hung up the phone and left the visiting room.

Ruth drove Abigail home from the prison in Northern California; and during the drive to the nearby hotel, Abigail looked out of the window and thought about how she "forgave" a person that she hated for nearly twenty years. She finally put "forgiveness" into the world, as her father wanted her to do for so many years; and then Abigail was finally "confined" to a hospital bed a few months later and she eventually lost more weight and had difficulties breathing. The cancer had "taken over" her body. She fought the disease the best that she could; and Ruth sat by her daughter's bedside, in the hospital; and during one afternoon, as she watched Abigail living with the aid of numerous machines, Ruth wondered what other horrible event could occur in her life.

Ruth was emotionally numb.

She endured some of the worst times that life had to offer and then she wondered where her "rotten" grandson could be at this very moment.

Marcus was living at various friend's places. Yeah he knew his mother was sick but all he cared about was getting "high" and selling drugs. And on one afternoon, Ruth was at her daughter's apartment cleaning when Marcus stumbled inside with his friends, Franklin, Rock and Skinny. She quickly kicked out his friends from the apartment and told Marcus to sit on the couch. He sat down and faced his grandmother who tried to tell him how sick his mother was and what could happen to her, and he tried to understand her and the "unfortunate" situation, but the drugs were frying his mind; and now his hands and arms and were nearly covered in tattoos of skulls and names of dead people and he was almost twenty years old and he was lost and he had nothing to lose.

Ruth knew Marcus was destined for an early death or a prison sentence, like his mother, and she begged her grandson to see his mother at the hospital. She gave him the address and the room number but none of that information mattered to Marcus and he left the apartment quickly after grabbing a few things from his room.

Ruth finally drove home and prayed. She no longer cared about her wealth. She had already received a ten million dollar advance for her third novel, *The After Life Part III.*

But none of that mattered.

Her life was becoming worse and during an afternoon prayer, she had asked God for a miracle to save her daughter and her grandson from the inevitable; but she feared she would lose them both.

Ruth cried while she prayed and felt Francis in the bedroom but she ignored the chill and the creaking floorboards and there was nothing that Francis could do right now.

She needed God.

She walked to the kitchen table and sat down by the window and drank a glass of Scotch; and her misery was starting over again, at sixty-three years old.

She continued to drink when she felt two hands touch her shoulders.

It was Francis.

She should have shivered or jumped from the chair.

But she didn't move because it was the same feeling she had "felt" on the first anniversary of his death when she took off her wedding ring in her bedroom; and now she was relaxed and the fear and anxiety left her body and although she couldn't see him or hear him, Francis said "I know everything has been so screwed up. I know you can't hear me but you have to trust me, Ruth. I'm here for you and Abigail, and I'm here for Marcus."

And then Francis was gone.

Ruth stood and poured the bottle of Scotch in the sink and walked to the bathroom and brushed her teeth and drove back to the hospital when it started to rain. She continued to pray "under her breath" for Marcus to visit Abigail.

She called Marcus on his cell phone when she arrived at the hospital.

His voicemail came on.

In a house in Venice, Marcus stood with Franklin, Rock and Skinny and a few other drug dealers in a bedroom. They were all "packing" a 9mm Smith & Wesson or a Glock pistol or a .38 Smith & Wesson; and on the bed were two suitcases filled with sealed bags of cocaine.

The time had come.

The guys in the room listened to a notorious drug dealer named Q who paced the bedroom. Q ruled many of Venice streets dealing drugs.

Q was forty-five years old and spent more than fifteen years in prison for various drug related charges and Q was the guy that knew distribution and also knew how to intimidate.

Every drug dealer in Venice knew about Q and they also knew about his quick temper; and when Q spoke, people listened; and right now he was saying "This is how this shit's gonna go down, so listen the fuck up. We roll up to security and everybodys' gonna act cool, 'cause their asses are in on this shit to. We do the exchange in the back and then we're outta there. We split the cash evenly. If something ain't right, nobody better put a cap in someone's ass until I say. Every one got that or you'll be dealing with me."

Now everyone in the room was "pumped" and they checked to see if their weapons were loaded and they left with two suitcases of cocaine. Marcus followed them outside on the dead lawn as it began to rain and the sky was becoming darker; and he watched a few guys that he didn't know put one suitcase of coke in the trunk of a blue Chevy Malibu and the other one in the trunk of the cherry red Monte Carlo. Franklin started up the blue Chevy Malibu and that is when he noticed Marcus standing on the dead lawn in the rain and Franklin finally said "Marcus, get your ass in here."

"I'm not going," Marcus said.

Everyone looked at Marcus and they all approached him and Q quickly asked "There a problem, homie?"

"No, there ain't no problem," Marcus said. "I'm just not going." Marcus was waiting for Q to punch him in the head or try to knock his ass out. Marcus had been in a few street fights before but never with someone as strong or big as Q, but Marcus didn't care. He was tired of pretending to be someone that he wasn't.

"Come on, Marcus. Stop being a bitch and let's go," Franklin said.

"I told you, I'm not going," Marcus said firmly as he looked directly at his friend.

And that is when Q pulled out his Glock and pointed it at Marcus' face and said "You're a fuckin' narc."

Franklin pulled out his .38 from his waistband and pointed it at Q's head and said "Put your piece down, homie. He's cool. We go way back."

"Your bitch here is a narc," Q said.

"He ain't a fuckin' narc," Franklin said. "He's just freaking out. That's all."

"I don't give a fuck. I think he's narc," Q said as he pushed the gun further in Marcus' face, but Marcus didn't flinch.

Franklin moved his .38 closer to Q's shaved head and said "I'll leave this up to you homie, if you want to end this right now or not."

"Let's hurry the fuck up!" Rock said quickly. "We gotta go!"

"He's right, man," Skinny said. "We gotta go!"

"So, what's it gonna be?" Franklin said to Q.

After a moment, Q lowered his weapon and so did Franklin and Q finally said to Marcus "You got lucky this time, bitch. Don't let me see your ass around here again."

Marcus waited for Q to suddenly end his life, but it didn't

happen. Marcus watched Q turn and enter the cherry red Monte Carlo. Marcus was about to leave when he noticed Franklin in the driver's seat of the blue Chevy Malibu. They nodded at each other and Franklin finally drove away along with the cherry red Monte Carlo. And that was the last time Marcus ever saw Franklin and Rock and Skinny. Marcus heard a few weeks later from someone who knew that Franklin was murdered by a drug dealer; and a few months later, Marcus heard from someone who knew that Rock and Skinny was arrested for "sales" and distribution" of "rock cocaine." Marcus believed that the police would come after him, but it never happened; and now Marcus walked along the wet streets in Venice, and he wasn't sure if he wanted to live anymore.

His life was a mess and it started to rain harder and the sky continued to darken, and Marcus walked into an alley and stood under a carport of a building and looked around and pulled out his 9mm and placed it under his chin and he started to cry as he placed his finger on the trigger; and then his cell phone rang. He snapped from his "trance of suicide" and finally lowered the gun and answered his cell phone and heard his grandmother yelling at him to get his "ass to the hospital." He said he would be there and hung up and he walked to the sewer and emptied the gun and tossed the bullets and the gun inside the sewer; and at that very moment, he remembered the location of the hospital and he got on the bus and sat in the back. He leaned his head against a window that rattled and he thought about Q shoving a gun in his face and he wondered if Q would ever find him, but he couldn't worry about that now. He tried to "clear" his mind from worry.

He got off the bus in Santa Monica and walked more than a block to the hospital and it was still raining steadily and he was nearly soaked when he entered the hospital and he rode the elevator to the second floor and noticed his grandmother in the hallway and she said "There you are! Your mother has been asking about you, and if you say anything smart to me I'm going to slap the shit out of you." And Ruth expected Marcus to grab her and call her a "bitch" and a "cunt" and pin her against the door and glare at her and threaten her with violence. However Marcus was too mentally exhausted to retaliate verbally and physically to anyone.

Marcus entered the room and noticed his mother who he barely recognized. It had been a few weeks since he saw her, but he was too high and busy making "real" cash to remember what his mother had said or looked like; and now his mother lay in bed, completely bald and barely able to live and breathe without the assistance of numerous machines.

He approached his mother.

It's true that Marcus never realized how sick she was or maybe he never wanted to know. He was a "bad ass" selling cocaine and getting "high" but he didn't care about anyone nor did he want to listen to anyone.

And now he sat on the side of his mother's bed as Abigail tried to speak and she softly said "Marcus, I want you to listen to me."

"I don't want you to leave, mom, I'm sorry. I'm sorry for everything," Marcus said. He wiped his eyes but he continued to cry. For many years, Marcus was the angry "rotten" son; but now he wanted to instantly erase those horrible moments and events.

"Marcus, promise me you'll never hate anyone again, okay?" Abigail asked. Her voice was weak and her lips were chapped.

"I swear. I'm sorry. I didn't mean to be like this," Marcus said.

"Marcus, promise me, promise me you'll never hate anyone again."

He finally nodded his head and he hugged his mother and kissed her on the cheek and he finally left the room and saw Ruth in the hallway. She was still very "upset" with her grandson but she knew this was a moment of forgiveness. She tightly hugged Marcus and said "I'm sorry." He lightly hugged her back.

Ruth entered the room and sat near the bed and grabbed her daughter's hand.

Abigail was silent and she could barely move.

She was fighting death and Ruth said "Abby, I'm sorry for how things turned out between us. You're right. I was jealous of you. It's not an easy thing to admit that a mother is jealous of her daughter. I was jealous that you took Francis' attention. I know it was wrong to feel that way. I know I had to have things my way." Ruth cried and was unable to restrain more than thirty years of feelings about her daughter. "I thought I could be a better mom than my mom, but I couldn't do it. I was just like her. I thought it would be easy to be a parent," Ruth continued. "I thought I knew everything. I was mean and angry and jealous; and I had an affair, and I'm sorry, Abby."

Ruth felt Abigail lightly squeeze her hand and Abigail softly said "It's okay, mom. You were great" and suddenly Abigail was gone.

The line on the heart monitor "flatlined" and the machine buzzed and so on.

Abigail's spirit left her body at thirty-eight years old and her spirit moved through white and yellow circles of light and everything was bright but within the brightness Abigail saw her father in the hospital room and he still looked the same as when she saw him living nearly twenty years ago; and Abigail was now wearing jeans and a T-shirt and she was healthy and attractive again and they finally hugged within the white and yellow circles of light.

"I don't want you to be scared, Abby," Francis said.

"I can barely see anything, dad. It's very bright here."

"It's okay, Abby," Francis said as he continued to tightly hug her daughter. "Everything will become clearer with time."

Abigail leaned back from his grasp and said "I know."

They both smiled knowing they would finally be together forever, in the after life.

CHAPTER 27

An hour after Abigail died in the hospital, Marcus told his grandmother that he would meet her at home. Ruth thought that he was leaving to sell drugs, but she was too busy discussing arrangements of Abigail's body with the nurses to worry what he was going to do. Ruth eventually drove home from the hospital and was already mentally "drafting" rules for Marcus since she would be responsible for him and she expected the worst.

Ruth remembered when Abigail told her that Marcus was "lost" when they had lunch together a year or two ago, at a café, in Brentwood; however Ruth didn't know at this very moment that Marcus was going to see Blue Sky. The rain stopped when Marcus reached her parent's apartment; and it had been a few months since he had spoken to her and he was unaware which classes she was attending at the community college, in Santa Monica.

She was trying to "move on" without Marcus, yet she still missed him and she missed the days of his smiles and their nights of "useless" chatter. She wanted to call him every time she wrote poetry on the bottom bunk bed; and she recently included him in one of her poems.

"He was a man of small dreams; but the world still spun

with hope.
His eyes were filled with darkness and shallow feelings;
but I loved him anyway.
Underneath his dark armor, there was something
shining in his heart."

And it was true, Blue Sky still believed that Marcus had "something shining in his heart," but she still believed that he was forever gone and she still believed that "someone" would "sweep her off her feet" one day; and she was determined to be loved and to be successful unlike her parents. Now it was nearly eleven p.m. when she turned off the TV in the living room when she heard a knock on the front door. She cautiously approached the door and peered through the peephole and couldn't believe who she saw in the hallway. She expected Marcus to be "coked up" and saying stupid shit with a gun tucked in his waistband.

The anger surged inside of her and she unlocked the door and swung it open and said "What are you doing here! I told you my father doesn't want you here! Don't you get it?" She was prepared for the cockiness and the arrogant attitude and all the other "shit" that came along with selling and using drugs and hanging out with thugs.

"I'm sorry," Marcus said as he wiped his eyes.

However Blue Sky was skeptical of his bullshit, yet she had never seen him like this before and asked "Do you know how to be a real man?"

"I can try."

And within the dim light of the hallway, they tightly hugged and kissed; and from that night, Marcus and Blue Sky began to "officially" date once again.

Marcus eventually completed his GED and they both attended community college together and Marcus studied business administration, as Blue Sky studied journalism and they both graduated together from Northridge State University. They moved into an apartment together in Calabasas, and they eventually bought a house in Agoura Hills.

And time moved forward.

Marcus purchased several businesses and properties throughout the San Fernando Valley and Blue Sky began to write for a national publication interviewing "political figures" and "community activists" and she traveled throughout the world as she became a broadcast journalist; and she became the first Hispanic woman to have her own nighttime political show on a "network" station; and Marcus continued to buy various properties and he eventually opened an "upscale" restaurant, in the valley, called Abigail's Cuisine.

In between their success, Marcus and Blue Sky got married and she gave birth to a boy named John and then a few years later, Blue Sky gave birth to a girl named Red Beam, and over the years their children had children.

And time moved quickly.

During the years of success and being a "loving" father, Marcus never forgot what his dying mother had told him to "never hate anyone again" and he shared that message with his children, John and Red Beam, and he taught them to "love everyone" and never to hate and let "God handle the rest." And before every meal, Marcus and Blue Sky sat around the table and prayed with their children.

And before Marcus and Blue Sky married and became wealthy and had children, Marcus moved into Ruth's house after his mother died. A day before Abigail's funeral, Ruth and Marcus searched through various boxes in her garage. Marcus discovered a folded piece of paper. He opened it and noticed partially faded words and he asked "What is this?"

"Let me see it," Ruth said. Marcus handed her the piece of paper and she looked at it and said "I don't believe it!"

"What, what is it?"

"It's your grandfather's eulogy. Abigail wrote it over twenty years ago. It's short but very memorable." She folded the eulogy and handed it back to her grandson. "I want you to read it tomorrow."

"I can't," Marcus said.

"What do you mean you can't? Of course you can," Ruth said. "It's just a few lines and it would make Abigail proud."

Marcus looked at the piece of paper and studied the partially faded words. The next day, in his suit, Marcus stood at the podium at his mother's funeral. His hand shook as he held the piece of paper and carefully read the eulogy.

> "*Birth and death are like a puzzle. What actually comes first? Who really knows? Every moment, every part of life feels out of order; but, in the end, life and death come together, within the after life.*"

THE END